The GULF

The GULF

HIGH CULTURE/HARD LABOR

Edited by Andrew Ross

(for Gulf Labor)

O/R

OR Books

New York · London

Published by OR Books, New York and London
Visit our website at www.orbooks.com

First printing 2015

Cataloging-in-Publication data is available from the Library of Congress.
A catalog record for this book is available from the British Library.

ISBN 978-1-68219-004-3 paperback
ISBN 978-1-68219-005-0 e-book

This book is set in the fonts Helvetica and Pobla.
Text design by Bathcat Ltd. Typeset by AarkMany Media, Chennai, India.
Printed by BookMobile in the United States and CPI Books Ltd in the United Kingdom.

Contents

Foreword

Sarah Leah Whitson

Today, in a region overwhelmed by war and seemingly intractable political and social problems, the systemic abuse and exploitation of millions of migrant workers may not seem the worst problem besetting the Middle East. But it has the advantage of being one of the easiest to fix, by applying readily available legal remedies and appropriately allocating costs. It is in fact one of the few areas where we have seen real progress and reform over the past decade. The collaboration of human rights organizations, artists, and academics to end this abuse and exploitation has become a model for globalized human rights activism, helping to improve the lives of migrant workers thousands of miles away from home and also upgrade some of the ethics and labor impacts of institutions, companies, and governments. It has allowed us to find our own strength in globalization, where the interconnectedness of economies, businesses, and institutions has created opportunities for activists to press for accountability.

It remains widely unknown outside the Gulf that approximately 15 million migrant workers, primarily from South Asia, but increasingly from Africa as well, make up the vast majority of the labor force in most Gulf states—and in some countries, the vast majority of the population. In the UAE and Qatar, migrant workers—white collar and blue collar—compose well over 90 percent of the work force and the population. Yet they have no voting, representation, or association rights (like much of the citizenry, of course), and no option of obtaining such rights, regardless of how many decades they have lived and worked there, or even if they were born there and never lived in their "home country."

In 2004, Human Rights Watch set out to examine abuses that had anecdotally appeared as news items. These were stories about tortured and sexually abused migrant domestic workers in Saudi Arabia, and also about masses of striking construction workers in the UAE. At that time, our focus was on individual cases of employer abuse, including unpaid or exceedingly low wages, poor housing conditions, and unsafe work environments, and the government's failure to protect these workers and sanction their abusive employers. But what we found was not only a problem of failed enforcement and protection by the state, but also a legal framework for labor importation that effectively encourages private-sector abuses.

A triangle of abuses fosters conditions in which exploitation thrives, often akin to forced labor or indentured servitude: the "sponsorship" system that grants all power over a worker's visa to their employer and bars them from changing jobs without their employer's consent; the nearly universal practice of passport confiscation by employers that limits the freedom of workers to return home; and the indebtedness of workers who owe thousands of dollars in recruiting fees. Under these conditions, workers find it difficult to escape from abusive employers, change jobs, or leave the country, let alone imagine how to repay the debts they owe at home. In these circumstances, the notion of "voluntary labor" has little meaning.

The asymmetry of the labor market—with each employer enjoying a captive labor pool and a bottomless supply of replacements facilitated by employment agencies operating in the workers' home countries—means there is little incentive for employers to respect workers' basic rights. This power imbalance makes it all too easy to find the cases of abuse that Human Rights Watch and others have documented: outright labor trafficking, including deception over jobs and wages; long hours with no days off or vacation; non- or under-payment of wages; dangerous working conditions; deplorable living accommodations; and few if any legal recourses.

The UAE and other Gulf governments could largely afford to dismiss our reports and our calls to end these abuses, but the international actors they courted could not. When the UAE launched its "Island of Happiness," the name of Saadiyat Island, Human Rights Watch directed our efforts toward global cultural institutions that would have a presence there, like the Louvre, Guggenheim, and New York University, reminding them of their stated ideals and values.

This strategy also enabled us to engage with and draw on the talents, insights, resources, and energy of the students and faculty of NYU and the artists associated with the Guggenheim and Louvre. Using the innovative strategies they developed as Gulf Labor they have built an important multi-dimensional model of activism to pressure these institutions to live up to their commitments, as described in fascinating detail in this book. The efforts of Gulf Labor have prevented these world-class institutions from sweeping their complicity in the exploitation of migrant workers under Abu Dhabi's desert sands.

Most significantly, these efforts have produced concrete results, with the private institutions and businesses involved in Saadiyat Island agreeing to a minimum set of commitments to protect worker rights, including the right to change jobs, an end to passport confiscation, and the refunding of recruiting fees. With independent monitors, to which the UAE authorities only reluctantly agreed after years of resistance, there is now a basic model in place that provides more labor protections than anywhere else in the Gulf. While enforcement with serious penalties against abusive contractors remains a problem requiring far greater vigilance, the commitments these institutions have made set an important precedent throughout the region and across business sectors. And the campaign has even led the UAE grudgingly to adopt some legislative reforms, including electronic payment of wages, changes to the sponsorship system that allow workers to switch jobs under limited circumstances, and greater supervision of work conditions by a vastly expanded pool of government inspectors.

Yet, at the same time, the UAE government has also tacked hard to the right, deciding to punish those who exposed the embarrassing abuses and who are monitoring the government's fulfillment of the promises it and private institutions have made. Starting in 2014, the government has banned many artists, journalists, human rights activists, and academics from entering or remaining in the country, while it has pursued repressive policies against the country's domestic political opposition and reform activists, jailing dozens. In so doing, the UAE has exposed itself and its academic and cultural partners to a separate set of important questions about their professed commitment to art, culture, inquiry, and learning, all of which depend on free expression and association. How they will have art without free-thinking artists? How will they have a leading university without critical scholars? And how will they have news, information, and public knowledge without inquisitive journalists and responsible human rights advocates?

In forcing these questions onto the agenda, Gulf Labor, Human Rights Watch, and other organizations have gone beyond pushing for critical reforms in migrant worker employment; we are also pushing for fulfillment of the promise that the UAE and its partners made about enlightenment in the country. In a modest way, our efforts as global activists can help make globalization work in the interests of those most affected—the millions of exploited workers in the UAE—and even in the interests of the UAE's citizens, who stand to gain most from a country that truly respects rights and freedoms, culture, and art.

Leveraging the Brand:
A History of Gulf Labor

Andrew Ross

The roaring wealth of the Persian Gulf states derives from high-yield petroleum reservoirs far beneath the desert sands. But the lustrous towers and grand villas that support the *de luxe* lives of the region's elites are not the direct result of slow organic decomposition underground. The gleaming cityscapes of Abu Dhabi, Dubai, Doha, and Bahrain are being assembled, at boomtown speed, from the hard-pressed labor of armies of migrant workers from India, Bangladesh, Pakistan, Nepal, and, increasingly, North and East Africa. Bound to an employer by the *kafala* sponsorship system, the laborers arrive, heavily indebted from recruitment and transit fees, only to find that their Gulf Dream has been a mirage.[1] Typically, the sponsoring employer takes their passports, houses them in substandard labor camps, pays them much less than they were promised, and enforces a punishing work regimen under the hot desert sun. Most of them find ways to endure the exploitation, but many fall prey to suicide, or die from overwork or the heat. If they voice their complaints or protest publicly, they are arrested, beaten, and deported.

The Gulf states are hardly alone in their dependence on tragically underpaid and ill-treated migrant workers. Every developed and fast developing country has its own record of shame. But these nations are in a league of their own. The opulent lifestyle of a minority—composed of citizens and corporate expats—is maintained by a vast majority (up to 90 percent in the United Arab Emirates and Qatar) who function as a servant class, with no rights and very little mobility, and whose compliant labor is

---

1. The *kafala* system, employed in all the Gulf Cooperation Council (GCC) states, requires all migrant laborers to have an in-country sponsor who oversees their visa and legal status.

secured through the fear of abuse and deportation. Their plight is so acute that, in recent years, the push to reform the cruel *kafala* system (instituted as a temporary guest program in the early 1970s) has become an international cause.[2]

By the end of 2014, the Gulf Cooperation Council (GCC), which comprises Bahrain, Kuwait, Oman, Qatar, Saudi Arabia, and the United Arab Emirates (UAE), was facing down a flood of overseas pressure to dismantle the *kafala* system. Spearheaded by Human Rights Watch, more than 90 human rights groups, many from the workers' countries of origin, signed a call for wide-ranging reforms of labor migration policies. Following allegations by the International Trade Union Confederation of "exploitative practices that may amount to forced labour," the International Labor Organization (ILO) launched an official investigation of the UAE.[3] Amnesty International released a report, titled *There is No Freedom Here*, on the treatment of political dissenters in the Emirates.[4] In response to the soaring death toll among the Nepalese working on Doha's construction spree, FIFA, the global football federation, was hotly petitioned by its European members to insist on labor reforms as a condition of Qatar's hosting the 2022 World Cup.[5] Investigative journalists from leading media organizations routinely filed front-page stories about the human cost of importing a workforce so vulnerable to abuse.[6]

Though its name did not always appear alongside those of the NGOs and high-profile advocacy groups, the Gulf Labor Coalition has played a key role in raising awareness of labor exploitation, especially in the UAE. An international network of artists and writers, energetically focused on Abu Dhabi's development of a new

---

2. Priyanka Motaparthy, "Understanding Kafala: An Archaic Law at Cross Purposes with Modern Development," *Migrant-rights.org* (March 11, 2015), http://tinyurl.com/lqjytvf.

3. David Batty, "UN Investigates Claims of Gulf State Abuse of Migrant Workers," *Guardian* (November 29, 2015), http://tinyurl.com/kmfrnut.

4. Amnesty International, "'There is No Freedom Here': Silencing Dissent in the United Arab Emirates," (November 18, 2014), http://tinyurl.com/nz7xkhp.

5. Owen Gibson and Pete Pattisson, "Death Toll Among Qatar's 2022 World Cup Workers Revealed," *Guardian* (December 23, 2014), http://tinyurl.com/o3bb489.

6. Glenn Carrick and David Batty, "In Abu Dhabi, They Call It Happiness Island," *Guardian* (December 21, 2013).

cultural zone on Saadiyat Island, Gulf Labor was able to do and say things that the more official organizations could not. Our creative approach to activism was inspired and innovative, and, in some respects, unique in the field of labor advocacy. More decisive was the position of our artist members as coordinators of cultural value, with some leverage over the politics of constructing museum branches of the Guggenheim and Louvre on Saadiyat.

While human and labor rights groups are denied entry into the UAE, and have only limited access in neighboring Qatar, the strenuous project of nation-building in both countries requires a degree of openness to producers of high culture. Art, after all, has become a status component of the amenity environment demanded by the GCC's affluent residents and visitors. Museums, galleries, and trade fairs are now obligatory landmarks for the global investor class. As the essential brokers of acquisitional prestige, cultural producers have to be courted, but only if they hold their tongues, and turn a blind eye to the daily suppression of basic rights. Because the constituencies it represents are both sought out and feared, Gulf Labor was probably in the right place at the right time. Over time, our members were regularly consulted by the NGOs, our reporting was cited in the media exposés, and the publicity generated by our actions reached a much wider audience than the communities of conscience who typically respond to reports about human and labor rights violations.

As for the impact on the artworld itself, *New York Times* art critic Holland Cotter, in his roundup of 2014's notable events, singled out Gulf Labor's campaign and the work of the Global Ultra Luxury Faction (a direct action spinoff). "The groups' action," he summarized, "has been carefully organized, effectively executed and persistent, as any protest that's going to work must be."[7]

The idea behind the Gulf Labor Coalition emerged from a 2010 conference (*Home Works Forum 5*) hosted by Ashkal Alwan, the Lebanese Association for Plastic Arts.

---

7. Holland Cotter, "Holland Cotter's Notable Art Events of 2014," *New York Times* (December 11, 2014).

The New York–based Lebanese artist and educator Walid Raad organized a panel to discuss Saadiyat Island, where Abu Dhabi's Tourism and Development Corporation (TDIC) was planning the mother of all luxury property developments. There was good reason for artists in the Middle East to pay attention. Saadiyat's plush real estate was to be sold on the premise that buyers could stroll to branches of the Guggenheim, the Louvre, and a new national museum partnered with the British Museum. To add to the cachet, a batch of lustrous starchitects—Frank Gehry, Jean Nouvel, Zaha Hadid, Raphael Viñoly, Tadao Ando, and Norman Foster—had been lured with princely sums to design the signature buildings.

On the face of it, Saadiyat looked like a real estate venture for globe-hopping elites, with top artworld brands thrown in for good measure. Yet the museums were also being planned as serious exhibitionary sites, each catering to contemporary art in some degree and, in the case of the Guggenheim at least, bent on acquiring a first-class collection of Arab and Middle Eastern art. While its brand was being purchased like any other pricey import, the Guggenheim Abu Dhabi was also viewed by many as a welcome asset for a region long bereft of major art institutions. "We have to begin somewhere," declared Zaki Anwar Nusseibeh, a UAE cultural advisor. "We know we cannot create culture overnight, so we are strategically building museums that in time will train our own people, so we can find our own voice. Hopefully, in 20 or 30 years' time, we will have our own cultural elite, so our young people won't have to go to London or Paris to learn about art."[8]

Raad had invited me to speak on his *Home Works* panel about my experience at New York University (NYU), where, through the faculty-student Coalition for Fair Labor, we had been pressing our administration to ensure fair labor standards in the construction of its new Abu Dhabi campus (NYUAD) on Saadiyat Island. Faculty had not been consulted about NYU's Abu Dhabi plan, and there were widespread concerns that the presence of a liberal arts college might be used as a showcase for free speech in a country where any criticism of the royal family is considered a criminal offense. Yet even if the right to academic freedom were assured (it was not secure at any other

8. Quoted in Carol Vogel, "A New Art Capital, Finding Its Own Voice," *New York Times* (December 4, 2014).

UAE educational institution), we concluded that it would be immoral to exercise that right in classrooms built or maintained by exploited workers.

When the NYU, Guggenheim, and Louvre plans were announced, Human Rights Watch had written to the leaders of each institution, advising them to take steps to guarantee improvements in worker conditions on their construction projects. None of the three responded. The NYU faculty and students who formed the Coalition for Fair Labor reasoned that an internal advocacy group was more likely to get results. In response to this pressure, in 2010, the NYU administration adopted a Statement of Labor Values that included labor standards and provisions that were superior to the regional norm.[9] Labor principles and regulations often look good on paper, but implementation and enforcement is another matter. Despite our efforts to push for an independent labor monitor, the Abu Dhabi authorities elected to choose a firm, Mott MacDonald, whose business in the region depends on good relations with the state. In a further conflict of interest, the company was awarded a lavish contract to oversee utility infrastructure on Saadiyat Island. In its capacity as labor compliance monitor, Mott had no incentive to look hard for violations, and it recorded little evidence of them in its yearly reports.

After the Saadiyat panel took place in Beirut, a few of the attendees (Walid Raad, Emily Jacir, Rene Gabri, Ayreen Anastas, Beth Stryker, and myself) decided to test the waters for a Guggenheim campaign. As with NYU, the goal would be to raise labor standards and practices by putting public pressure on a high-profile brand name. The museum had already approached galleries with a view to acquiring works for its collection, and so the opportunity arose to raise the issue by blocking permission for the sales. Several artists agreed to do so, and the names of others were gathered soon afterwards. Since they stood to forsake a good deal of revenue from any sales, their commitment entailed considerable personal sacrifice. A letter signed by 43 artists was sent to the Guggenheim in June 2010, and the first of many meetings over the course of the next few years was convened with officials, including museum director Richard Armstrong and Nancy Spector, deputy director and chief curator.

---

9. NYU and Executive Affairs Authority of Abu Dhabi, *Statement of Labor Values* (first posted February 3, 2010), http://tinyurl.com/q573wv6.

Model of Saadiyat Island in the TDIC headquarters—Guggenheim in the foreground (Credit: Gulf Labor)

From the outset, the Guggenheim leadership pledged its sympathy with Gulf Labor and its goals, and, privately at least, declared its willingness to pursue beefed-up employment policies with its partner TDIC. In September 2010, TDIC made public its Employment Practices Policy for all of its projects on Saadiyat, followed by the TDIC/Guggenheim Statement of Shared Values.[10] Though they were slightly weaker than the NYUAD Statement of Labor Values, these documents included solid provisions related to, among other things, the payment of recruitment fees, freedom of movement for workers, health and safety provisions, accommodations, monitoring of wage payments, and rest and leisure time for workers. In response, Gulf Labor pushed for the appointment of a non-profit monitor, visibly independent of ties to contractors or to Abu Dhabi authorities, to enforce these provisions. In June 2011, PricewaterhouseCoopers (PwC)—decidedly not on Gulf Labor's recommended list— was commissioned by TDIC to oversee labor compliance among the subcontractors engaged on Saadiyat projects.

In the interim, little progress had been made in talks between Gulf Labor and the Guggenheim. Our perception was that the museum's capacity to take decisive action was heavily constrained by the terms under which the franchising and licensing of the Guggenheim identity was contracted to TDIC. As with NYUAD, the purchase of the use of the brand name also entailed tight UAE control over all aspects of the delivery of the buildings and their infrastructure. Consequently, Gulf Labor decided to make its letter public and announce a museum boycott at the 2011 March Meeting of the Sharjah Biennial. The petition brought attention to the moral quandary faced by artworld professionals who might be approached with a commission from the Guggenheim Abu Dhabi: "no one should be asked to exhibit or perform in a building that has been constructed and maintained on the backs of exploited employees." The boycott petition caught the attention of the artworld, and more than 2,000 artists, curators, and writers signed up. Notably, Gulf Labor has never sought to "police" the terms of non-cooperation with the museum. Signatories choose how they will interpret their own solidarity; some have extended their embargo to all branches of the

---

10. TDIC, *Employment Practices Policy* (first posted September 23, 2010), http://tinyurl.com/qzeuxh5.

museum, and others to the Louvre Abu Dhabi, in the absence of a serious counterpart campaign on the part of French artists.

The boycott went public at the height of the Arab Spring. In response to a request for GCC intervention in March 2011, the UAE sent troops to put down a popular insurgency in Bahrain. A few weeks later, Jack Persakian, artistic director of the Sharjah Foundation, was dismissed in the wake of Emirati complaints about a work by Algerian artist-activist Mustapha Benfodil that had been included in the Biennial. Under the aegis of the Sultan's daughter Sheikha Hoor al-Qasimi, the Foundation had become the UAE's most progressive advocate for the arts, and so this act of censorship was a profound setback for the regional and international arts community. In response, a "Sharjah Call for Action," which proposed a boycott of the Biennial, collected more than 1,500 signatories.

In the years that followed, the Sharjah Foundation restored its reputation as a GCC haven for open aesthetic expression, in part by soliciting the involvement of the region's most virtuoso artists, including many Gulf Labor boycott signatories. But the Persakian incident, among other skirmishes, was a stark reminder that institutional guarantees of speech protection could always be overruled by the insistence of local elites on strictures governing what sorts of material can be exhibited, spoken, and performed. At the same time, artists with precarious livelihoods—like underpaid academics—were prone to a more familiar form of censorship: the market lure of being bought off. After all, Gulf money has purchased everything else, including some of the most prized real estate in the world's financial capitals. Speech and expression are easier to buy, and much cheaper, than chunks of Mayfair or Central Park South.

As the sentiment underlying the Arab Spring spread to the Gulf, the outbreak of open speech was nipped in the bud. On April 11, Ahmed Mansoor, an engineer and human rights advocate, and Nasser bin Ghaith, an Emirati economist and lecturer at the Sorbonne's Abu Dhabi branch, were arrested for their pro-democracy activities. Three more arrests followed, with dozens more interrogated by police, and the subsequent trial of the "UAE Five" attracted international condemnation. The five were released from prison following a 16-day hunger strike, but the crackdown has left a palpable chill over public expression of dissent. In the wake of his release, Mansoor was attacked and beaten, and deprived of some of his assets.[11] In the years that followed, investigative journalists who wrote exposés of conditions in UAE labor camps were deported or denied entry. Human Rights Watch (HRW) pioneered this kind of investigation with its 2006 report, *Building Towers, Cheating Workers*.[12] An HRW researcher, Nicholas McGeehan, was barred from re-entry in 2013 after conducting field research on Saadiyat Island sites, and Sarah Leah Whitson, HRW's regional director, was also barred from entry. The results of that research were eventually published in February 2015, and they centered on labor violations in the construction of NYU Abu Dhabi and the Louvre.[13]

By early 2013, the workforce on Saadiyat had multiplied and construction of the Louvre and NYUAD, along with hotel and villa projects, was picking up pace. As the year progressed, accounts of worker resistance trickled out, though many more went unreported. Almost 7,000 employees of Arabtec, the largest construction company in the UAE and a major subcontractor on the Louvre project, went on strike in May of that year. They were housed in four different labor camps in Dubai and Abu Dhabi, including on Saadiyat Island itself, and so the strike required close coordination. Workers were warned that they faced arrest and deportation if they did not go back to work. As many as 700 were eventually sent home after periods of detention. The Arabtec strike was followed in June by a work stoppage by several hundred Al-Reyami workers, some of them employed at NYUAD. A series of strikes and disturbances in the Saadiyat Accommodation Village (SAV), a model labor camp built to house all workers employed on TDIC projects, culminated in a violent confrontation between Pakistani and Bangladeshi workers in August.[14] Not long afterward, a two-day strike

---

11. Mansoor's plight is described in Molly Crabapple, "Slaves of Happiness Island," *Vice* (August 4, 2014), http://tinyurl.com/mocmf74.

12. HRW followed this up in 2012 with a report entitled *The Island of Happiness Revisited*, and in 2014 published a report on the abuse of female domestic workers, *I Already Bought You*.

13. Human Rights Watch, *Migrant Workers' Rights on Saadiyat Island in the United Arab Emirates* (February 10, 2015).

14. Shane McGinley, "Mass Brawl at Arabtec Labour Camp Leaves 40 in Hospital," *Arabian Business* (August 22, 2013), http://tinyurl.com/nx6qko5.

by BK Gulf employees stopped work at the NYUAD site. Housed in Camp 42 in Jebel Ali, Dubai, and in the Aldar camp on Yas Island, the strike leaders were rounded up by riot police, many wearing balaclavas and swinging batons, and were detained in Dubai Central Prison, where they were beaten and eventually sent home without a dirham in their pockets.[15] In the weeks following, hundreds of BK Gulf workers were rounded up and transferred to confinement in Camp 42 before being terminated and deported. In this way, the labor camp was effectively transformed overnight into a detention facility.

In October 2013, at the Venice Biennale, Gulf Labor launched its *52 Weeks* project. Each week, one of an international array of artists, writers, and activists was asked to submit a work, a text, or an action. Almost all of the contributions are reproduced in the dossier at the end of this volume. The breadth and quality of the submissions show how widely the issues resonated. In addition, *52 Weeks* broadened the tactical scope of the campaign, allowing the commissioned artists to make connections with other struggles relating to labor and the political economy of the artworld.

No Debt is an Island, a November 2013 contribution to *52 Weeks*, traced the connections between debt extracted from workers in their home countries and the Emirates, and the debt burden of students and artists in the US. The project included a call for action in February 2014, which became a point of origin for G.U.L.F. (Global Ultra Luxury Faction), a Gulf Labor spinoff devoted to direct action. The two February G.U.L.F. actions, which took place at NYU and at the Guggenheim in New York, drew together activists from NYU's Coalition for Fair Labor, Occupy Museums, and Gulf Labor. The latter action, which took place inside the museum, was the first of four "occupations" that occurred over the course of 2014.

Each occupation was planned to imitate the style of the exhibition showing at the time, and to expose the workings of the institution by calling out the leadership and trustees. The first three were conducted as performances in the spirit of the museum's Italian Futurist show, and included the hanging of quasi-Futurist graphics and man-

---

15. Tom South and Archie Bland, "Dubai Workers for British Firm Beaten by Police Over Strike," *Independent* (May 25, 2014), http://tinyurl.com/mf8djt4.

NYUAD workers sharing a small room in downtown Abu Dhabi
(Credit: Sergey Ponomarev/The New York Times/Redux)

ifestos. Number two included a spectacular drop of thousands of petro-dollars, while the fourth one aligned Gulf Labor's new campaign phase, Countdown, with the museum's *Countdown to Zero* exhibit. This last one was accompanied by a protest, called *Eat Up! Speak Up!*, outside the Guggenheim's annual fundraising dinner: "Guests will be feasting royally at $75,000 tax-deductible tables. On the other side of the world, Guggenheim Abu Dhabi's migrant workers are being exploited while having meager rations on their plates and very little time to prepare their meals after a punishing 12 hour work day."

In March 2015, Gulf Labor sent a new set of proposals to the Guggenheim leadership. These included the establishment of a Bonus and Debt Settlement Fund to give each Guggenheim Abu Dhabi worker an additional 2,000 USD, the average amount of the recruitment debt burden in the UAE; a living wage for workers in Abu Dhabi, to help compensate for severe wage depression and pay inequalities; and the freedom to associate and collectively address grievances, to help protect against the growing cycle of intimidation, imprisonment, and deportation. In its response, the Guggenheim Foundation insisted that meeting these demands lay "outside the Guggenheim's range of authority," because "they are matters of federal law." Yet there is nothing in UAE labor law to prevent an employer from paying a living wage or compensating workers for recruitment fees. In fact, the Employment Practices Policy (EPP) on Saadiyat Island specifically instructs them to do so.

The intransigence of this response from the Foundation capped five years of inaction on the museum's part. To mark the occasion, G.U.L.F. mounted its most ambitious occupation on May Day. Once again, the props for the action were synchronized with the aesthetics of the museum's current exhibition (by On Kawara). Solidarity messages were prepared specifically for the security guards, who were being paid a mere $11 an hour, and thousands of pamphlets were circulated for the purpose of public education. This time, the action had the public support of a host of labor and human rights groups. The primary goal, to hold the central floor of the museum, was achieved, and the authorities decided to shut down the museum (allegedly for the first time ever). While the occupation continued for the rest of the day, the Guerrilla Girls, the Taxi Drivers Alliance, and other South Asian solidarity groups demonstrated outside the museum. In another, more public display of intransigence, the museum's directors decided they would make no effort to engage with those in occupation; as demonstrators, we were treated as if we were hostage-takers. One week later, to mark its first activity as an official participant in the Venice Biennale, Gulf Labor collaborated with G.U.L.F. on a dramatic occupation (by boat) of the Guggenheim's museum on the Grand Canal. As a result, the request for a meeting with trustees was better received.

G.U.L.F. was formed to escalate the pressure on the museum over its complicity in migrant worker abuse on Saadiyat. But it also aimed at exposing the role played by museums in showcasing, laundering, and magnifying wealth accumulation among the ultra-luxury class whose gravitational pull exerts more and more influence over the artworld. Christie's ended 2014 with the highest-ever total for an art auction, grossing 852.9 million USD for only 75 lots in its November 12 sales event in New York.[16] Its October Dubai auction far exceeded estimates, and set 19 new records for sales of regional artists. Fairs like Art Basel and ArtBasel Miami are incubators for high-end shopping orgies now that the social status of hedge fund managers and other financial tycoons has to be confirmed through blue-chip art acquisition. Many of the purchases end up in freeports, the tax-free storage facilities sprouting up in Switzerland and other countries, where they can be privately exhibited by dealers and collectors for re-sale to other members of the 1 percent club.[17] All of this conspicuous consumption has given rise to a new wave of museums built to house private collections: Walmart heiress Alice Walton's Crystal Bridges Museum of American Art in Bentonville, Arkansas; François Pinault's Palazzo Grassi and Punta della Dogana in Venice; and Eli Broad's new museum in downtown Los Angeles. By one estimate, there are as many as 350 private contemporary museums in 46 countries (48 in the US, and six in Beijing alone).[18]

These collections and buildings often draw on public resources to glorify the private owner of the plunder. This pattern of extraction dates from the museum-

16. Dan Duray, "Christie's Contemporary Art Sale Nets $852.9 M., All-Time Auction Record," *Art News* (November 12, 2014), http://tinyurl.com/k7r9ryj.

17. "Freeports: Über-Warehouses for the Ultra-Rich," *Economist* (November 23, 2013).

18. Scott Reyburn, "New Report Builds a Profile of the Elusive Art Collector," *New York Times* (January 16, 2015).

building craze of the 1990s, though it has recently become a more direct transfer of public funds into private pockets. In the course of that decade, large-scale art venues were funded as drivers of urban renewal, and many of them ended up boosting land value, rents, and tourist revenue in select cities. A contemporary example is the proposed allocation of more than 130 million euros of taxpayer money (along with a prime harborfront chunk of public land) to a Guggenheim branch museum in Helsinki. Local opposition to the funding plan has taken root in every sector of Finnish society, where the arts are still viewed as a vital public component of the welfare state. On the other side, advocates of the museum saw an opportunity to replicate the "Bilbao Effect" (evoking the success of the Gehry-designed Guggenheim Bilbao to attract tourism to the depressed Basque region of Spain) by strengthening the city's brand in the global competition for attention and investment.

As part of its March week of action, G.U.L.F. issued a press release from the Guggenheim announcing a call for the ethical redesign of the Abu Dhabi branch. The spoof, curated on a new website (www.globalguggenheim.org) that captured a good deal of traffic to the official museum sites, was resurrected in a different, more serious format later in the year. In response to the polarization of public debate around the proposed Guggenheim Helsinki, G.U.L.F. co-sponsored an alternative design competition—The Next Helsinki (www.nexthelsinki.org)—launched at the same time that the Guggenheim's official competition closed in September 2014. Working with the Finnish arts organization Checkpoint Helsinki and the New York architecture group Terreform, and drawing on the expertise of an international jury, G.U.L.F. and its partners called for a wide range of submissions that acknowledged artistic expression as an everyday activity infusing the urban fabric.[19] This expansive vision of art and urbanism was in marked contrast to the Guggenheim's exhibitionary Gehry-style box—an exclusionary act of quarantine, answerable, increasingly, to the artworld marketplace or to a tourist trade driven by the circulation of blockbuster shows. The competition attracted 220 entries from more than 42 countries, and the volume and quality spoke to a hunger for alternatives to the superstar museum

---

19. Oliver Wainwright, "Helsinki v Guggenheim: the backlash against the global megabrand is on," *Guardian* (September 11, 2014), http://tinyurl.com/m8groer.

typology. A public announcement of the shortlist in April 2015 highlighted the divide between the respective design philosophies of the two competitions.

Another Gulf Labor spinoff, Who Builds Your Architecture? (WBYA?), took on the starchitect paradigm in other ways. Formed to press the architecture profession on its ethical responsibilities toward those who erect its buildings, WBYA? Coordinates an ongoing series of workshops, panels, exhibits, and presentations focusing on the role of construction workers in the building process. The profession's neglect was highlighted by Zaha Hadid's widely scrutinized comment about worker protections at her al-Wakrah stadium in Doha; "I have nothing to do with the workers. . . . It's not my duty as an architect to look at it. . . . I have no power to do anything about it."[20] At the time of her comment, Nepalese workers were dying in large numbers (more than a thousand estimated deaths in two years) due to heat exposure and exhaustion from the speed-up demanded by Qatar's nation-building campaign, which will be capped by World Cup stadia like the al-Wakrah.

Since Gulf Labor first met with Guggenheim officials in 2010, its dialogue with the museum has been intermittent but ongoing. At times, we were also in direct communication with TDIC spokespersons, though that dialogue often took place through public statements and press releases. Shortly before the first G.U.L.F. action, and in response to our criticism of the second PwC monitoring report, TDIC issued another invitation to visit the SAV (the first visit was conducted in 2011, during the Sharjah Biennale). In March 2014, a Gulf Labor team spent a day at the village and in discussions with TDIC officials. Clients and other foreign dignitaries are routinely taken to the SAV for visible assurance that Saadiyat workers are well treated and housed in this well-equipped, showpiece facility (some would call it a Potemkin village). Our tour afforded us a close-up view of the careful techniques used to promote the facility itself, which boasts ping-pong tables, art workshops, and a well-manicured cricket pitch, but has the feel of a detention camp. Constructed, according to

20. Quoted in James Riach, "Zaha Hadid Defends Qatar World Cup Role Following Migrant Worker Deaths," *Guardian* (February 25, 2014), http://tinyurl.com/me5y4cz.

ILO guidelines, with a capacity for 20,000 occupants, it is typically half-empty because subcontractors have to pay a high premium to house their workers there; indeed, for many, the accommodation costs are higher than what they pay their workers. Despite the EPP regulations that require SAV residence, many Saadiyat workers can be found in much less adequate accommodations on the mainland, far from the construction sites.

Over several days, our team visited these more informal labor camps to inter-view workers in environments that were not heavily surveilled. Unannounced visits to migrant labor camps are guaranteed to attract suspicion pretty much anywhere you go, and in the UAE, the authorities are particularly sensitive to unofficial inspections of this sort. Even so, it was disquieting to discover that we were followed everywhere by a car, whose driver clearly wanted us to know he was there. It took a day to figure out that our whereabouts were being tracked through a cellphone.

It did not take us long to confirm, from spot interviews, what investigative teams from Human Rights Watch, the *Guardian*, and the *Independent* had found. Work-ers offered ample testimony about violations of the TDIC and NYUAD labor values, including wage theft, substandard housing, confiscated passports, compulsory over-time, and harsh punishments for any expression of grievances. Mott McDonald and PwC had only interviewed workers in their employers' offices or in the model villages, and had not ventured off-island to the cruel archipelago of labor camps that encircles Abu Dhabi and Dubai. Moreover, the monitors' reports made little or no mention of labor unrest. Our team collected details about the BK Gulf strike, which was later cor-roborated and reported in a front page *New York Times* story about labor compliance violations on the NYUAD campus project.[21] In a first, the newspaper was not printed in the UAE on the day the story appeared. Further reporting drew attention to a con-flict of interest involving NYU board member Khaldoon Khalifa Al Mubarak, who also happened to be the chief executive of the Mubadala Development Company, com-missioned to oversee the construction of the campus.[22] In the wake of the *New York*

---

21. Ariel Kaminer and Sean O'Driscoll, "Workers at N.Y.U.'s Abu Dhabi Site Faced Harsh Conditions," *New York Times* (May 18, 2014).

22. Andrew Ross Sorkin, "N.Y.U. Crisis in Abu Dhabi Stretches to Wall Street," *New York Times* (May 26, 2014).

Recreation time in Saadiyat Accommodation Village—wall image from inside the facility (Credit: Gulf Labor)

Times article, co-author Sean O'Driscoll, the only UAE-based journalist who was brave enough to cover the plight of migrant workers, was deported, but not before bribes were offered to him by high-ranking officials to plant positive stories about the UAE in the international press.[23] Writing under a pseudonym, O'Driscoll had co-authored many of the big investigative stories about UAE worker abuse, and his deportation deprived us of an invaluable local source.

In the course of our own camp visits with O'Driscoll, we found many workers like Ganesh, whose story is worth recounting briefly here. We spoke with him and his work mates into the early morning hours, in a makeshift restaurant in the Al Quoz industrial area near Dubai. Despite frequent power cuts, the staff still managed to put decent Punjabi food on the table. Slightly built with a dazzling smile, Ganesh switched between Hindi and English to explain his predicament. Owed a year's worth of wages by the manpower firm that brought him from Nepal, he was unable to leave the UAE because his sponsor, Robodh, had his passport. His labor visa had expired, and he was surviving on canteen credit and illegal work stints. Paying off recruitment debts had consumed his first two years of hard labor in the UAE. During that time, his family's subsistence farm had been at his creditor's disposal. "Three or four out of ten lose their land," he reckoned, "when they can't repay on time." Far from being an incidental by-product of the recruitment system (from which rapacious middlemen extract yes their cut), debts like those incurred by Ganesh are key to the entire labor regime. No one can get to the Gulf without taking on debts, and no one would work for such low wages and under such poor conditions unless they were under the gun to pay them off.

Ganesh's next decade in the UAE was spent scratching out thin remittances to send to his wife and children in the Himalaya foothills. On some work projects, he was housed three hours from the construction site. To put in a mandatory 12-hour shift, "I had to wake up at 4 am," he reported, "and then had to cook my dinner after I returned at 10 pm." Today, he is a much weaker and thinner man than when his original recruiter asked him to run around with a 90 pound cement bag to prove he could make the grade. A year after we met with him, he still had not been paid.

---

23. Sean O'Driscoll, "How Speaking Irish Saved My Life on the Run from United Arab Emirates Police," *Irish Central* (March 13, 2015), http://tinyurl.com/mljssj5.

Taking Gulf Labor testimony in a Musaffah labor camp, Abu Dhabi, March 2014 (Credit: Gulf Labor)

In May 2014, Gulf Labor issued a report based on our team's findings (See pp. 150–70). Despite the establishment of labor values and provisions, chronic problems persisted: workers' wages on Saadiyat had remained at very low levels; the persistent issue of recruitment fees had not been resolved; grievances went unheard; and off-island living conditions were well below standard. The team was impressed by some aspects of the SAV, but concluded that the social isolation and high-security nature of the facility is not a good model to be followed in the UAE in general. The report also recommended a relocation fee program for paying off recruitment debts; adopting an Abu Dhabi living wage for all Saadiyat workers; establishing workers' councils to maintain communications with, and channel grievances to, the UAE authorities; and reforming compliance monitoring methods.

The NYUAD campus opened in September, though shoddy installation of the cooling system made it all but uninhabitable for the first several months. The Abu Dhabi authorities had commissioned Nardello, a New York–based investigative firm, to look into the worker abuses documented by Gulf Labor, the *New York Times*, and other newspapers. Nardello's report, issued in April 2015, revealed that a third of the workers (10,000) engaged in construction of the campus had been excluded from the NYUAD protections regarding fair wages, living conditions, and debt reimbursement.[24] This "exemption" was applied to small subcontractors whose work fell below a $1m threshold or was completed in less than a month, but its existence incentivized larger firms to break subcontracts into smaller portions in order to avoid compliance costs. So, too, only a handful of workers had their recruitment fees reimbursed, due to the university's narrow interpretation of the stated requirement to discharge these debts.[25] While the report verified many of the allegations made by Gulf Labor, the *New York Times*, and others, it made no mention of the police violence directed at striking workers. In response, the NYU administration pledged to reimburse the workers who had been disenfranchised from the protections, though it was by no means clear how they would be located.

---

24. Nardello & Co., *Report of the Independent Investigator into Allegations of Labor and Compliance Issues During the Construction of the NYU Abu Dhabi Campus on Saadiyat Island* (April 16, 2015), http://tinyurl.com/nceunzm.

25. Stephanie Saul, "N.Y.U. Labor Guidelines Failed to Protect 10,000 Workers in Abu Dhabi, Report Says," *New York Times* (April 16, 2015).

GUGGENHEIM DIRECTOR RICHARD ARMSTRONG'S
ANNUAL SALARY: $612,550

MIGRANT CONSTRUCTION WORKER'S
ANNUAL SALARY: $1500

GUGGENHEIM ABU DHABI:
MODERN ART, MADE POSSIBLE BY MODERN-DAY SLAVERY.

ITUC campaign against Dior for its sponsorship of the Guggenheim (Credit: ITUC)

In March and May of 2015, Gulf Labor teams returned to the UAE for another round of field research. The Louvre project was nearing completion and work was expected to begin on the primary phase of the Guggenheim Abu Dhabi. My own participation in the March trip was blocked when I was denied permission to board a flight at JFK airport. Unlike the NGO investigators, I am an NYU professor, whose academic freedom and rights of smooth passage to the UAE is supposed to be guaranteed by NYU's agreement with its Emirati partner. The resulting scandal generated a very public debate about the hollow nature of these guarantees on the part of NYUAD and the museums.[26] The incident clearly demonstrated that promises of academic or artistic freedom on the part of university or museum administrators mean little when they can so easily be overridden by the autocratic exercise of state authority. In addition, a private investigator had been hired to interrogate academic acquaintances about myself and *New York Times* journalist Ariel Kaminer. The exposure of the investigator's activities cast even more public suspicion over the effort by UAE authorities to block access and suppress coverage of labor abuses.[27]

In the lead-up to the May field trip (which coincided with the Sharjah March Meeting), Ashok Sukumaran was denied a visa to travel to the UAE, and then Walid Raad was turned back at the Dubai airport. Despite efforts to intercede by the leadership of both the Guggenheim and the Sharjah Foundation (the former concluded that the issue was "outside our sphere of influence"), the travel bans on these longstanding Gulf Labor members were not overturned.[28] In some ways, this repressive response was evidence that, far from promoting liberalization of speech, the presence of the museums and the university appeared to be generating exactly the opposite effect.

---

26. Andrew Ross, "Professor Non Grata: Andrew Ross on Collusion and Delusion," *Chronicle of Higher Education* (March 18, 2015), http://tinyurl.com/qxtmbh5; Stephanie Saul, "N.Y.U. Professor Is Barred by United Arab Emirates," *New York Times* (March 16, 2015), http://tinyurl.com/kxqm4om.

27. Jim Dwyer, "Murky Inquiry Targets Critic of N.Y.U. Role in Abu Dhabi, and a Reporter," *New York Times* (March 26, 2015).

28. Noelle Bodick, "Gulf Labor Artists Walid Raad, Ashok Sukumaran Barred from U.A.E.," *BlouinArtinfo* (May 14, 2015), http://tinyurl.com/lsnl5wc; Gulf Labor, "More Members of Gulf Labor Denied Entry and Turned Away From the U.A.E.," (May 15, 2015), http://tinyurl.com/qano7g4.

Since the NGO investigators had already been barred from entry, some members of the Gulf Labor team were in a unique position to gather interviews and document conditions. Some of the team had previously visited deported workers in India, in December 2014, and were able to take testimony about their harsh treatment at the hands of the UAE police and their ejection from the country with barely a rupee in their pockets. The field trips in March and May documented a range of forced labor practices and added to the archive of exploitation. The evidence gathered by the teams flatly contradicted the rosy propaganda pumped out by UAE authorities for publication in state-approved media like *The National*, the Emirates English-language daily.[29]

The wealth and *de facto* power of Emirati elites is immense, and the board members of NYU and the Guggenheim are equally rich and influential. How did Gulf Labor persevere in the face of such formidable adversaries, and why has it achieved some measure of success? Campaign strategy was an important component. The tactics of the coalition have been diverse and well-considered, and they are discussed in more detail in other chapters of this volume. But there were also some large-scale factors and conditions operating in favor of our tactics.

Over the course of the last decade, Western high-culture institutions have been following in the path of corporations that went offshore 20 years before. The underlying motive—to beef up their balance sheet—is more or less the same, but the rationale for operating overseas has to be presented as more than a monetary undertaking. More often than not, these initiatives are couched in rhetoric about spreading the virtues of Western-style liberal arts, which at times can sound little different from the 19th-century credo of the *mission civilisatrice*. When quizzed about the appearance of being in bed with authoritarian rulers—the preferred destinations of many of these institutions are China and the Persian Gulf states—administrators will insist

29. Editorial, "Workers Offer Another Side to the Labour Story," *The National* (March 23, 2015), http://tinyurl.com/nutevrk; Anwar Ahmad, "Special Report: Abu Dhabi Invests in Worker Comfort," *The National* (March 23, 2015), http://tinyurl.com/q8tky3n.

that their presence allows them to "lead by example." Moreover, institutions with reputations as "leaders" do not expect to have their decisions challenged from their rank
and file employees. Yale University administrators, for example, were surprised to
field criticism from faculty members following Yale's agreement to a joint venture
with the National University of Singapore; the faculty cited Singapore's "history of
lack of respect for civil and political rights." And NYU's John Sexton has faced down a
barrage of criticism for his expansionist efforts, some of which fed into faculty votes
of no confidence in his presidency.

But the rhetoric of the civilizing West also creates an opening to challenge the
basic terms of debt peonage that underwrite workers' contracts in the UAE. Prominent, PR-sensitive outfits like NYU, the Guggenheim, the Louvre, and the British
Museum (chief consultants to Saadiyat's Zayed National Museum) are susceptible to
the tarnishing of their brand. The elevated cultural standing of their names and their
institutional missions is wholly incompatible with the taint of labor and human rights
abuse—they cannot afford to be associated with such tawdriness.

Fifteen years ago, anti-sweatshop activists used the same tactic of shaming
global brands like Nike and the Gap in order to publicize labor abuses in the offshore
factories of the apparel industry. Just as the garment brands tried to deflect responsibility further down the subcontracting chain, so too have these high-profile educational and cultural institutions. Across the board, their alibi boils down to a simple
claim: *We have little control over what the subcontractors do or pay.* It took many years
of campaigning and legal pressure to force the apparel brands to accept some liability
for abuses that occur all the way down the chain. Unlike garment factories, however,
which can be moved overnight to more obscure locations, the museums and the NYU
campus are there to stay, offering long-term leverage to activists. And while apparel
manufacturers have little internal accountability to their users, universities have obligations to their faculty and students, and museums are answerable to public ethics
upheld by the more conscientious factions of the artworld.

Nor are these cultural bodies quite like corporations, bent on repatriating their
offshore profits as quickly as possible. There's no question that their fiscal managers
and boards are all too happy to take the loot. To bring the Louvre to the Gulf, Abu
Dhabi authorities agreed to a 1.3 billion USD package, including 520 million USD

for use of the name alone. The bankrolling of NYU Abu Dhabi is estimated to be in the billions. But how do administrators combat the perception of selling out? How do they make the arrangement palatable to the museums' constituency, and to the faculty and students of the university, all of whom may find any mention of hard cash to be distasteful? Delivering a high-caliber cultural or educational product is different from manufacturing a shoe that will pass some minimal quality standard. Maintaining the good will of all the participants in a cultural process is a challenge at the best of times, and it is even more arduous if their resident cynicism about monetizing also has to be overcome. Ultimately, no matter how much time and money is invested in these efforts, they can easily run aground when some endemically corrupt association surfaces.

Economically, it would not be difficult to treat the UAE's workers well. The issue is not money—the Emirates are awash with resources—but power. The *kafala* system is serviceable to Gulf elites because it ensures that a large and vulnerable servant class is readily at hand to perform all required tasks. Recruitment debt is central to the system—no one would labor under such conditions unless they had to pay off the debt. The employer-sponsors who keep passports and who withhold wages are the labor regulators, and the threat of deportation is a persuasive enforcer against those who voice grievances. Yet workers still do organize and resist. Every week, a protest or strike action breaks out.

Despite the bans and deportations, the cause of the advocates and activists is growing in strength, and the workers' rights groups in source countries are applying ever more pressure on the recruitment networks. The construction of Saadiyat Island will be an ongoing target for years to come, the 2020 World Expo in Dubai is on the horizon, and the build-out of the 2022 World Cup infrastructure in Qatar has already proven to be a major point of leverage. By the time the first ball is kicked, we are convinced that the *kafala* system will be defunct, relegated to the swollen historical archive of heinous labor practices.

Gulf Dreams for Justice: Migrant Workers and New Political Futures

Paula Chakravartty and Nitasha Dhillon[1]

Since 2006, migrant workers have launched a spate of labor actions and strikes in the UAE. The profiling of these actions by independent journalists, scholars, and workers' advocates, combined with mounting evidence about the mistreatment and deaths of workers building the World Cup infrastructure in neighboring Qatar, has attracted heightened global scrutiny of the plight of the workforce underpinning the Gulf states' growth. Of the roughly 22 million migrants who make up the majority populations of the six Gulf Cooperation Council (GCC) countries, South Asian workers have been the primary contributors to the region's pell-mell development since the second oil boom of the 1970s. In the UAE, up to 90 percent of whose nine million residents are migrants, "low-skilled" workers from India make up the largest population (between 2.2 and 2.8 million), followed by workers from Pakistan (900,000–1.2 million), Bangladesh (700,000–1 million) and the Philippines (470,000–680,000).[2] Workers from Nepal, Indonesia, Kenya, Nigeria, and elsewhere in the Middle East and North Africa account for smaller portions. These numbers reflect a notable spike after the speculative real estate boom began in 2002, when the Gulf's investors returned to

---

1. We wish to thank Amin Husain, Zachary Lockman, Stephanie Luce, Vasuki Nesiah, Parimal Sudhakar, and Sher Singh for ongoing conversations that have helped shape our research and writing. We also wish to thank Andrew Ross for his patience and editorial guidance.

2. These figures are compiled from: *Total Migrant Stock at Mid-Year by Origin and Destination 2013*, United Nations Department of Economic and Social Affairs—Population Division (2013); Binsal Abdul Khader, "Indian Worker Pensions in UAE Soon," *Gulf News* (May 26, 2013), http://tinyurl.com/nfyahyb. For further discussion, see Froilan T. Malit Jr. and Ali Al Youha, "Labor Migration in the United Arab Emirates: Challenges and Responses," *Migration Policy Institute* (September 18, 2013), http://tinyurl.com/n49h49w.

the region following September 11 and a decade-long steep escalation of crude prices. Dubai became the region's growth icon, symbolized by a wave of "international mega–real estate projects" aimed at global elite investors.[3]

The developers' appetite for cheap sources of labor in this period was insatiable. But just as the 2008 financial crisis disproportionately hurt African American and Latino home owners targeted by risky "sub-prime" loans in the US, the popping of the Gulf's real estate bubble took its worst toll on the five million (out of an estimated 22 million) migrant workers, who lost their jobs overnight and were sent home.[4] Throughout this decade of boom and bust, working conditions and wages for an already precarious and indebted workforce—one that despite its size is not covered by the 1990 International Convention of the Rights of All Migrants because the host governments insist that they are "temporary workers"—have significantly deteriorated. Moreover, following the Arab Uprisings in 2011, GCC states, fearful of internal instability, have ramped up the "securitization of immigration policy" to further curb labor militancy.[5]

In this chapter, we seek to deepen understanding of migrant workers as active participants in the evolving political struggles over *their* futures and *our* solidarities. Given constraints of space we focus on male migrant workers but recognize that the largely feminized domestic workforce is an equally important component of the story that is also drawing global attention for reform and redress. We write not only as scholars and activists, but also as migrants from India to Canada and the US (via, in one of our cases, Qatar). While ours are migrant stories of middle class/caste privilege and gendered differences, we begin by recognizing that international migration itself is a relative privilege. In this sense, the workers in question do not become migrants only when they leave India to work in Dubai or Doha. They become migrants when they leave their home villages because neoliberal reforms have meant lack of land to

3. Omar Al Shehabi, "Histories of Migration to the Gulf," in Abdulhabi Khalaf et al. (eds.), *Transit States: Labour Migration and Citizenship in the Gulf* (London: Pluto Press, 2015), pp. 3–38.

4. ILO estimate, cited in Michelle Buckley, "Construction Work, 'Bachelor' Builders and the Intersectional Politics of Urbanisation in Dubai," in Khalaf et al. (eds.), *Transit States*, pp. 132–52.

5. Abdulhadi Khalaf, "The Politics of Migration," in Khalaf et al. (eds.), *Transit States*, pp. 39–56.

cultivate, decline of paid work in their hometowns, and the desperate need to service debts that are calculated bets on the promise of their "Gulf Dreams" for dignity and a better life for their families. To make sense of the material futures imagined by India's migrant workers to the Gulf we have to better understand the conditions of urbanization, migration, and mobility within post-liberalization India. This larger context of migration will help explain why the spate of labor protest in the Gulf calls for a politics of *solidarity* and not one of *rescue*.

First, we will offer a brief overview of the history of Gulf capitalism and its racial and gendered division of labor. Then, drawing on field research in the Gulf and in India, we will summarize a series of interviews conducted across four states in India in 2014–15 with labor activists and migrant workers returned from the Gulf. In this section, we also draw on a second series of interviews with Indian, Pakistani, and Bangladeshi workers in the UAE.[6] With each of the interview sets, we share some of the details of individual migrant work experience, while presenting the collective experience and vision(s) for social justice that were shared by both India- and UAE-based workers. The objective here is not simply a clearer understanding leading to more effective strategies of resistance or policy reform, but rather to build a necessary foundation for any shared understanding of the meaning of solidarity itself, which is a prerequisite for collective liberation.

Beyond Orientalist rescue

The segregation of millions of permatemp "bachelor builders"—with no formal rights to association or representation—into spatially isolated labor camps has brought international shame upon the GCC countries.[7] But what differentiates the conditions of these migrant workers from the plight of undocumented workers in the United

---

6. Interviews and documentation in both India and the UAE were conducted by Nitasha Dhillon and Amin Hussein. Additional research was collected, translated, and transcribed in collaboration with the Delhi-based Society for Labour and Development.

7. Buckley, "Urbanisation in Dubai" (2015) considers the common term "bachelor builder" to provide a thoughtful analysis of the gendered and racialized dimensions of migrant work experiences in the Gulf.

States and Europe? They, too, face insecurity, racialized violence, and scant protection of their labor rights, especially since national governments in the global North have progressively restricted the terms of migration and enforced harsh policies of detention and deportation for "low-skilled" non-white migrants.[8]

The local particularities of the GCC's *kafala* work-permit sponsorship system are often framed by homegrown advocates of nation-building as a matter of "cultural difference." Criticisms of the system by "outsiders" (Gulf Labor or its NGO allies) are typically deflected as a form of ethnocentric insensitivity toward Arab cultural norms. By contrast, Western institutions, like NYU, the Guggenheim, and the Louvre, are warmly welcomed as proponents of liberal values and norms—freedom of speech, cross-cultural dialogue, and labor standards—through their very presence in the region. Yet in some of the outsiders' campaigns and in much of the Western media reportage, *kafala* is depicted as a form of "modern-day slavery" by summoning up stock images of anonymous suffering and calls for abolition from the West. This genre of criticism trades on two troubling Orientalist assumptions. First, that *kafala* is a premodern patronage system outside of liberal democratic norms. And second, that the migrant workers, driven to desperation by conditions in their home countries, are passive victims in need of rescue (by Western activists). Both of these need to be challenged if meaningful solidarity is to be forged between workers and transnational advocates.

Instead, as researchers and activists within the region have shown, *kafala* is best understood as a modern, and especially lucrative, visa-trading system.[9] The political compact that separates migrants from citizens within the GCC is not a product of pre-modern cultural difference. Instead, as scholars of "Gulf Capitalism" have established, the vast wealth from oil and natural gas produced largely for global markets enables the Gulf's ruling elites to "rent" foreign working classes, insuring against political demands that citizens might make. The enormous wealth gener-

---

8. Didier Fassin, "Policing Borders, Producing Boundaries: The Governmentality of Immigration in Dark Times," *Annual Review of Anthropology* 40, pp. 213–26.

9. For more discussion and an overview of the variation in the sponsorship system across Gulf states and reforms implemented, see Priyanka Motaparthy, "Understanding Kafala: An Archaic Law at Cross Purposes with Modern Development," *Migrant-rights.org* (March 11, 2015), http://tinyurl.com/lqjytvf.

ated from oil and gas is central to the means by which the ruling classes in the GCC maintain their autocratic power, protected in no small part by the United States and Western allies. Adam Hanieh argues that the "institutional arrangement of citizenship and differential laws for resident populations" allows for a spatial structuring of class "that has underpinned the process of state formation itself—enabling the Gulf's ascension as a core zone within the global economy."[10] This generates a "double exclusion": migrants are excluded from citizenship, while citizens are excluded from the private labor market.[11] Looking to circumvent political demands by the 10 to 15 percent of the population made up of nationals, Gulf monarchies, in collusion with Western interests, have "marginalized citizens from productive labor" as insurance against political dissent.[12] Designing and enforcing a system of "permanent temporary migration" to meet a broad range of economic demands has resulted in a racialized discrepancy in wages between migrant nationalities, high rates of exploitation, and a built-in instrument separating citizens from workers, for disciplining potential labor unrest.[13] In practice, *kafala* has become a for-profit, privatized sponsorship system that allows states to delegate oversight of migrants to either individual nationals or, more commonly, to a chain of South Asian brokers and middlemen who manage recruitment in the home countries and in the Gulf itself.[14]

The involvement of South Asian middlemen in the Gulf's visa trading system speaks to the sharp racial and class hierarchies segmenting Gulf migrants. At the top are white North American and Western European "expats," followed by non-national Arab and Asian professionals who are considered "migrants," even though

10. Adam Hanieh, *Capitalism and Class in the Gulf Arab States* (Denver: Palgrave McMillan, 2015); Adam Hanieh, "Overcoming Methodological Nationalism: Spatial Perspectives on Migration in the Gulf Arab States," in Khalaf et al. (eds.), *Transit States*, pp. 57–78.

11. Mohammed Dito, "Kafala: Foundations of Migrant Exclusion in GCC Labour Markets," in Khalaf et al. (eds.), *Transit States*, pp. 79–100.

12. Al Shehabi, "Histories of Migration to the Gulf," in Khalaf et al. (eds.), *Transit States*.

13. Hanieh, *Capitalism and Class in the Gulf Arab States*.

14. Neha Vora, *Impossible Citizens: Dubai's Indian Diaspora* (Durham: Duke University Press, 2013); Anjali Kamat, "The Men in the Middle," *Dissent Magazine* (Spring 2015), http://tinyurl.com/k53x34b.

many of them belong to multi-generational families and were born in the Gulf. The "middlemen" who broker the visa-trading system directly with migrant workers come from this group. Next down the ladder are South and East Asian "clerks" (office workers across various sectors), followed by the large majority of South and Southeast Asian manual and service workers, including the mostly female domestic labor force. The stark disparities within this hierarchy are perhaps more rigidly codified in the Gulf than elsewhere, in terms of uneven wages, ability to sponsor family members, access to housing and services, social status, surveillance of movement, and overall job security.[15] But to understand the particularities of the *kafala* system, we have to look far beyond local occupational structures.

The US and other Western powers have directly contributed to shaping the modern political architecture of the region, using the oil monarchies of the Gulf to subsidize the "carbon democracies" of the West.[16] This record casts doubt upon the idea that the GCC's exploited migrant workers can be liberated by Western values alone, whether transmitted through museums, universities, or oil companies. In his 2009 book *America's Kingdom: Mythmaking on the Saudi Oil Frontier*, Robert Vitalis shows how the Arabian American Oil Company (ARAMCO), an amalgamation of Western firms, implemented a Jim Crow colorline characteristic of American segregation in the postwar labor camps of Saudi Arabia. Responding to labor unrest in the sector, ARAMCO organized the camps on a racialized basis, with work, compensation, and housing segregated along ethnic lines in clear parallel to the treatment of African American workers in the US and non-White workers in the oil industry from South Asia and the Arab world.

The contradiction between Washington's promotion of Cold War democracy and freedom and ARAMCO's design and enforcement of the racial division of labor transplanted from the "original American empire" did not go unnoticed. Vitalis

---

15. Anh Nga Longva, "Neither Autocracy nor Democracy but Ethnocracy: Citizens, Expatriates and the Socio-political System in Kuwait," in Paul Dresch and James Picatori (eds.), *Monarchies and Nations: Globalisation and Identity in the Arab States of the Gulf* (London: I.B. Tauris, 2011); Neha Vora, *Impossible Citizens*; Neha Vora, "Expat /Expert Camps: Redefining 'Labour' Within Gulf Migration," in Khalaf et al. (eds.), *Transit States*, pp. 170–97.

16. Timothy Mitchell, *Carbon Democracy: Politics in the Age of Oil* (New York: Verso, 2011).

excerpts an oil worker's compelling testimony from a 1949 issue of a Pakistani newspaper: "Their color distinction and racial discrimination coupled with their haughtiness and high-handedness was at the root of every maneuver and machination devised to degrade and insult us."[17] For workers like these, the claim that US political and corporate interests promoted social uplift, let alone freedom, clearly rang hollow.

ARAMCO's segregated labor camps, as documented by Vitalis, were largely made up of Saudi and other Arab workers. The large-scale use of non-national, non-Arab workers through the *kafala* system employing a dominantly South Asian workforce in the region began on a significant scale only in the 1970s. Prior to that, labor unrest and strikes had led to the nationalization of Saudi oil, with Saudi national workers incorporated into public sector employment and migrant workers from Yemen, Egypt, and other parts of the Middle East and North Africa replacing local workers in the oil industry. But the post-1973 oil boom saw a significant growth in numbers of South Asian workers.[18] Saudi Arabia can be distinguished from other GCC countries, like Bahrain and Oman, both of which had ties to the subcontinent that predate European colonialism. What the Saudi case makes particularly explicit is that the racialized division of labor so characteristic of the Gulf today has deep colonial and neocolonial roots. American and European notions of white supremacy and European privilege continue to shape the institutionalization of racial hierarchies in the region, even as they are reinforced today by Arab and Asian forms of racial superiority.

The turn to an overwhelming majority South Asian labor force in the Gulf, beginning in the 1970s and accelerating through the 1990s, is often explained by the lower relative wages and higher numbers of reserve workers from the subcontinent. But this is only part of the story. The GCC states' initial preference in the 1960s for workers from Yemen, Egypt, Sudan, Jordan/Palestine, and Syria also shifted in large part because of political concerns. By the 1970s, leaders in the region were wary of

---

17. Robert Vitalis, *America's Kingdom: Mythmaking on the Saudi Oil Frontier* (New York: Verso, 2009), p. 102.

18. S. Irudaya Rajan and K.C. Zacharia, "Kerala Emigrants in the Gulf," *Middle East Institute* (February 2, 2010).

leftist pan-Arab political sensibilities, insurgent labor activism, and the growth of pro-Palestinian sentiment, among other non-economic factors

During the 1991 Gulf War, Palestinian and Yemeni workers were deported *en masse* from several GCC states because they were suspected of supporting Iraq's invasion of Kuwait.[19] In the 1990s, governments of sending nations in South and Southeast Asia began to actively promote labor migration as an export strategy, with Bangladesh, the Philippines, Pakistan, and Sri Lanka competing with India over contracts for migrant work in the Gulf. Seeking to diversity its predominantly Indian labor force, the UAE government passed a law in 2005 decreeing that contractors must "source workers from at least three countries." This prompted economic managers in the sending countries to promote their own "heat-resistant workers," who could endure long hours through their exceptional "strength and stamina."[20] Following in this vein, embassies and consulates from the source countries, with the exception of the Philippines, have done very little to protect the well-being of the fellow citizens they help to send to the Gulf.

In the next section, we turn to the lived experience of South Asian workers who continue to pursue their "Gulf Dreams" for a better life in the face of the structural constraints discussed above. While researching this topic, we observed that migration to the Gulf has shifted from the northern states of Uttar Pradesh (UP) and Bihar and away from Kerala, which had accounted for the highest numbers of migrants to the region since the 1970s. This shift reflects changes within the Indian economy—a reminder of the need to understand migration more broadly than the process of crossing national borders. We also found that these larger patterns of migration and mobility have led to new claims for dignity in both India and the Gulf region. Gulf dreams are not only an aspiration of individuals; they feed into a widely held collective imaginary. The dream is rooted in and across communities with long experience of members journeying abroad, sending remittances back,

---

19. Andrzej Kapiszewski, "Arab versus Asian Migrant Workers in the GCC Countries," *United Nations Population Division—Department of Economic and Social Affairs* (Beirut: UN Department of Economic and Social Affairs, May 15–17, 2006).

20. Buckley, "Urbanisation in Dubai," p. 142.

often trapped in cycles of debt, and, in many cases, fighting back against seemingly insurmountable odds.

Returned migrants and political possibilities

Labor migration to the Gulf has persisted alongside a resurgence of internal labor circulation within India over the past 25 years of economic liberalization. Despite impressive rates of economic growth in this period, by conservative estimates 300 to 450 million Indians continue to live in the most extreme poverty, and those in the bottom half of India's economy face a choice between stark poverty at home and a highly precarious mobility. The reserve army of informal labor seeking work and shelter make up a "nomadic workforce" who remain "outsiders in the area to which they have been recruited on a temporary and casual basis, and are treated as transients by those who make use of their labor power."[21] India's own construction boom in the last two decades has been concentrated in specific cities and towns and it has been staffed by this floating workforce from villages and regions in decline—agricultural workers "escaping often much harsher conditions of economic and social inequality."[22]

These internal migrants face rock-bottom wages and precarious work conditions in locations where the local language and culture is just as foreign (sometimes more so) than what they might find in Qatar or the UAE. Migration therefore includes a more expansive geography of mobility, which, in India, comprises people "migrating to cities, to the Gulf, to irrigated areas, to coffee plantations or simply commuting daily to non-agricultural jobs nearby."[23] This new mobility has also seen what anthropologist Jan Breman has called the emergence of "new claims for dignity," based on

21. Jan Breman, *Outcast Labour in Asia: Circulation and Informalization of the Workforce at the Bottom of the Economy* (New Delhi: Oxford University Press, 2013), p. 3.

22. John Harriss, "Middle-class Activism and the Politics of the Informal Working Class: A Perspective on Class Relations and Civil Society in Indian Cities," *Critical Asian Studies* 38.4 (2006), p. 10.

23. Priay Deshingkar and John Farrington, *Circular Migration and Multilocational Livelihood Strategies in Rural India.* (New Delhi: Oxford University Press, 2009)

assertions of caste, community, gender, and class interests.[24] Though they speak different languages and belong to distinct castes and ethno-religious traditions, migrant workers in India's urban centers have engaged in both spontaneous and organized efforts around a range of demands for improved housing, education, wages, and worker representation.[25] If we are to understand and support labor actions in the Gulf by South Asian workers, it therefore makes sense to see these two worlds of migration as closely connected.

Keeping this in mind, we shaped our research on returned migrant workers with conversations and engagement with labor researchers and activists who drew connections between the upsurge in worker protest in the Gulf and economic restructuring within India itself. Before our trips to Kerala, Telengana, UP, and Bihar to conduct interviews with returned migrants, we spent some time in the Gurgaon and Okhla industrial zone, about 30 miles outside of Delhi in the state of Harayana. This has been the site of a series of labor protests and actions, beginning in 2010, over wage disparities between temporary (mostly migrant lower-caste) and salaried workers who were often unified in actions against management. These workers struggled for parity in wages (the difference being approximately 100 USD a month) and the formation of a new union that would represent both contract and permanent workers. Two years of largely self-organized struggle culminated in a controversial incident in July 2012, when a manager died in a clash with protesting workers at a Maruti Suzuki plant in Manesar, 30 miles outside of New Delhi. According to testimony by workers involved, "this was not some action by a group of 20 or 50 workers, but rather thousands of new and old, permanent and temporary workers participated in the revolt."[26] State police responded with great force, factories throughout

---

24. Jan Breman, *Footloose Labor: Working in India's Informal Economy* (New Delhi: Cambridge University Press, 1996); Breman, *Outcast Labour in Asia*.

25. Breman (1996) and others studying migration and urbanization in post-liberalization India point also to the potential for ethno-nationalist and reactionary populist mobilizations within migrant and between competing migrant communities in Gujarat, Mumbai, and elsewhere.

26. Sheena Jain, "An Account of Factory Workers Activities Today: Maruti Suzuki Cars, Manesar, India," *Tidal* (January 3, 2015), http://tinyurl.com/knygb52.

Interviewing returned migrant workers in the village of Narayanpur Siwan, Bihar (Credit: Gulf Labor)

the region were shut down, and more than 140 workers were "rounded up" from surrounding villages and jailed, while 1,800 contract workers and more than 500 permanent workers were fired.[27]

Mainstream Indian media has paid very little attention to the plight of these workers, and focused instead on how the Maruti Suzuki incident might affect future foreign investment. As for the migrant workers we met in the same industrial zones in 2014 and 2015, making everything from garments to electronics and cars, their primary focus remained on the Maruti Suzuki workers' legacy of self-organizing. As it was much more useful as a source of news and information than the dozens of 24 hour news channels blasting out the same business-friendly message, we followed the distribution of a Hindi-language monthly broadsheet called the *Faridabad Majdoor Samachar* (Workers Newpaper), produced by independent labor organizers and distributed to workers at central street crossings across multiple industrial zones in Harayana and the National Capital Region (NCR).[28] We gathered testimony about women garment workers who had intentionally produced pants with the left leg longer than the right, in order to financially damage the manufacturer who refused to meet their wage demands. Throughout our encounters and conversations with workers and labor organizers, we found that the experience of travel away from family, friends, and community was difficult for them to bear, especially when wages and exploitative conditions of work were perceived as "unfair" or beneath their dignity.

From the standpoint of this first group of circular migrant workers it was surely a matter of privilege that allowed someone to aspire to "Gulf Dreams." Not surprisingly, our subsequent interviews with returned migrants revealed a common refrain—"I went because I could earn more." To do so, they had to first accept the risky burden of recruitment debt—a form of "leveraged labor"—in hopes of financial gains over the long term. Almost all the workers we interviewed had taken on debts, ranging from

---

27. Rakhi Sehgal, "Notes from the warfront: Maruti workers 'on trial': Rakhi Sehgal," *Kafila.org* (August 21, 2012), http://tinyurl.com/myc5atv; Anumeha Yadav, "Maruti Strikes," *Himal Southasian* (March 27, 2015), http://tinyurl.com/ppa8ceg.

28. *Faridabad Workers Newspaper*, http://faridabadmajdoorsamachar.blogspot.com/.

100,000 to 200,000 Rupees (1,600 USD to 3,000 USD), in addition to outlays for the cost of air travel.[29] Most of our interviewees took anywhere from two to four years to pay off these debts, depending on whether the loans were contracted from banks, migrant associations, or from informal money lenders who charge much higher rates of interest. We found that, while all workers go to the Gulf with the goal of making more money—and if they are successful they stay for several years—they tend to have very little to show for it upon their return. Only the lucky few might have earned a slightly improved home or a surplus for weddings or school for their children. Indeed, the promise of economic benefits for their children was a common point of reference for almost everyone, but all our interviewees also spoke about the steep emotional costs of being away from their children, spouses, and aging parents for long stretches of time. In this equation, time away is exchanged for wages, but the wages don't turn into savings or capital; in most cases, they are fully expended on daily living and the cost of raising a family at home.

We began our research in Kerala, the state that has seen the highest migration rates to the Gulf, followed by Telengana, another region in the south with relatively high rates since the 1970s. But we were also interested in speaking to workers from the northern states of Uttar Pradesh and Bihar, which have seen, since 2011, the fastest growth rate in "low-skilled" immigrants to the Gulf.[30]

In the Kannur district of Kerala, we met with Mani, a carpenter who had worked for Al-Reyami, a large subcontractor building doors and windows for NYU's campus on Saadiyat Island. He was initially recruited from his home town

---

29. These amounts are very close to estimates by other researchers. See, for example, the discussion of recruitment debt and "leveraged labor" of workers in the post-financial crisis Kerala by Michelle Buckley, "From Kerala to Dubai and Back Again: Construction Migrants and the Global Economic Crisis," *Geoforum* 43.2 (2012), pp. 250–59.

30. The geographical spread of migration from India to the Gulf is changing. For the first time, 2011 statistics show that Kerala holds the second rank in terms of absolute numbers of immigrant workers to the Gulf. Around a quarter of the emigrant workers came from Uttar Pradesh, followed by Kerala (13.8 percent), Andhra Pradesh, Bihar, Tamil Nadu, Rajasthan, Punjab, and West Bengal. Other states individually constituted less than 1 percent of the immigrant workforce. (Naresh Kumar, "Recent Trend and Pattern of Indian Emigration to Gulf Countries: A Diaspora Perspective," *Population Association of America: 2014 Annual Meeting Program* (Boston: PAA, 2014))

by a "high-ranking" employee of the firm. In June 2013, Mani was one of eight workers who participated in an action involving hundreds of workers in Abu Dhabi, Dubai, and Jebel Ali. In the aftermath, Mani and the eight others who were identified as "strike leaders" were summarily rounded up and deported. Asked whether he had ever organized an action before, his definitive answer was no, nor was he comfortable using the term "strike." He told us that he and his fellow workers had not been paid for three to four months, despite repeated complaints to management. In response, Al-Reyami shifted the blame by claiming it was NYU that was late in making payments. Workers in his labor camp discussed what to do as the non-payment of wages dragged on. More than 300 workers from his camp alone decided they would not board the buses that took them from the labor camp to NYU's Saadiyat worksite. "What else can one do if they are not getting paid for their work?" he pointed out. "You do not work."

As a foreman, he felt responsible for the workers under him and wondered why the pay of the "office workers" at Al-Reyami had not been withheld, since they made higher salaries than the manual workers. It was also clear to us that Mani felt comfortable participating in this labor action in large part because his recruitment debt was paid off (he had been in the UAE for seven years). As a semi-skilled worker (carpenter) he had some opportunity for work after he was deported, and, when we met him, he had set up a small carpentry shop in his hometown. Despite this level of economic stability, he felt financially insecure and wished to return to the Gulf but only with his family—technically impossible given the firm restrictions on migrant workers. Although he had endured "miserable accommodations and poor food," he could "work all the time" there. It was this sheer abundance of available paid work that made the Gulf so desirable, albeit not at any cost.

Many of the returned Keralite migrants we interviewed had come, in the course of their UAE stints, to assume managerial positions over other Indian workers from other states as well as other South Asian workers. Hailing from a state where more than 90 percent of the population is literate, educated, and multi-lingual, Keralites like Mani, who take on the role of foremen speaking English or Hindi and Arabic, are often the primary interface between "low-skilled" and "no-skilled" workers and management. Kerala has a long history of skilled migration in sectors like nursing and white-collar office employment.[31] But as the cost of living, in India, has increased exponentially over the last decade, workers at every skill level have been taking on recruitment debt "for better jobs" overseas. The middle class migrants, with denser networks of transnational contacts, often pay an agent to find them more lucrative employment in the Gulf, and many spoke about turning to the Non-Resident Keralite Associations for help "during difficulties." In our conversations with returned migrants, stories of grievances were less common than expressions of pride at having worked overseas and delivered enhanced opportunities for their children and, in some cases, their communities as a whole.

But the overseas experience of the Keralite migrants is only one part of the Gulf story. As K.K. Kannan, a labor organizer with the Center of Indian Trade Unions (CITU) with 20 years of knowledge in the region, told us, "Kerala is the Gulf for most North Indians." He explained that the construction sector in Kerala was increasingly employing workers from West Bengal, at pay rates as low as 250 rupees (3 USD) a day. Kannan highlighted a much broader circuit of migration, whereby economically distressed workers came from Bengal to replace the more educated Keralite migrants moving to the Gulf.

From Kerala we traveled to Hyderabad, capital of the new state Telengana (formerly Andhra Pradesh), also a major source of Gulf migrant labor. In the nearby village of Narsingapur, we interviewed 15 returned construction workers who had traveled to the Gulf between 2003 and 2013 on tourist visas handled by local agents. They were part of a large undocumented workforce that grew throughout the region during the real estate boom until 2009, and continues to exist at the shadowy margins of the visa-trading system today. Even after labor reforms targeting the undocumented workforce in the UAE, researchers estimated that there were some 135,000 such workers in 2013.[32]

For their visa and travel fees, these workers had borrowed against their small plots of land. Unlike their counterparts in Kerala, they were all agricultural workers

31. K.C. Zachariah, B.A. Prakash, and S. Irudaya Rajan, "The Impact of Immigration Policy on Indian Contract Migrants: The Case of the United Arab Emirates," *International Migration* 41.4 (October 2003), pp. 161–72.

32. Malit Jr. and Al Youha, "Labor Migration in the United Arab Emirates."

with little education or skills training, and they engaged in various modes of cyclical migration in search of paid work. Most came from self-identified "backward caste," or *Dalit*, communities, whose low status in the Indian caste hierarchy is a source of new political claims for economic justice and recognition. They included workers like Ramesh (28), Ganesh (30), and Sidirimalu (54), who each reported taking on steep debts (1,500–2,500 USD) to get to the Gulf without "proper papers," because their families had either lost their land or were "struggling" to survive. Middlemen had promised higher wages than those offered through the official recruitment channels, but they reckoned that the intense stress generated by their undocumented circumstances had canceled out the value of the additional pay. Most of the Telengana workers had their passports confiscated by the middlemen, and found themselves competing for new gigs every two weeks at *chawks* (informal labor marketplaces). Forced to subsist as daily laborers, constantly on the lookout for the next job, they had rented small rooms, usually shared by anywhere from five to 15 men, in informal labor camps or private tenement buildings. All testified to the recurrent experience of wage theft and underpayment, which meant that few had returned home with any savings to speak of. The Telengana region has hosted neo-Maoist, left-wing, and radical caste-based political movements going back decades. However, none of the workers we spoke with had become involved in work stoppages or other labor actions in the Gulf. It became clear to us that the fear of imprisonment and deportation for this group of workers was compounded by the debt they had incurred, and that they wanted to avoid at all costs the stigma of returning home worse off than when they had left.

Our research in India ended in the northern states of Uttar Pradesh and Bihar, where more recent migration corridors to the Gulf have opened up. In districts and villages located nearby or within the "Maoist Belt" across North and East India, which have seen an ongoing armed insurgency by tribal and other marginalized communities, our conversations with returned migrants took a different turn. Several interviewees discussed instances of involvement in both unorganized and organized modes of protest as well as a more general sense that the potential for slightly higher wages in the Gulf was not enough to compensate for the insecurity and humiliation associated with the harsh labor conditions. In the district of Azamgarh, close to the Hindu holy city of Varanasi, we spoke with workers who identified themselves as

Sidirimalu from Narsingapur Village, Telangana (Credit: Gulf Labor)

belonging to Muslim "backward caste" communities, having worked largely in construction in Qatar between 2007 and 2014. Mohammad, a 32-year-old who had spent eight years in Doha in two separate stints, had originally been recruited for a job as a personal driver. On arrival in Doha, he was instead assigned work as a bus driver shuttling other workers for a steel-welding company engaged on various projects, including constructing stadiums for the FIFA World Cup. In addition to long hours of driving, Mohammad would also be expected to do construction work on the site at times and was not paid for either overtime or extra work. He told us that he often felt like a *"Ghulam"* (the Hindi/Urdu and Arabic word for slave) in the way he was treated by his sponsor: "This time when I went, I could not bear it. It's better to live in your own country. You earn less, you eat less but it's better. Over there it doesn't feel good and our lives have little value."

In Bihar, we went to one of the frontlines of the struggle between the Maoist insurgency and the national government's heavily militarized response. In the village of Narayanpur in the Siwan district on the Nepal border, we met with four workers, all from "backward caste" communities, who, like their counterparts in Telengana, had worked as unskilled laborers in construction in Abu Dhabi and Dubai. They had also taken on high-interest loans to pay off the 2,000 USD recruitment fees demanded by agents who offered them contracts promising wages of 1,000 AED (275 USD) a month; in Abu Dhabi and Dubai, they were paid only 800 AED a month. All four of these workers subsequently participated in spontaneous actions and strikes, sparked by a decline in wages, poor quality of food, and limited access to clean water. Like Manu in Kerala, 25-year-old Ansari had taken a full five years to work off his debt, and offered a straightforward explanation for the reasoning behind the strikes: "We go there to work to make money and if we do not get the wages which is our right it's only obvious to strike or resist." In 2013, fed up with unpaid wages and unmet demands about quality of food, about 50 of the 500 workers in his labor camp refused to go to the work site. Their supervisors took note of those who spoke the most; they were "not called for duty" over the course of the following weeks, and eventually, over a span of two months, were "sent back home." Ansari had no desire to go back to the Gulf, but others in Naraynpur were more ambivalent, and reported that they might consider returning.

Ansari from Village Narayanpur in Siwan, Bihar (Credit: Gulf Labor)

The foregoing sample of returned Gulf migrants across four states offers a snap-shot of the larger uneven and variegated processes of globalization underway in India. Without making unwarranted generalizations, we can say that, after comparing the experiences of these returned migrants with the labor conditions for circular migrants working in India's industrial zones, we need to think more relationally about the experience of mobility and informalization of work overall. Taking part in labor actions in the Gulf is a high-risk decision, unlikely to be taken by those who were still tethered to recruitment debt or working under even more precarious conditions as undocumented migrants. P. Naraswamy, the chairman of the Palamoori Migrant Labour Union (PMLU) in Hyderabad, which has one of the longest histories of working with Gulf migrants, told us that, despite worsening conditions for most "low-skilled" migrants in the region, people from Telengana and elsewhere continue to "Dream, dream, dream. . . . A dream that exists because of the promise of white-collared jobs and making a lot of money in the Gulf." Outside of Kerala, however, we heard very few stories from migrants who had "moved up" the chain from "low" or "semi-skilled" manual labor to office work or into self-employment, even after their return from multiple three-year stints in the region.

The PMLU's main tasks at hand included intervening in cases of imprisoned undocumented workers and sexual assault of domestic workers in the Gulf, and repatriating the dead bodies of migrant workers that arrive in Hyderabad from the Gulf countries, sometimes as many as ten a day. Naraswamy echoed the sentiments of the Kerala and Delhi labor organizers, that the Indian government did very little to protect the rights of a vulnerable workforce in the Gulf. Indeed, they held government agencies directly responsible for failing to enforce ILO conventions on responsible recruitment practices.[33] In the last few years, a number of independent labor groups, working in conjunction with the ILO and other international labor organizations, have pressed the Indian government for stronger regulation on recruitment. Meanwhile, the recent spate of labor actions in the Gulf has not surprised labor researchers and activists in other parts of India. As Hare Ram, a civil liberties activist and

---

33. For the ILO convention on recruitment (C-181), see ILO, "C181 – Private Employment Agencies Convention (1997)," http://tinyurl.com/lj96z32.

Hindi-language journalist who works in Bihar, pointed out, most of the workers in this area came from more politicized backgrounds. "They would resist in Dubai and Abu Dhabi against unjust treatment," he observed, "just as they would in another state in India where they might have to seek work."[34]

Amplifying the voices of workers in Abu Dhabi

We followed our research in India in 2014–2015 with a shorter and more con-strained—in terms of workers' comfort to speak with us freely—field visit to Abu Dhabi in March of 2015. Our visit coincided with a sizable, and media-savvy, strike of 500 construction workers engaged on Dubai's Fountain View project, which blocked traffic in one of the city's main arteries near the world-famous *Burj Khalifa*. Once again at issue were arbitrary wage cuts, of approximately 100 USD per month, along with the denial of overtime work and extra pay.[35] Our interviews with returned migrants in India found average wages at around 250 USD per month, while the report published by Nardello found that the average wage for NYU's workforce of 30,000 was 217 USD per month.[36] A difference of 100 USD per month was therefore significant for workers who had the additional pressure of recruitment debt to con-tend with. While riot police were called within an hour of the protest, workers told us that such actions are "inevitable," since they were being "pushed" too far. Given our trip's proximity in time to the strike and the publicity generated by a travel ban imposed on one of our research team (and editor of this volume), we knew that it would be difficult for workers to meet with us at their work sites or at labor camps,

---

34. Hare Ram Mishra is one of two additional research assistants hired by the Delhi-based Society for Labour and Development to conduct interviews with workers in Bihar and UP, who accompanied us on these inter-views in January 2015.

35. Rory Jones, "Construction-Worker Pay Dispute Resolved, Say Dubai Authorities," *Wall Street Journal* (March 10, 2015), http://tinyurl.com/k6t3p9q.

36. Nardello & Co., *Report of the Independent Investigator into Allegations of Labor and Compliance Issues During the Construction of the NYU Abu Dhabi Campus on Saadiyat Island* (April 16, 2015), http://tinyurl.com/nceunzm.

as security had tightened and everyone we spoke with knew stories of other workers who had been jailed or deported.

Taking suitable precautions, we conducted interviews at cafes or restaurants in Abu Dhabi with 35 workers, most of them Indian, Pakistani, or Bangladeshi, employed on construction projects across the island, which included building the island's extensive infrastructure. We followed the workers' everyday existence outside of the work site, which included informal settings like the "Bengali market" that pops up once a week at the periphery of the Mafraq Workers City (Abu Dhabi), providing everything from haircuts to prepared food. Based on these interviews and our observations, this section offers a brief overview of the conditions of work and life in two labor camps: Mafraq Workers City and the Saadiyat Accommodation Village (SAV).

Four Punjabi "low-skilled" workers ages 21 to 24, who had been hired to build the cooling plant for the Louvre, were being paid 1,200–1,500 AED (327 USD to 408 USD) per month including overtime, and all had recruitment debts that were being slowly paid off. Even though TDIC's employment policies stipulate that all employees engaged on its Saadiyat projects are to be housed on the island, all four workers were living in Mafraq Workers City, far beyond Abu Dhabi's urban fringe. Because the quality of the food at Mafraq was so poor, they generally paid private caterers for meals, which cost them an additional 60 USD to 160 USD per month. In other words, almost half their income went to cover costs for food. Their typical work day began at 5 am and ended around 8 pm when they returned to Mafraq, exhausted from physically demanding work. Three hours or more were spent on travel time, which left only one precious hour to talk with their coworkers while trying to procure and eat a "decent meal."

Those of our interviewees who were housed in the SAV, and who therefore did not have the three hour commute, nonetheless all testified that they would prefer to live elsewhere. While they were physically closer to the work site, the village was heavily guarded, with "nothing around" it, and they had to adhere to a strict 10 pm curfew. The SAV, which housed some 6,000 workers, was surrounded by checkpoints and gates at every entrance, barring all unauthorized vehicles. Workers who wished to visit Abu Dhabi "to eat or on a day off" were forced to wait for hours at these checkpoints. The Louvre workers we spoke with complained about feeling "trapped in

Bengali Friday market, Mafraq Workers City, Abu Dhabi (Credit: Gulf Labor)

the desert far away from regular life." In addition to the surveillance and isolation, they testified to lower than expected wages (for example, two workers in their early 20s from Peshawar in Pakistan were being paid 1,200 AED (326 USD) per month, including overtime) and repeatedly brought up the issue of substandard food. Without exception, all the SAV workers complained that the provisions on offer were like "feed to animals." Some reported that the food had been "decent" initially—"for a couple of weeks"—but deteriorated soon after, and many alleged that "chemicals" were used in the food to hasten preparation and preservation. They noted that there was no overall effort on the part of management to provide "fresh food" for "three meals a day."

From the evidence of these conversations and media coverage of labor actions going back to 2011, it appears that the deteriorating quality and rising costs of food relative to stagnant wages had pushed many of these workers to breaking point. Many had concluded that the "Gulf Dream" of a better life, if not for themselves then for their families, would never materialize. Everyone we spoke to, in both India and the UAE, wanted us to know that they were proud of their labor—they had sought as much work as possible—because of the scarcity of regular paid work in their villages and home towns. But they had expected to be paid as promised, and to be treated with some basic dignity, even in their very precious hours off from labor and sleep. We concluded that these experiences, collectively endured over the course of a decade, were not breeding acceptance by a "docile workforce," but had instead prompted unforeseen modes of resistance and organization.

The tight social bonds generated by migrant networks had nurtured new kinds of labor leaders. Some, like Mani in Kerala, acted out of responsibility for workers under them, while others were politicized by migrant struggles in India, Pakistan, and elsewhere. Their organizing efforts were reinforced in no small part by free social networking software (WhatsApp was the most popular platform) and by the ubiquity of mobile phones, the only instrument of communication that was not subject to employer surveillance and control. Accounts of the strikes and stoppages circulated far beyond Abu Dhabi and Dubai, throughout the home communities of Kerala, UP, and Bihar. They resulted in the deportation of some, but also in noticeable improvements in wages, food, and accommodations for others. The UAE's official media organs seldom reported strikes, and regularly published stories about workers who were grateful for the opportunity to live the Gulf Dream. But the migrants were part of their own media underground, and it broadcast a rather different story.[37]

Solidarity looking forward

We began this chapter by noting that the unprecedented protests in the UAE commanding global attention should inform our own strategies of solidarity. We then provided a broader historical context for the modern workings of the lucrative *kafala* sponsorship system, and the complicity of Western governments and corporations in designing and propping up the racist segregation of the region's "permanent temporary" low-wage workforce. In the shadow of the ongoing "War on Terror," our efforts at solidarity targeting political reforms in the Gulf must be particularly critical of this history and the current mobilization of human rights in the service of empire.

In turning to the lived experiences of migrant workers themselves in India and the UAE, we showed that a person does not become a migrant only when they cross a national border. The broader, uneven experience of mobility and skewed terms of globalization within India and throughout South Asia have consequences in places like the UAE. While dispossession from land and through debt were universal conditions pushing people to seek work and shelter away from home across India, differences between workers based on class, caste, and community networks ultimately shaped both their material well-being and their political visions.

We believe it remains urgent to continue to use our leverage as transnationally based artists and scholars to hold US and European museums and universities accountable in their home countries for the abuses against human dignity of workers thousands of miles away. In March 2015, Gulf Labor issued a letter to the Guggenheim leadership supporting concrete demands made by workers who have engaged in labor actions.[38] These demands included a living wage for all workers employed by

---

37. For an interesting example, see the Saudi rap video on migrant labor abuse circulated through the independent Arabic online video network Telfazll. ("Saudi Rap Video Highlighting Migrant Abuse Goes Viral," *Migrant-rights.org* (February 28, 2015), http://tinyurl.com/l5opa3m)

38. For details of the exchange between Gulf Labor and the Guggenheim, see Gulf Labor, "Guggenheim

the museum, a debt compensation fund, and measures to ensure meaningful worker representation and association. On the first two points, we found in our interviews, both in India and the UAE, that workers earned approximately 250 USD a month and had paid between 1,500 USD and 2,000 USD in recruitment debt. The 250 USD figure was also the estimated median income in a much larger study on labor reform in the UAE,[39] confirming that our findings were reasonable and representative of overall wage stagnation, if not decline, for the majority of low-skilled workers in the Gulf since 2009. In workers' own estimates of a fair, or "living," wage, taking into account the dramatic increase in the cost of living in home countries, the sum that emerged as the consensus figure was 2,000 AED, or approximately 550 USD, per month. Labor organizers in India in all four visited states, as well as in Delhi and Gurgaon, emphasized the need to reform the punishing terms of recruitment debt, especially for migrant workers coming from socially and economically marginalized communities who often earned the least monthly income and paid the highest interest rates. They were equally concerned about the Indian government's lack of meaningful intervention on the behalf of migrant workers' rights in the Gulf and also in "rehabilitation" (finding paid work) when they returned home. We support the fledgling efforts by independent labor unions and labor rights organizations in India and the ILO to organize around these issues transnationally.

Beyond these important pragmatic tactics for reform, we want to close this chapter by suggesting broader and more difficult goals for a project that must rethink new modes, and unearth existing forms, of solidarity. The interrelatedness of struggles must be a key principle going forward, along with the insight that freedom from oppression requires a liberation that is collective and all-encompassing. Living up to these principles demands that we examine how we are each implicated in the causes with which we engage. In the case of the South Asian migrant workers in the Gulf, for example, those participating in the work of activism and solidarity might be both

Responds, Nothing Has Changed," *Gulf Labor Artist Coalition* (April 23, 2015), http://tinyurl.com/qcrtoae.

39. Suresh Naidu, Yaw Nyarko, and Shing-Yi Wang, "Worker Mobility in a Global Labor Market: Evidence from the United Arab Emirates" (February 2015), http://tinyurl.com/p43zeew.

exploiters and exploited, depending on their own caste/race, class, and gendered positions. The same can be said of the workers we met in Kerala, who are often acting as foremen and project managers over other South Asian migrant workers in Abu Dhabi in the service of their common employer. Moreover, we must acknowledge that, as writers and artists, we hold on to, and reap the benefit of, material privileges that would not exist but for past and continuing oppression along race/caste, class, gender, or nation-state divides. While we use these privileges to speak out, we must always be careful to avoid reproducing privilege—an easy slip.

Such awareness and attention opens up new political possibilities of coalition that do not rely on rescue or victimhood, but rather on the recognition of debts owed.[40] For example, expanding the notion of "debt" to include non-financial obligations to one another, as opposed simply to lenders, might be one way of re-imagining solidarity. As one of Gulf Labor's *52 Weeks* contributions (*No Debt Is An Island—A Solidarity Initiative*) put it:

> There, on the "Island of Happiness," Abu Dhabi's showpiece real estate venture, his [the migrant worker's] bonded labor is now linked to the "indenture" of the American students. Their respective financial obligations are connected to, and amplified by, Abu Dhabi's over-leveraged boom economy, which rests on an ever-growing carbon debt. "No Debt Is An Island" is a solidarity initiative that aims to trace the chain of debt that sustains the fortunes of the international art market, the global aspirations of Anglophone higher education, and the ascent of the Gulf petroleum states.[41]

Most students and artists in the US do not experience the dynamics of precarity and debt in the same ways as security guards and janitorial staff—primarily people of

---

40. This line of argument is drawn from the context of the racialized politics of the "sub-prime" financial crisis in Paula Chakravartty and Denise Ferreira da Silva, "Accumulation, Dispossession, and Debt: The Racial Logic of Global Capitalism—An Introduction," *American Quarterly* 64.3 (September 2012), pp. 361–85.

41. This is from a collaboration between MTL and Andrew Ross. See "Week 10. NO DEBT IS AN ISLAND," *Gulf Labor Artist Coalition* (December 18, 2013), http://tinyurl.com/qjnu6rb.

color—who maintain the institutions in which we contemplate artistic treasures and conduct intellectual exchange. Similarly, many of the "bachelor builders" in the Gulf might themselves be privileged relative to the reserve army of circular migrants in towns and cities across India. Our challenge is to establish a truly ethical foundation for a "coalition" that encompasses so many different members across the globe. In this process we must work to locate solidarity not on the basis of *helping* the migrant worker, but on a clear understanding that we are complicit in the conditions that force a worker to leave his or her home, that we benefit from their exploitation, and, conversely, that the betterment of the workers' conditions is a prerequisite for the betterment of our own. Such solidarity requires constructing a coalition of equals.

Art out of Joint: Artists' Activism Before and After the Cultural Turn

Gregory Sholette[1]

End page from An Anti-Catalog, Artists Meeting for Cultural Change *(1977) (Sholette Archives)*

1. The author wishes to express special thanks to the following people, who contributed historical reference material for this essay: Karl Beveridge, Carole Conde, Carol Duncan, Jerry Kearns, Suzanne Lacy, Loraine Leeson, Marc Léger, Lucy R. Lippard, Florian Malzacher, Alan Moore, Beverly Naidus, Rasha Salti, Jeffrey Skoller, Dan S Wang, John P. Weber, Carol Wells/Center for the Study of Political Graphics (CSPG), and to editor Andrew Ross.

This essay sketches a history of artists who, in response to external events, chose to abandon, at least for a time, their studio practice in favor of more direct political action. While my primary focus is on the years of the post-war "cultural turn" between 1965 and 1989, the genealogy of such actions stretches back at least to the painter Gustave Courbet and his involvement in the Paris Commune in the late 19th century, and continues today with groups such as Liberate Tate and Occupy Museums and artists in Syria and Egypt's Tahrir Square revolution who asked themselves whether or not there was even time to make art under such demanding circumstances.[2] The tendency I focus on accelerated considerably after the late 1960s through informally organized art-based collectives like Black Mask, Guerrilla Art Action Group (GAAG), Red Herring, PAD/D, Guerrilla Girls, Gran Fury, and Critical Art Ensemble, all of whom eschewed the white box for the public sphere. This same lineage of self-directed activist culture also includes the Gulf Labor Coalition (GLC), an informally organized alliance of artists, writers, and academics focused on pressuring the Guggenheim Foundation to improve sub-standard labor conditions in Abu Dhabi where immigrant workers are constructing another spectacular Guggenheim Museum designed by Frank Gehry. GLC's practice aggressively ignores established rules regarding the non-partisanship and objectivity of researchers, as well as classical notions of aesthetic disinterestedness.

This fierce noncompliance with research and artistic norms also emerged among cultural producers at earlier moments of crisis, almost as if the experience of extreme political duress forces us to bump up against the limits of our assigned stations. For artists, whose social mentality pivots on the belief that art is self-directed labor and thus free and without limits, this external bump is a particularly jarring experience. Occasionally the jolt leads down the path toward radicalization, though it always involves some degree of disruption regarding familiar assumptions about one's field

---

2. With the post-war rise of mass-consumerism, "culture," according to Michael Denning, began to be understood as no longer solely the property of an elite, but something in which the entire population could participate. "Suddenly after 1950 everyone discovered that culture had been mass produced like Ford's cars; the masses had culture and culture had a mass." (Michael Denning, *Culture in the Age of Three Worlds* (London: Verso, 2004), p. 2)

of professional activity. Inevitably, gatekeepers of a given discipline attempt to manage these dislocating moments. When artists engage in direct political action, the artworld tends to respond with renunciation or denial.

In perhaps all other vocations save for journalism, where objectivity is considered paramount, and the priesthood, where a concern with the afterlife is supposed to trump worldly injustice, an individual's social or political activism is understood to have little or no assumed impact on his or her professional identity. Doctors cross borders in order to care for disaster victims, lawyers establish NGOs to assist victims of injustice. No one concludes that a commitment to liberal social change alters the application of battlefield triage or standard litigation procedure. However, when cultural producers become politically engaged, allegations fly about professional deformation. Moreover, while priests and journalists are threatened, or even assassinated, for siding with impoverished victims of injustice, artists are more typically chastised for perverting their talents toward propagandistic ends. Serious culture, so the orthodox position insists, must remain in its proper place: detached, disinterested, and depoliticized. And if an artist is compelled to engage in social criticism, it must always take place within the formal vocabulary of art, not politics. This latter point was driven home to the GLC in 2011, when Guggenheim staff members called for an end to the group's Abu Dhabi boycott while simultaneously suggesting that we instead express our opinion through works of art.[3]

Confronted with this advice, we heard a reverberation of Hans Haacke's seminal encounter with the Guggenheim in 1970, when the museum canceled his exhibition on political grounds. In the words of director Thomas Messer, Haacke's piece about corrupt real estate ownership in New York City was "an alien substance that had entered

---

3. Needless to say, the alleged "radicality" of institutional critique was never so deeply compromised as it seemed at that moment, although earlier confrontations with mainstream museums had similar outcomes. For example, when the Art Workers' Coalition challenged, in the late 1960s and early 1970s, the ideological neutrality of art, the cold warrior art critic Hilton Kramer proclaimed in a *New York Times* editorial that "the time has come for all of us who believe in the very idea of art museums—in museums free of political pressures—to make our commitments known; to say loud and clear that we will not stand for the politicalization of art that is now looming as a real possibility." (Hilton Kramer, "Do You Believe in the Principle of Museums?" *New York Times* (January 18, 1970), D25)

the art museum organism." Critics who consider it perfectly natural that an artist produces ultra-luxury commodities affordable only by .01 percent of the population, are quick to condemn politically active artists as professionally corrupt. For example, Hilton Kramer denounced Deborah Wye's 1987–88 Museum of Modern Art (MoMA) exhibition of political graphics, *Committed To Print,* in the *New York Observer* under the headline, "Show of Political Prints at MoMA Echoes the Bad Taste of the 1920s." For all intents and purposes, Kramer was red-baiting the museum, which never again hosted a large, explicit exhibition of confrontational works of political art.

If social activism by doctors and lawyers does not impair or diminish medical or legal expertise, then what is it about the labor of artists and cultural producers that leads to charges of professional deceit so onerous that it tars the very identity of what it means to be an artist? After all, if direct political engagement is out-of-bounds to serious visual artists, then a large branch must be lopped off the trunk of art history. And yet, perhaps this is not such a loss? The record of artist-initiated solidarity and direct action suggests that a subtler interpretation is in order.

In 1965, Bob Dylan released his hit single "Subterranean Homesick Blues," containing the memorable line—*you don't need a weatherman to know which way the wind blows*—that inspired the radical SDS splinter group Weather Underground. In that year, the United States military occupied the Dominican Republic, allegedly to thwart a communist takeover, and President Lyndon Johnson sent the first official combat troops to Vietnam. SDS marched on Washington to call for an end to military action in Southeast Asia, racially-charged riots erupted in Watts, Los Angeles, and, in California, Filipino-American farm workers walked off grape fields to protest labor conditions, initiating a multi-year boycott led by Cesar Chavez and the United Farm Workers. And one early spring day that same year, civil rights demonstrators were savagely beaten by state troopers in Selma, Alabama causing March 7 to be renamed "Bloody Sunday."

Unquestionably the wind was shifting in radical and radicalizing directions. Throughout the 1960s, loosely organized coalitions brought cultural producers together with student protesters, striking workers, feminists, gays, and civil rights activists in acts and campaigns of political and artistic solidarity. But as art and politics colluded and collided with each other, panicked tradition-bound cultural institutions and artworld patrons pushed back against this dangerous blurring of categories.

The Black Panther newspaper frequently carried a UFW fundraising
coupon to send support directly to the UFW. Emory Douglas was the
BPP Minster of Culture and most likely designed this graphic (1973)
(Credit: © 2015 Emory Douglas / Artists Rights Society [ARS], New York)

1965 is a key year in this history because it witnessed the emergence of the first overtly politicized post-war artists' collective: Artists and Writers Protest Against the War in Vietnam. In an open letter published in the *New York Times*, the group called on others to "End Your Silence." The missive was signed by almost 500 writers and artists, including musicians John Cage and Morton Feldman, pop artist Roy Lichtenstein, and abstract painters such as Georgia O'Keefe, Elaine de Kooning, Lee Krasner, and Mark Rothko, none of whom were known for making explicitly political art.

> *We are grieved by American policies in Vietnam. We are opposed to American policies in Vietnam. We will not remain silent before the world. We call on those who wish to speak in a crucial and tragic moment in our history, to demand an immediate turning of the American policy in Vietnam to the methods of peace.*[4]

This public show of opposition to military action in Vietnam was followed by the collaborative construction of the Peace Tower in Los Angeles in 1966, a 58-foot steel tower covered with 400 anti-war artworks, standing in a dirt-filled lot between Hollywood and downtown Los Angeles. One year later, Angry Arts Week took place in New York, involving Bread and Puppet Theater and members of Black Mask as well as Leon Golub and Max Kozloff. The group produced a show called "The Collage of Indignation," which was exhibited at NYU's Loeb Student Center.[5] On the West Coast, Angry Arts included members of the Longshoreman's Union, long associated with progressive politics. In the borderlands to the south, groups of artists associated with the Chicano Movement, or *El Movimiento*, including the Royal Chicano Air Force, generated posters, performances, direct actions, and murals in support of the UFW grape boycott. One group of migrant farmers formed Teatro Campesino, a political

---

4. "End Your Silence," *New York Times* (April 18, 1965), Section 4, E5, cited in Francis Frascina, *Art, Politics and Dissent: Aspects of the Art Left in Sixties America* (Manchester: Manchester University Press, 1999), p. 50.

5. An excellent account of these projects and programs is found in Lucy R. Lippard, *A Different War: Vietnam in Art* (Seattle: Real Comet Press, 1990).

theater troupe that initially used flatbed trucks as mobile stage sets in order to reach workers directly in the fields.[6]

More militant tactics soon emerged. A 1966 manifesto from the anarchist collective Black Mask/Up Against the Wall Motherfuckers proclaimed: "a new spirit is rising. Like the streets of Watts we burn with revolution. We assault your gods. DESTROY THE MUSEUMS—our struggle cannot be hung on the walls."[7] Across the Atlantic, the Situationist International's affiliation with striking university students in the events of May 1968 was a high-profile illustration of how artists were exceeding the limits of their studio practice in order to directly engage in political action. Situationist-inspired slogans ("The society that abolishes every adventure makes its own abolition the only possible adventure," or, "To Hell with Boundaries") scrawled on city walls by militant students underscored the sense of societal impasse. Under the Situationist banner, artistic production was transformed into an array of ideas, organizational platforms, and political actions that influenced the practice of Conceptual Art, which was emerging at approximately the same time, and also the later (mid-1980s and early 1990s) work of tactical media activists such as Critical Art Ensemble, the Yes Men, Electronic Disturbance Theater, and the Zapatista Networks in Chiapas, Mexico.[8]

In 1969, a boycott was organized against the 10th São Paulo Biennial in protest of Brazil's repressive military regime, while, in New York City, the Art Workers' Coalition (AWC) was founded. Among its core group was Conceptual artist Hans Haacke, who remains active today in GLC. Initially, AWC functioned much like a trade union that viewed museums, their boards, and their top administrators as a *de facto* managerial class who effectively represented not artists or the public good, but the interests of the commercial art market. AWC took on the task of revealing this class conflict by staging protests outside MoMA, the Met, and the Guggenheim museums. Among the

---

6. See Alicia Gaspar de Alba, *Chicano Art Inside/Outside the Master's House: Cultural Politics and the CARA Exhibition* (Austin: University of Texas Press, 1998).

7. Black Mask no. 1, November 1966, cover printed in Alan W. Moore, *Art Gangs: Protest and Counterculture in New York City* (Autonomedia: New York, 2011).

8. See Nato Thompson and Gregory Sholette (eds.), *The Interventionists: Users' Manual for the Creative Disruption of Everyday Life* (Cambridge: MIT Press, 2004).

demands formally presented to these institutions were a call for a royalties system whereby collectors would pay artists a percentage of profits from the resale of their work and a request that the museums "be open on two evenings until midnight and admission should be free at all times."[9] Before AWC disbanded in 1971, its members marched in support of striking staff at MoMA, called on museums to set aside exhibition space for women, minorities, and artists with no gallery representation, and stridently protested the war in Vietnam, thus seeking to leverage their status as cultural producers to achieve social, political, and economic reforms for artists and also to advance a conception of society more broadly. Member Lucy R. Lippard summarized AWC's tactically focused critique of established art institutions as follows:

> As a public and therefore potentially accountable institution, the Museums were targeted in order to make points not only about artists' rights but also about opposition to the war in Vietnam, to racism and eventually sexism, and about the institutional entanglement of aesthetic with corporate finance and imperialism.[10]

In 1970, Artists and Writers Protest joined forces with the AWC in a mass letter-writing campaign calling on Pablo Picasso to withdraw his anti-war canvas *Guernica* from MoMA, where it still hung at the time. Later that year, New York's Attorney General shut down *The People's Flag Show* at Judson Memorial Church, an exhibition that included Abbie Hoffman and a range of artists protesting the war in Southeast Asia. Three participating artists were arrested on charges of "Desecration of the Flag."[11] In the UK, the

---

9. Similar groups to AWC emerged at or about the same time in Atlanta, Georgia, in Buenos Aires, Argentina, and in Canada, where this 1969 organizational legacy remains alive today as the Canadian Artists' Representation/*Le Front des artistes canadiens* (CARFAC). Indeed, the contemporary advocacy group Working Artists for the Greater Economy, or W.A.G.E., and their ongoing campaign to standardize artist's fees within the US not-for-profit artworld is modeled in part on CARFAC. See Gregory Sholette, *Dark Matter: Art and Politics in the Age of Enterprise Culture* (London: Pluto Press, 2011), p. 134.

10. Lippard is cited in Julie Ault (ed.), *Alternative Art New York* (Minneapolis: University of Minnesota Press, 2003), p. 79.

11. See Bradford D. Martin, *The Theater in the Street: Politics and Performance in Sixties America* (Amherst:

community arts movement had radicalized over the course of the 1960s, and in 1970, a group of artists led by Gustav Metzger marched on the Tate Gallery under the name of the International Coalition for the Liquidation of Art. Their intent was to debate with museum "visitors and staff about the complicity of museums in racism, sexism, war," while demanding "equal representation of women, ethnic minorities, and greater decentralization of culture."[12] The following year, and clearly under the influence of AWC, Mary Kelly, Kay Fido, Margaret Harrison, and Conrad Atkinson founded the Artists Union, among whose goals was to establish resale rights for all British artists.[13] Self-interest by artists recognizing their status as a type of worker typically evolved to other levels of protestation. Robert Morris and Poppy Johnson had initiated a one-day shutdown of all New York museums under the heading of the *New York Art Strike Against Racism, War and Repression* in 1970 to protest Richard Nixon's bombing campaign in Cambodia, among other war-related outrages; Metzger would later call on artists to cease making art altogether, between the years 1977 and 1980.[14] In 1979, Goran Đordevic called for an art strike, citing "the art system's unbroken repression of the artist and the alienation from the results of his practice," and Stewart Home would later promote *The Art Strike 1990–1993*. But in none of these instances was anything sustainable generated, making these attempted withdrawals from the artworld not significantly different from Lee Lozano's 1969 *General Strike Piece* and 1971 *Boycott Piece*, which are far more intellectually engaging projects that ultimately led the artist to turn her back on the New York artworld altogether with *Dropout Piece* (begun c.1970), in which she pledged to

[g]radually but determinedly avoid being present at official or public "uptown"

University of Massachusetts Press, 2004), pp. 151–53.

12. John A. Walker, *Left Shift: Radical Art in 1970s Britain* (London: I.B. Tauris, 2002), pp. 30–32.

13. Walker, *Left Shift*.

14. Julia Bryan Wilson, *Art Workers: Radical Practice in the Vietnam War Era* (Berkeley: University of California Press, 2011); cf. Gabriel Mindel Saloman, "On Hiatus: The Imminent Impossibility of the Art Strike," *The Journal of Aesthetics & Protest* 9 (Spring 2015), http://tinyurl.com/ohlbvy5.

functions or gatherings related to the "artworld" in order to pursue investigation
of total personal & public revolution.[15]

And yet before her death from cervical cancer in 1999, several prominent galleries featured retrospectives of her work.

In 1970, the Mexican art collective *Proceso Pentágono* was invited to participate in the 10th Biennale De Paris, and decided to publish a "Biennale counter-catalogue" as a subversive protest against Operation Condor, a CIA-led terror campaign targeting leftist students and workers across South America. According to historian Rubén Gallo, when the Biennale organizers got wind of this project, director Georges Boudaille sent a laconic letter to the groups informing them that the upcoming exhibition was "an artistic event and not a political one," and urged them "to behave professionally."[16] Meanwhile, back in New York, an AWC faction calling itself Guerrilla Art Action Group (GAAG) staged a mock gun battle in front of MoMA to protest the fatal shooting by National Guard troops of unarmed anti-war student protesters at Kent State University. GAAG carried out numerous direct actions inside MoMA to protest the wartime draft and the lack of representation of artists of color, utilizing tactics similar to those of Liberate Tate in recent years. Similar direct action was carried out in Toronto, as artists chained themselves to the doors of the Art Gallery of Ontario to protest mercury pollution coming from the nearby Reed Paper Company's mill. Eventually members of GAAG were refused entry into the MoMa, while in Canada Reed later compensated First Nations people for heavy metal contamination after years of public protests by both artists and activists.[17]

---

15. Sarah Lehrer-Graiwer, *Lee Lozano: Dropout Piece* (London: Afterall Books, 2014); cf. Lucy R. Lippard, "Escape Attempts," from the introduction to *Six Years: The Dematerialization of the Art Object from 1966 to 1972* (New York: Praeger, 1973).

16. See Rubén Gallo, "The Mexican Pentagon: Adventures in Collectivism during the 1970s," in Blake Stimson and Gregory Sholette (eds.), *Collectivism After Modernism* (Minneapolis: University of Minnesota Press, 2006).

17. Karl Beveridge points out that the late filmmaker and artist Joyce Wieland actually demonstrated against a 1976 exhibition entitled *Changing Visions* thatshe was part of in order to call attention to environmental damage caused by the paper mill, who also happened to be sponsoring the show. (Email to Author, February 9, 2015)

Cultural producers strongly supported the anti-war movement, but they also organized in support of striking workers, and in solidarity with numerous liberation movements that emerged in the late 1960s and 1970s. In 1974, the UK Artists' Union presented a show, *United We Stand: Exhibition in Solidarity with the Miners* at the miners' union headquarters in London, while artists protested the exclusion of women one year later outside the exhibition *Condition of Sculpture* at the Hayward Gallery. That same year, Mary Kelly collaborated with the Berwick Film Collective on a feature-length movie, *Nightcleaners,* about London's female janitorial workers. The film was intended to be part of a unionizing campaign and not a work of gallery art.[18] In 1976, artists picketed the Whitney Museum to denounce an exhibition celebrating the US bicentennial, which comprised (with only one exception) works by white men that were drawn solely from the collection of billionaire philanthropist John D. Rockefeller III. The group Artists Meeting for Cultural Change formed in angry response, and produced *An Anti-Catalog,* which probably represents the first substantial interpretation of American art from a socially contextualized perspective rather than a formal or biographical one.[19] And in 1977, London-based Conrad Atkinson was among a group of professional artists who designed banners for May Day labor demonstrations, while the Camera Work Collective engaged in street battles with police as squatters in Lewisham were being evicted.[20] That same year in Los Angeles, artist Leslie Labowitz worked with Women Against Violence Against Women (WAVAW) and the National Organization of Woman (NOW) to successfully force record companies to cease using offensive, sexist imagery in their advertisements. The campaign was carried out through a combination of boycott tactics and publicly performed demonstrations (Labowitz and fellow artist Suzanne Lacy called them "media performances") staged specifically to attract mass news coverage. These projects prefigured the work

---

18. See Walker, *Left Shift*, p. 137.

19. *An Anti-Catalog* is available for free download at http://www.darkmatterarchives.net/.

20. See Walker, *Left Shift*, pp. 204–7. Squatters recently moved back into Lewisham—see Sarah Trotter, "Squatters Invade Lewisham Royal British Legion Headquarters," *Bradford Telegraph and Argus* (June 9–10, 2014), http://tinyurl.com/omuau8z.

Ikon *journal featuring Art Against Apartheid exhibition (1986) (Sholette's Archive)*

of tactical media artists in the 1990s.[21]

Acts of solidarity and direct action by artists continued into the 1980s. At the start of the decade, French Fluxus artist Ernest Pignon-Ernest and Spanish writer and artist Antonio Saura initiated Artists of the World Against Apartheid. To honor the boycott of South Africa, which had been in place since the Sharpeville Massacre of 1960, they curated a traveling exhibition to educate audiences about the racial injustice in that country. The collection would be donated to South Africa following its liberation from apartheid.[22] A similar initiative had been undertaken in 1973 by two Chilean exiles, who organized a collection of some 1,800 works of art into the Resistance Museum in Solidarity with Salvador Allende. This later inspired Rasha Salti and Kristine Khouri to curate the International Art Exhibition in Solidarity with Palestine, which opened in Beirut in 1978.[23]

In 1981, a hundred artists demonstrated against an all-white, all-male exhibition at the Los Angeles Contemporary Museum of Art (LACMA), wearing photographic masks of museum director Maurice Tuchman. Even mainstream art critic Christopher Knight wrote indignantly:

> *After a decade of neglect of contemporary art in general and L.A. art in particular, for LACMA to re-emerge into the field with an exhibition of artists whose rise to prominence was benignly assisted by common racist and sexist attitudes*

---

21. See Carolyn Bronstein, *Battling Pornography: The American Feminist Anti-Pornography Movement, 1976–1986* (Cambridge: Cambridge University Press, 2011), p. 167.

22. Rhetoric by Western businesses about labor conditions under South African apartheid in the 1970s is echoed today by indifference toward the plight of migrant workers in the Gulf. In 1972, a *Fortune Magazine* article celebrated South Africa's cheap labor, arguing that, "South Africa has always been regarded by foreign investors as a gold mine, one of those rare and refreshing places where profits are great and problems small. Capital is not threatened by political instability or nationalization. Labor is cheap, the market booming, the currency hard and convertible." Cited in Gay W. Seidman, *Beyond The Boycott: Labor Rights, Human Rights, and Transnational Activism* (Russell Sage Foundation: 2007), p. 49.

23. Salti recently organized an exhibition about the International Art Exhibition in Solidarity with Palestine for the Museum of Contemporary Art in Barcelona, entitled *Past Disquiet* (http://tinyurl.com/ounlkoc). Notably, the 54 Venice Biennale special edition that took place between October 1974 and 1975 was organized under the title *Libertà per il Cile* (Freedom for Chile), to recall the 1973 coup against Salvador Allende.

The Committee Against Fort Apache (CAFA) protesting in the South Bronx in 1981 (Credit: Jerry Kearns)

(especially when racism and sexism were highly visible concerns of the Los Angeles art community in the intervening decade) serves to reopen old wounds rather than celebrate an artistic heritage.[24]

On the East Coast a boycott was called against the film *Fort Apache the Bronx* (1981), an urban exploitation movie starring noted liberal actor Paul Newman that was set in the crumbling South Bronx. Opponents from the Puerto Rican and Black communities formed the Committee Against *Fort Apache* (CAFA). The cultural significance of these protests attracted the attention of *Artforum*'s editors, who invited artist and CAFA member Jerry Kearns to submit a piece on the protest in collaboration with critic Lucy Lippard. But when their essay "Cashing in a Wolf Ticket" was delivered, the noted art magazine initially refused to publish the piece because the authors openly sided with the boycott activists. Eventually "Wolf Ticket" went to press, but only after *Artforum* added a disclaimer alerting readers to the fact that the opinions expressed by Kearns and Lippard were not those of the journal's editors. This addendum may be the only instance of such a disclaimer ever printed in the journal. Between 1976 and 1980 Kearns was also active in the Cultural Committee of the National Black United Front and Amiri Baraka's Anti-Imperialist Cultural Union, where he used photography to document boycott actions, stop work tactics, police brutality, and courtroom testimony. These were predominantly African American organizations to which belonged not only Kearns, but also three other white former members of *Fox Magazine*, a politically focused offshoot of the UK-based Art & Language collective that published between 1975 and 1976.

By the middle of the decade, President Ronald Reagan had launched a not-so-covert war in Central America aimed at overthrowing the revolutionary Sandinista government of Nicaragua and targeting leftists in neighboring Guatemala, Honduras, and El Salvador. In response, the New York–based artists' collective Group Material collaborated with an El Salvadorian support group to curate an exhibition for a popular urban dance club, and the Political Art Documentation/Distribution collective paraded a giant blue, inflated Pac Man beast with the features of Uncle Sam in front of the White

24. Christopher Knight writing in the *Los Angeles Herald Examiner* (August 19, 1981), cited in Stacey Allan, "Protest at the Los Angeles county museum, 1981," *East of Borneo* (July 13, 2012), http://tinyurl.com/o9nypo4.

House. In 1984, Leon Golub, Lucy Lippard, Doug Ashford, John P. Weber, and others organized *Artists' Call Against Intervention in Central America*, which brought together artists, alternative spaces, small commercial dealers, and even a few major art galleries in a consciousness-raising mobilization focused on Reagan's policies south of the border.[25]

Artists' Call may have been the last major art project of this period in which the notion of solidarity between cultural workers and a social justice campaign was central to the very conception of the operation. It was the last time that groups of professionally trained, high-profile artists acted beyond their immediate set of interests as cultural workers, women, African Americans, Latinos, or LGBTQ individuals. Notwithstanding the significance of later groups, such as Gran Fury and the Guerrilla Girls, the focus of artist engagement in direct protest in the later 1980s was considerably narrowed, limited to countering injustices directed at specific social groups that overlapped with the population of artists as opposed to addressing systemic inequities or ideological structures endemic to contemporary capitalist society. While many individual artists participated in actions organized by ACT UP (AIDS Coalition to Unleash Power), it seems that in the aftermath of the fall of actually existing socialism, a different paradigm of activist art began to emerge, at once less ideologically romantic and more pragmatic, in which acts of tactical public intervention were directed at correcting particular offenses, or sometimes even understood as interventionist ends in themselves. And although some artists remained committed to broader change by working with or in tandem with the counter-globalization and pro-environmentalist protest campaigns such as the Global Justice Movement, the artworld backed away from notions of wholesale social and political confrontation and change.[26] Gone was the cultural

25. See Ault (ed.), *Alternative Art*, p. 71.

26. The anti-globalization "movement of movements," as it was sometimes called, gave birth to an impressive array of cultural activities, but most if not all of this imaginative work remained off the radar screen of the mainstream artworld, as well as much of the so-called alternative art scene as well. Valuable overviews of this social movement culture can be found in George McKay (ed.), *DiY Culture: Party & Protest in Nineties Britain* (London: Verso, 1998); Notes from Nowhere (ed.), *We Are Everywhere:The Irresistible Rise of Global Anticapitalism* (London: Verso, 2003); Josh MacPhee, *Realizing the Impossible: Art Against Authority* (Oak-

drive to imagine an ecstatic revolutionary event such as May 1968 or an alternative future in which social justice prevailed over oppression and militarization. In the 1990s and 2000s, most "engaged" artists directed their attention at everyday life experience, or cultural identity. Two dominant theories at the time were Nicolas Bourriaud's Relational Aesthetics and Tactical Media (TM). Though incompatible in many respects, both concepts eschewed ideology, including that of the Left. TM theorists David Garcia and Geert Lovink once alluded to Marxism as "vaporware": a software product announced with much fanfare that never actually materializes, although it is never officially abandoned either.[27]

TM itself did not last long, holding out only until a globally integrated system of electronic surveillance was implemented after the terrorist attacks of September 11, 2001. With the post-9/11 Patriot Act–empowered investigation of Critical Art Ensemble co-founder Steven Kurtz starting in 2004, followed by the high profile tribulations of journalist and WikiLeaks co-founder Julian Assange in 2010, the espionage conviction of Chelsea (Bradley) Manning, and the self-exile of National Security Administration whistleblower Edward Snowden to Russia in 2013, many of the electronic loopholes TM exploited, such as RTMark's fake George W. Bush campaign website gwbush.com and denial-of-service attacks on servers carried out as a form of digital "sit in," have become impossible to accomplish while remaining clandestine, if not actually crimi-nalized along the lines of Pirate Bay, identity theft, and Internet hacking.[28]

These technological and ideological shifts were followed by a second blow: the crushing weight of capital's faltering economic system and the 2007–8 economic melt-down, which pushed artists into an ever more precarious existence alongside many

---

land: AK Press, 2007).

27. "Our hybrid forms are always provisional. What counts are the temporary connections you are able to make. Here and now, not some vaporware promised for the future. But what we can do on the spot with the media we have access to." (David Garcia and Geert Lovink, "The ABC of Tactical Media," *Nettime.org* (May 16, 1997), http://tinyurl.com/ng3f77)

28. More about the Steve Kurtz investigation can be found at the Critical Art Ensemble Defense Fund website: www.caedefensefund.org; see also RTMark, which was the artistic predecessor to the Yes Men, at: http://www.rtmark.com/.

other types of uneducated service employees, but also overeducated creative workers. Their virtual proletarianization in recent years has only added insult to injury. The cultural agency that has emerged since is far less sanguine about the power of culture to change anything. Contemporary artist Pedro Lasch puts it succinctly. Noting that in May of 2006 the *New York Post* extensively covered the food and fashion associated with Cinco de Mayo celebrations in the US and Mexico, even though, at that same moment, unprecedented mass demonstrations by undocumented workers were taking place across the United States, all of which the paper ignored, Lasch concludes: "I once thought that when you win the battle of culture, you win the battle of politics. It's just not true."[29] One response to this reality check is that direct action, which has witnessed a sporadic coming and going among artists over the past century or more, is now emerging again as both institutional critique and identity politics have yielded little substantial change in the artworld. Thus we see today more and more acts of embodied resistance by artists in opposition to an entrepreneurial political economy in which a multitude of Master of Fine Arts (MFA)–credentialed art professionals vie for an ever thinner slice of the art market pie (valued at 47.42 billion euros in 2013).[30]

What, then, has changed since the end of the cultural turn in 1989? And what is it about the social position of cultural producers that still makes their occasional involvement in direct action appear such a fraught and problematic retreat from "proper" artistic practice?

Throughout the post-war era, the influence that artists and other cultural producers felt they possessed helped empower them to focus on political and social circumstances not directly tied to their own professional working conditions. It was as if the passionate expression of a novelist, painter, playwright, or musician could,

29. Pedro Lasch, in a personal correspondence (March 15, 2015). Lasch was a participating artist in Gulf Labor's *52 Weeks* campaign (2014).

30. Alexander Forbes, "TEFAF Art Market Report Says 2013 Best Year on Record Since 2007, With Market Outlook Bullish," *artnetnews* (March 12, 2014), http://tinyurl.com/mlvj6bx.

when amplified by the mass media, stand on equal footing with statements issued by corporate chiefs or heads of state. Acting as public intellectuals, cultural producers demanded that national leaders, as well as museum directors, live up to democratic ideals. No doubt this sense of empowerment was also due to the prominent role that culture played in the Cold War itself. Recall the words of John F. Kennedy shortly before he was assassinated, which paved the way for the establishment of the National Endowment for the Arts:

> The artist, however faithful to his personal vision of reality, becomes the last champion of the individual mind and sensibility against an intrusive society and an officious state. . . . Artists are not engineers of the soul. It may be different elsewhere. But democratic society—in it, the highest duty of the writer, the composer, the artist is to remain true to himself and to let the chips fall where they may.[31]

The "elsewhere" Kennedy referred to was, of course, the socialist bloc, and his assurances regarding absolute artistic freedom in the West were central to the ideological theater of the Cold War. Not surprisingly, state support for individual artists collapsed precipitously following the break-up of the USSR.

Of course, acts of solidarity between cultural producers and oppressed groups long preceded the wrenching realignment of the Cold War, but with a key difference: prior to the Cold War, artists put their talents at the service of well-defined anti-capitalist political movements and parties. The involvement of early 20th-century artists in radical Left politics, including the founding of the Soviet Union but also in post–World War I Germany, is well known. More obscure, perhaps, is the 1913 Paterson Silk Strike and Pageant, in New Jersey, USA. Members of the International Workers of the World, including Elizabeth Gurley Flynn and John Reed, joined forces with painter John Sloan and members of the Greenwich Village *avant-garde* to produce a large-scale spectacle in Madison Square Garden. The event included throngs of

31. President John F. Kennedy, *Amherst College Convocation Address* (October 26, 1963), transcribed by Amherst College Archives and Special Collections from the audio recording of JFK's speech, http://tinyurl.com/n5j6njf.

immigrant workers who reenacted scenes of factory life inside the New Jersey silk plant they were striking against. Participants called for support of the work stoppage with its demand for an eight-hour work day, but as strikers played themselves, police and industrialists simultaneously moved back and forth from theater rehearsals to actual picket lines.[32] After the formation of the Communist Party USA's John Reed Clubs in the late 1920s, the involvement of artists and writers in organized political groupings came to pervade cultural life for the next decade. Convinced that artists were just another type of exploited laborer suffering from the chaos of capitalism's 1929 collapse, left artists formed their own union in 1934. Painter Stuart Davis, one of its first presidents, declared that its members had "discovered their identity with the working class as a whole."[33] In 1936, the American Artists' Congress was founded as part of the Communist Party's Popular Front, and sent an Artists and Writers Ambulance Corps to fight in the Spanish Civil War.

The great upheavals of the 1930s (and 1960s) resulted from extraordinary political and economic circumstances, and helped to create that existential bump which results in greater solidarity between populations most at risk. Perhaps we are seeing a third such movement today in the continuum of direct actions generated by the GLC, W.A.G.E., Debt Fair, Liberate Tate, and Occupy Museums as well as the increasing use of boycotts by artists not only toward the Guggenheim Abu Dhabi, but in Moscow, Sydney, São Paulo, and in solidarity with the Palestinian Academic and Cultural Boycott of Israel.

Yet an important difference between the early 20th-century forms of solidarity and those of recent years is the absence today of an ideological counter-narrative to capitalism, and the ever-diminishing belief that cultural producers bring something extraordinary to the underprivileged masses via the elevated benefits of serious art. Cultural politics is becoming just plain politics, and the legacy of the post-war cul-

---

32. See "Chapter Nine: Blurring the Boundaries Between Art and Life," in Nicolas Lampert, *A People's History of the United States: 250 Years of Activist Art and Artists Working in Social Justice Movements* (New York: The New Press, 2013).

33. Andrew Hemingway, *Artists on the Left: American Artists and the Communist Movement, 1926–1956* (New Haven: Yale University Press, 2002), p. 87.

tural turn appears to have persuaded artists that they are simply one type of producer among others. Is it possible to rekindle, or re-hack, in a self-critical way, the symbolic power art once had as an expression of freely directed labor? If so, the task is not to wield it solely for cultural producers or their elite audiences, but instead to turn it outward toward whole populations that are increasingly caught in the cruel cycle of precarity.

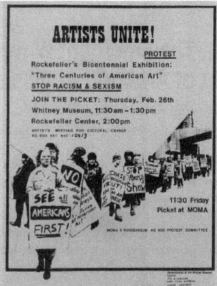

End pages from An Anti-Catalog, Artists Meeting for Cultural Change (1977) (Sholette Archives)

The Emergent Wave of Artworld Activism

Guy Mannes-Abbott

"How is protest articulated?" German artist Hito Steyerl asked that disarmingly simple question back in 2002.[1] For artists who also want to be effective activists, the answer to her question is increasingly complex because it also requires a biting articulation of our present world. On the one hand, as the artworld and economic globalization increasingly merge, artists become implicated in the systemic humanitarian and ecological violence of global elites. On the other, the value their work generates and the credibility it grants offer strategic leverage over institutions that are actively complicit with the same systems.

The artists and writers of Gulf Labor have utilized that kind of power to protest the exploitation of "forced labor," according to the ILO's definition, in the construction of the Guggenheim Abu Dhabi (GAD) and other cultural outposts on Abu Dhabi's Saadiyat Island. The institutions involved—the British Museum, Guggenheim, NYU, and Louvre—once represented civil, liberal, and even revolutionary[2] values in contestable degrees, but are now indisputably in the vanguard of a frontier-capitalism. Each has reduced itself to a brand in the winner-takes-all spectacle distorting our common world and imperiling the biosphere. In the largest sense, we could say that the Gulf Labor

---

1. Hito Steyerl, "The Articulation of Protest," *republicart.net* (September 2002), http://tinyurl.com/m4kd8qh; reprinted in Will Bradley and Charles Esche (eds.), *Art and Social Change: A Critical Reader* (London: Tate Publishing, 2008).

2. See Guy Mannes-Abbott, "Utopian Dust Versus Perfumed Amplification: Object Lessons from Saadiyat Island and Gehry's Guggenheim, Abu Dhabi," *Ibraaz* (June 26, 2014), http://tinyurl.com/nu4xql6.

campaign is also aimed at the socio-political, culturo-ethical recomposition of what Jason Moore has called the "capitalocene."[3]

My aim here is to situate Gulf Labor within related and emergent forms of protest in the artworld. Doing so will differentiate forms of art as well as activism from a developing economic globalization that instrumentalizes this artworld for narrowing purposes. The sample of protests that I analyze are all linked in some way to the problematic funding of art-museum extensions and new cultural institutions: the activism of Platform in London, which highlights the sponsorship of art and culture by corporations that threaten human existence; G.U.L.F.'s creative interventions at the Guggenheim in New York, which have supplemented and stimulated the campaigning of Gulf Labor's coalition; and the protests over sponsorship at Biennials in Sydney and São Paulo during 2014, which challenged Australia's abuse of asylum-seekers and Israel's war crimes, respectively.

A good place to begin is the planner's vision for Abu Dhabi's Saadiyat. In 2007–8, TDIC's Masterplan for Saadiyat's Cultural District promised to deliver "the largest concentration of cultural venues anywhere in the world: four enormous museums, a five-stage performing arts centre" within a decade.[4] Appearing alongside the global cultural brands was a wearyingly predictable cluster of starchitects enlisted to build these spectacular "culture-shops": Norman Foster, Frank Gehry, Zaha Hadid, and Jean Nouvel. In addition, there would be "a Biennial Park of 19 multipurpose venues arrayed along a man-made canal" designed by emerging global names, including "Russia's Yuri Avvakumov, New York's Hani Rashid, the UK's David Adjaye, China's Pei-Zhu and Korea's Seung H-Sang," as well as a seemingly tokenistic Emirati: Khalid al Najjar.[5]

3. Jason Moore, *Capitalism in the Web of Life* (London: Verso, 2015).

4. Youssef Rahka, "Hatching Saadiyat," *The National* (April 24, 2008), http://tinyurl.com/kxx6uk2.

5. *Ibid.*

Thomas Krens, the Guggenheim's brand-expanding deal-maker, trumpeted Saadiyat's capacity to shake up the (old) world. "The collection of national pavilions in the Park [Giardini] at the Venice Biennale," he declared, "is really a snapshot of what the world was like in the 1930s."[6] In fact, as Jonas Staal has pointed out, it's more settled and insidiously commercialized than that. "The first countries to host the World's Fair—the United Kingdom (1851), the United States (1853), and France (1855)—occupied powerful positions comparable to those of the first countries to secure a permanent national pavilion on the grounds of Venice's Giardini: the colonial powers of Belgium, Germany, and the United Kingdom (all in 1907)."[7]

Krens continued: "131 art biennales already existed around the world . . . but . . . none has a longer history than Venice. If you looked at the origin of the biennale concept, you can include São Paulo and Documenta. And then you ask, 'What works?'"[8] An odd choice of words from a man whose attempts to extend his museum's brand failed in so many locations. "The thinking," he went on, "was that Abu Dhabi had to improve that situation by discarding the national pavilion model in favor of a more global, curatorially-driven one."[9]

Krens was proposing an expanded geography and more varied curatorial origins to replace the model of national pavilions acting as cultural embassies, arcades, or shop windows for the old world. Yet since São Paulo had rather belatedly joined this shift in 1998, by 2007–8, "the anachronism of staging a world's fair for art" already really lived on "only in Venice."[10] Not surprisingly, the "vision" for Saadiyat would be not only better, but bigger: some 65,000 square meters of exhibition space versus

6. Thomas Krens and Rem Koolhaas, "After Bilbao—Thomas Krens' vision for Abu Dhabi as a 'cultural destination'," *Al Manakh* 12 (2007), pp. 334–36.

7. Jonas Staal, "Art. Democratism. Propaganda," *e-flux journal* 52 (February 2015).

8. Krens and Koolhaas, "After Bilbao."

9. *Ibid.*

10. Charles Esche, "Making Art Global. A good place or a no place?" in Rachel Weiss et al., *Making Art Global (Part 1): Havana Biennial 1989* (London: Afterall, 2012).

"the overall Venice Biennale space which is around 50,000 square meters."[11] In the years since the financial crisis of 2008–9, the masterplan timeline has been stretched out and most of the grand museum projects remain unfinished, while the original "vision" of a Biennial Park of pavilions, designed as flexible educational and commercial spaces, seems to have dropped out of sight entirely.

Saadiyat's pavilions were intended to mediate between the museums and the District,[12] a paradise of "luxury" retail and leisure for the kind of global tourist who might pick up an apartment or villa to store their shopping—cars, clothes and artist's video-editions—at the end of a long weekend. In bee-keeping terms, the word "pavilion" refers to the middle hive in a collateral system. What does it tell us that in no time at all such an expanded collateral system became unnecessary? That "what works" now is an unremarked continuity of experience between retail and cultural boutiques?

Perhaps this is not simply a manifestation of the directionality of the artworld but a familiar experience for so many of us in so many parts of the globe. Trade fair or national embassy, arms or art-sales, cultural legacy or political cover, mall or museum, architect or slave-driver—these distinctions are blurred in a single, increasingly totalized, collateral system.

Gulf Labor's coalition operates in, and shares this context with, a range of other forms of artworld protest. To protest effectively has required not only persistent precision-targeting of the Abu Dhabi government-owned vehicle of TDIC, not to mention its favored contractor Arabtec (the government owns a controlling stake in Aabar, the majority owner of Arabtec). It has also entailed pressuring the New York–based Guggenheim Foundation, whose current director, Richard Armstrong, has been at pains to extend Krens's overweening legacy, adding portentousness to the former's vulgarity. Armstrong insists that his GAD will be a beacon of civilized values, "transformative of the cultural landscape of the region and the world."[13] Statements like this

---

11. Krens and Koolhaas, "After Bilbao."

12. The District is the name of Saadiyat's vast elite-brand mall—see http://tinyurl.com/mvorz4g.

13. Simeon Kerr, "Labour abuse claims overshadow Guggenheim Abu Dhabi show," *Financial Times* (November 3, 2014), http://tinyurl.com/mzv6clx.

sit uneasily alongside the record of human rights abuses in the construction of Abu Dhabi's glittering monuments.

Two-dimensional protesting is inadequate in an era of globalization. What's required is to aim *everywhere*, strategically. To protest at every point in the chain, up, down, and throughout the collateral system, challenging every complicit element. Old-fashioned public protests and bad publicity at home and, if loud enough, then also abroad. Chasing down individual starchitects and holding them to account, while exposing exploitative contractors and myriad sub-contractors. And, last but not least, vigilant research to reveal what is going on behind shiny PR screens and to follow through at the level of international law.[14] When UAE officials finger individuals and organizations that offer critiques as shadowy, interfering "foreign agents," protest must cross borders to force engagements with the issues.

Emergent forms of protest therefore require precision about a globalized world, with its machinery of political and military supports and its social, humanitarian, and ecological costs. Art's new co-dependency with global corporations directly implicates or involves debt bondage, crimes against humanity, and climate-driven devastation. Exposing and reforming this intimate arrangement is the challenge of our time. If that seems extravagant, let me describe some of the ways that artists have begun tackling these issues at this scale of engagement.

One such example is the Free For All campaign. Initiated in the late 1990s and fronted by Richard Hamilton, it was aimed directly at the political economy of institutions. Under the rubric of a National Campaign for the Arts, artists, musicians, and actor unions formed a coalition to protest against charging admission to the core collections held by UK national institutions (including the Victoria and Albert Museum and National Portrait Gallery). The call was predicated on the 1948 Universal Declaration of Human Rights: "Everyone has the right freely to

---

14. GL's May 2014 Report formed a substantive part of the ITUC complaint to the ILO, which GLC members were instrumental in, too—International Labor Organization (ILO), "Decision on the 14th Item on the Agenda: Reports of the Officers of the Governing Body Fifth report . . ." (November 13 , 2015), http://tinyurl.com/no98ypk; cf. David Batty, "Call for UN to Investigate Plight of Migrant Workers in the UAE," *Guardian* (September 13, 2014), http://tinyurl.com/lpq5lsg.

participate in the cultural life of the community, to enjoy the arts and to share in scientific advancement."

The focus on institutional funding and cultural access has been transformed in the intervening years, largely because private money now out-muscles public at the national institutional level. That shift is reflected in the work of Platform, "an NGO that combines art, research and education in projects that are often aimed at addressing the environmental and human rights abuses of the oil industry."[15] Founded to investigate the relationship between British Petroleum (BP) and the Tate, Platform launched a campaign[16] in 2010 to coincide with the Tate's celebration of 20 years of support from BP, and hosted a series of performance protests by Liberate Tate and others.

Today, BP sponsors the Tate, the British Museum, the Royal Opera House, and National Portrait Gallery to the tune of some £2 million a year. The Tate won't say, but Platform members presume that the museum receives a quarter of that, or £500,000 a year (0.4 percent of the Tate's overall funding).[17] The Tate and the British Museum have never charged entry to core collections, but the former claims that oil money has been "instrumental in Tate developing access to the Tate Collections"[18]— this despite free access being linked to governmental Grant-in-Aid funding. While the Tate has resisted brand-extension abroad, the British Museum is a beneficiary of "forced labor" on Saadiyat in its capacity as advisor to the Zayed National Museum, in return for which it received millions of pounds of Abu Dhabi oil money for its own new wing in London.[19]

---

15. "Tate fears that 'protests might intensify' over BP sponsorship," *Platform* (September 19, 2014), http://tinyurl.com/l4wveaa.

16. "Unprecedented coalition from the arts condemns BP-sponsorship of the Tate," *Platform* (June 28, 2010), http://tinyurl.com/psfhona.

17. "Tate fears," *Platform*.

18. Matilda Lee, "Platform: attempting to drive a wedge between the Tate Modern and BP," *The Ecologist* (February 18, 2011), http://tinyurl.com/oqwc4qz.

19. The British Museum hides behind corporate financial sensitivity, but a reliable source described a dedicated London staff of 20 and an FOI request that I made in November 2013 conceded a £3 million gift. In 2013, the *Economist* estimated the British Museum's contract was worth "as much as £10m a year."("Temples

Labour Power supermarket, from Guy Mannes-Abbott, "Companions" (2014)

Labour Power restaurant, from Guy Mannes-Abbott, "Companions" (2014)

Restricted to operating on home soil, the Tate still solicited funds from petro-quarters to finance its status-marking physical extension. The lion's share (£143 million) of the £215 million cost came from private sources, including "Elisabeth Murdoch, banker John Studzinski, and one of Studzinski's good friends, Tate's Chair of Trustees and former Chief Executive of BP, Lord John Browne."[20] Browne is also a partner in Riverstone Holdings, which owns Cuadrilla—a fracking company widely criticized for its blind pursuit of fossil fuels at the expense of renewables and the environmental damage it causes, including water contamination. He has been a major asset in raising cash from billionaire connections who are often also collectors and donators of works in lieu of tax.[21] In aligning itself with global corporate developers like Lend Lease,[22] the museum chose "commercial sensitivity" over public interest and ethical transparency.

There are two aspects to this. First, the ethics of art funding, which requires transparency—something that "needs to become a protocol" rather than simply the object of protest and struggle.[23] On this point, Platform's persistence was rewarded in January 2015 when the Information Commissioner's Office ruled to force the disclosure of sponsorship deals, and revealed how little the Tate had sold its credibility to BP for.[24] Liberate Tate celebrated by dropping petro-pound notes (equivalent to BP's annual contribution) from the Members Room into the galleries below. Second, there is the larger issue of ethical art funding: whether the Tate should, as it obviously

of Delight," *Economist* (December 21, 2013), http://tinyurl.com/k9gvufr)

20. "Tate, Big Oil, and the savage inequality of capital," *Platform* (December 1, 2014), http://tinyurl.com/p4gly6t.

21. *Ibid.*

22. The ICO ordered that a secret financial viability agreement at the heart of a major regeneration project between Lend Lease and London Borough of Southwark be made public. ("Heygate FOI Appeal Decision—Tribunal Delivers Verdict," *35% Campaign* (May 10, 2014), http://tinyurl.com/mt6zglu)

23. Charles Esche, cited in Rachel Spence, "Who Funds the Arts and Why We Should Care," *Financial Times* (September 19, 2014), http://tinyurl.com/jvfw8x5.

24. Mark Brown, "Tate's BP Sponsorship was £150,000 to £330,000 a Year, Figures Show," *Guardian* (January 26, 2015), http://tinyurl.com/ktmthyg.

could, say no to corporations that are working hard to destroy our common world.

The nexus of "dirty" private money and unashamed brand-promotion has been a central target of Gulf Labor's strategies from the beginning. Increasingly, direct action is part of the mix. In early 2014, activists with roots in Occupy Wall Street added their autonomous voices and bodies to the Guggenheim protests. G.U.L.F. (Global Ultra Luxury Faction) is a "coalition of groups (and) autonomous off-shoot of Gulf Labor Coalition" whose members embrace an "artistic vision" with "a global dimension that both encompasses and surpasses migrant workers as bonded labor in Abu Dhabi."[25] According to Amin Husain and Nitasha Dhillon, "for us, the most relevant forms of art involve creative direct action . . . that challenge the institutional frames of museums, galleries, festivals and academic establishments."[26]

In a series of high-profile actions, G.U.L.F. has artfully rained petro-dollar bills within New York's Guggenheim, projected Illuminator statements across its exterior, picketed a $75,000-a-table fund-raising dinner,[27] established an alternative competition for a Guggenheim Helsinki, and staged a spectacular occupation of the Peggy Guggenheim museum in Venice.[28] Operating in New York, Husain, Dhillon, and others "are provided a unique opportunity to leverage the visibility" of the Guggenheim, while building knowledge about the labor economy of the city's own artworld institutions; indeed, museum staff instructed to expel them confided information about their own exploitative conditions of employment.[29] According to Noah Fischer, "G.U.L.F actions are made to function on two edges: to create maximum visibility and to make it structurally difficult for the institution itself to function."[30] For example,

25. Nate Christensen and John Warner, "The Art of Resistance: Labor, Debt, and G.U.L.F.'s Guggenheim Campaign," *Jadaliyya* (May 16, 2014), http://tinyurl.com/oy67gox.

26. *Ibid.*

27. Mostafa Heddaya, "Protestors Unfurl Three-Story Banner in Guggenheim Museum," *Hyperallergic* (November 5, 2014), http://tinyurl.com/pevq9w5.

28. The Next Helsinki, http://www.nexthelsinki.org.

29. Christensen and Warner, "The Art of Resistance."

30. Noah Fischer, private correspondence with the author (January 2015).

when the group hung agit-prop works on the walls during a Futurist exhibition, furious calls were generated from protective collectors. G.U.L.F. concluded: "we let these collectors tell the museum that the *status quo* cannot continue."[31]

In March 2014, members of Gulf Labor came together from all over the world—Australia, India, the US, and Europe—to conduct field research in the UAE's labor camps and to meet with TDIC officials. Sustained conversations with the latter revealed that no serious attempts had been made to address issues like recruitment fee indebtedness, which is key to conditions of forced labor. Subsequently, GLC compiled a report· that garnered wide publicity and significantly contributed to the ITUC's formal 2014 complaint to the ILO about forced labor at Saadiyat and elsewhere in the UAE.[32]

Early in March 2014, I arrived in Abu Dhabi from Sydney, where I'd given a talk about Gulf Labor in the midst of a dramatic protest by artists against the Biennale's financial links to the mandatory detention of asylum seekers.[33] In the lead-up to the Biennale, Reza Barati, a Kurdish-Iranian architect detained in a camp on Manus Island, Papua New Guinea, had been killed during a crack-down on inmates protesting their conditions.[34] Transfield, the company that runs the camps (and which supplied patrolling warships to the government), was also the founder and ongoing sponsor of the Biennale of Sydney. A significant body of artists, including Martin Boyce, Nathan Coley, Deborah Kelly, Libia Castro, Olafur Olafson, and Ahmet Ogut, wrote to the Biennale's Board claiming "responsibility for our own participation in a chain of connections (both) ethically indefensible and in breach of human rights."[35]

---

31. *Ibid.*

32. Cf. note 14, above.

33. The talk and related radio interviews were spontaneous, in that I was in Adelaide and Sydney touring my book, *In Ramallah, Running*. The talk can be viewed here: http://tinyurl.com/mnplvxk.

34. Paul McGeough, "Someone's son, someone's brother: Reza Barati, An Architect Who Had Hopes for a Better Life," *Sydney Morning Herald* (March 1, 2014), http://tinyurl.com/qfktlkp.

35. "An Open Letter to the Board of Directors, Biennale of Sydney" (February 19, 2014), http://tinyurl.com/qdwlt2j.

Ongoing "participation" would amount to "an active endorsement, providing cultural capital for Transfield."[36] Ögüt describes the Board's response as "misleading . . . and intransigent."[37] Having requested that the administrators "withdraw from the current sponsorship arrangements with Transfield."[38] Ögüt, himself a Turkish Kurd, and several other artists announced their withdrawal from the Biennale.

My Sydney talk about Gulf Labor took place in a Biennale venue while plans were being laid to heavily "secure" the looming mega-event against a fast-galvanizing protest. Within two days, Luca Belgiorno-Nettis, the chair of the board, resigned, taking his financial ties to Transfield with him. He has since divested his private and commercial interests in the systemic persecution of asylum-seekers.[39] Transfield Holdings, the trust that financed the Biennale, cut its own financial involvement in Transfield Services too. The government's policy of detaining "illegal" asylum-seekers in extraterritorial camps and of privatizing these operations remains unchanged.

Ögüt rejoined the Biennale, and struggled to find a Transfield-free venue to show his politically-sensitive installation. "We felt that everyone is responsible for his or her immediate sphere of influence and for us as artists this included the Biennale of Sydney."[40] Transfield's involvements predated the 2012 Biennale[41] and an earlier, more strategic boycott might have impacted the policy by leveraging the Biennale's credibility. Yet the 2014 protest was effective because artists rejected the double-bind that enables institutions and Biennials to show engaged or worldly art without recognizing their own entangled responsibilities.

---

36. *Ibid.*

37. Marisa Mazria Katz and Ahmet Ögüt, "Editor's Letter—April 2014," *Creative Time Reports* (April 1, 2014), http://tinyurl.com/qchy2mu.

38. "An Open Letter."

39. Andrew Taylor, "Biennale Artist Takes Some Credit for Transfield Share Sale," *Sydney Morning Herald* (September 12, 2014), http://tinyurl.com/nk7yqo9.

40. Ahmet Ögüt and Zanny Begg, *Broadsheet* 43.2 (2014).

41. Matthew Kiem, "Should artists boycott the Sydney Biennale over Transfield links?" *The Conversation* (February 12, 2014), http://tinyurl.com/mkrctn7.

A related protest at 2014's São Paulo Bienal drove this point home in the context of further massacres of the besieged refugee population in Gaza by Israel's armed forces. When alerted to the use of official Israeli contributions for the general funding of the Bienal, participating artists responded with a show of unity and in the Boycott, Divestment, and Sanctions (BDS) spirit of solidarity with Palestinian civil society.[42] Rather than offer themselves as cheap sacrifices by staging a mini-boycott, "we decided to stay and fight," in the words of Tony Chakar.[43] An open letter opposing the use of "Israeli cultural sponsorship" to whitewash "ongoing aggressions and violations of international law"[44] was signed by 176 of 199 participating artists. The Bienal curators supported the letter, adding that "sources of cultural funding have an increasingly dramatic impact on the supposedly 'independent' curatorial and artistic narrative of an event."[45]

In São Paulo, the protesting artists, who included Palestinians, succeeded in making their point. In response, the Fundaçao Bienal São Paulo agreed to "clearly disassociate" Israeli funding from the general sponsorship of the exhibition. What is the overall lesson that emerges from the Sydney and São Paulo protests? That it is no longer possible, even if it were acceptable, to separate the creativity on display from the organizational infrastructure that hosts the artworks. Participating artists are increasingly unwilling to lend credibility to abhorrent sponsors or related efforts to whitewash crimes against humanity.

---

42. The international campaign for boycotts, divestment, and sanctions against Israel was launched in 2005; see "Palestinian Civil Society Calls for Boycott, Divestment and Sanctions against Israel Until it Complies with International Law and Universal Principles of Human Rights," *BDSMovement.net* (July 9, 2005), http://tinyurl.com/3fnrncc.

43. Tony Chakar, "WOOHOO!!!!!! SÃO PAULO BIENAL ARTISTS DISASSOCIATE FROM ISRAELI FUNDS," *Facebook (September 1, 2014)*, http://tinyurl.com/nl5gf4q.

44. Mostafa Heddaya, "São Paulo Biennial Participants Demand Organizers Return Israel Funding (Updated)," *Hyperallergic* (August 28, 2014), http://tinyurl.com/pzyxpar.

45. "São Paulo Biennale Curators Respond to Artists' Demands to Refuse Israeli State Funding," *ArtLeaks* (August 30, 2014), http://tinyurl.com/o3vv9eu.

*

In summary, the objects of protest I have described here include: exclusion of non-elites from their heritage; laundering of fossil-fuel profits by national institutions; deliberate exploitation of forced labor to refinance and expand a cultural brand; mandatory detention of asylum-seekers in breach of international law; and acute and chronic war crimes conducted with routine impunity by an occupying state.

Traditionally, artists have not chosen to engage these issues as part of their working lives, even if they have at times in their artwork. Yet these working lives are increasingly implicated by the decision of artworld institutions to accept money generated through violations of international law. Gulf Labor's campaign has drawn a line in the Saadiyat sand, demonstrating why it is no longer acceptable to ignore this practice. In response, mainstream art critics perceive an artworld "trend" to "politicize everything" but have failed to understand the nature of the protests, or misread the underlying connections between exhibition, infrastructure, and worldly context.

Of course all of the circumstances sketched here breed complexity, and rarely is a simple response also right, with the obvious exception of the artists who faced urgent dilemmas in Sydney and São Paulo. What we are witnessing is an emergent wave of creative, political responses to the hard-nosed, self-loving appetite for gold—no matter the consequences for human and other life forms on a patently precarious planet.

The appearance of a newly creative ethics is a beautiful thing, a utopian impulse free of old-fashioned theoretical obscurity and too-tightly mapped ends. The logic of economic globalization is producing a totalized planet: dead in more ways than one. Any resistance to that juggernaut, every creative challenge to it, each of these unrewarded, instinctive fight-backs and expressions of dissent is all that change can be and a demonstration of the negotiability of seemingly untouchable structures and processes. Champions of the latter rightly fear the vocalization of what it means to reclaim our common world.

Who Builds Your Architecture?—An Advocacy Project

Mabel Wilson, Jordan Carver, and Kadambari Baxi

Over the past three years, we have been directing the question "Who builds your architecture?" to professional organizations, architectural firms, and architects, and can report that it has largely been met with silence or polite evasion. Those architects who did respond to our query often cited "contractual constraints" as precluding their intervention in the exploitation of workers who construct their designs. This rationale categorically casts the problem of responsibility outside the purview of the profession. It echoes the response offered by Pritzker Prize–winning architect Zaha Hadid when the *Guardian* newspaper asked her to comment on the deaths of migrant workers on Qatar's construction sites, where she has been commissioned to design the flagship stadium project for FIFA's 2022 World Cup. "I have nothing to do with the workers," she declared, before quickly transferring responsibility for their plight to the authority of the state: "I think that's an issue the government—if there's a problem—should pick up. Hopefully, these things will be resolved." Hadid expressed her deep concern over the deaths in the Iraq war but asserted that, just as she could not intervene in that conflict, architects like her were not obligated to guarantee the fair treatment of construction workers. "I'm not taking it lightly," she added, "but I think it's for the government to look to take care of. It's not my duty as an architect to look at it."[1]

Hadid's choice of the word "duty" illustrates the risk adversity and class divisions that characterize the prevailing mentality of the construction and design industries. Like many of her defenders, she was highlighting the fact that architects'

---

1. James Riach, "Zaha Hadid Defends Qatar World Cup Role Following Migrant Worker Deaths," *Guardian* (February 25, 2014), http://tinyurl.com/nrx3995.

WBYA? workshop at Studio X, New York City (Credit: WBYA?)

contractual obligations are at the service of the project's owner and do not extend to the contractors and workers engaged in realizing their designs. While this might seem a technical distinction, it shields architects from claims that they have any sort of legal responsibility toward construction workers. The word "duty" points to a very carefully defined accountability that minimizes risk to architects and insulates them over the course of the construction process. But it also reflects the perceived class distinctions drawn between the intellectual labor of the design professional and the physical labor necessary to erect the building.

Hadid is only one of the many prominent architects and firms of various sizes working on projects in countries whose governments have poor records on human rights and labor laws. Frank Gehry, another Pritzker winner, has long been a target of Gulf Labor criticism as the architect for the Guggenheim Museum in Abu Dhabi. In contrast to Hadid, Gehry hired Scott Horton, a prominent human rights lawyer, to consult about protecting the well-being and rights of the workers constructing the Guggenheim project.[2] On the other hand, Gehry has readily admitted that, as far as ideal clients go, perhaps "the best thing is to have a benevolent dictator—who has taste!"[3]

To better understand these kinds of declarations by leading architects, we need to analyze how the global supply chain of the construction industry produces buildings—not simply how buildings are conceived by architects but also how they are materialized by a network that mobilizes architects, construction workers, and a host of other actors. This requires an approach that deploys the representational tools and techniques of architecture along with a critical analysis that explains and makes visible architecture's entanglements with geopolitical and economic structures. The agency of the architect, by definition, is a delicate balance. Unlike artists, architects are hired not just for their creativity and design capabilities, but also in the service role of interpreting and executing a project within a framework established

2. Anna Fixsen, "What Is Frank Gehry Doing About Labor Conditions in Abu Dhabi?" *Architectural Record* (September 25, 2014), http://tinyurl.com/ocpgyn9.

3. Benjamin Pauker, "Epiphanies from Frank Gehry," *Foreign Policy* (June 24, 2013), http://tinyurl.com/pblm2zb.

by a client's needs and desires. At the same time, international-scale projects, often presented as cultural centerpieces for a city or state, garner international prestige by exploiting the image of so-called "starchitects," and thus provide a platform for architects to expand their role beyond form-maker, problem-solver, and service provider. But we cannot expect architects to shoulder this responsibility alone, nor to resolve the ethical challenges that arise from these outsize projects. In their efforts to ensure fair treatment of the migrant construction workers building the Guggenheim Museum in Abu Dhabi, the artists and activists of Gulf Labor have shown that many points of pressure are needed to shift the networks that coordinate all of the actors and resources in the building of these large-scale projects.[4] In alignment with the Gulf Labor campaign, Who Builds Your Architecture? (WBYA?), the titular name we have adopted as a reminder to our colleagues and ourselves, has been asking how architects can be most effective in bettering the conditions of workers employed in building their designs.

Who is building?

For 30 years, urbanization in various regions around the world has functioned as a lucrative terrain for surplus-capital generation, a growth facilitated by the internationalization of finance markets. "The property market," writes David Harvey "[has] absorbed a great deal of surplus capital through new construction."[5] The rise of the industrializing BRICS nations (Brazil, Russia, India, China, South Africa), along with myriad forms of resource extraction and debt financing to facilitate public and private investment, has meant that urban development is now a primary vehicle for generating profit and wealth. The construction sector, which is flooded by development financing on the construction end and mortgage financing on the business and consumer end, has become so large and profitable that its wealth functions as a leading

---

4. For a summary of Gehry Partners' statement on treatment of construction workers, see Fixsen, "What is Frank Gehry Doing?"

5. David Harvey, *Rebel Cities: From the Right to the City to the Urban Revolution* (London: Verso, 2013), p. 12.

economic indicator for many national economies. The downside to this was brought into dramatic relief in 2008 when the global economy collapsed due to the large-scale default of American mortgage payments. The payments themselves were indicators of the housing market bubble that had been propping up the US economy through a complex financing system linking the economies of individual home construction and the securitization of mortgage debt traded on a global scale. Similarly, in China, whole cities remain empty as a result of optimistic town planning and an economy predicated on construction and urbanization.[6] The overabundance of housing and real estate stock, and the resulting slowdown in new construction, has triggered an economic slowdown in China, whose housing market recently hit a 24-year low.[7]

Both the planning of whole cities in African countries by the Chinese government and the construction of factories in Mexico's duty- and tariff-free *maquiladora* zones by US companies typify how large-scale construction projects become the vehicles of cross-border government-brokered economic expansion.[8] Public and private investment has also been channeled into nation-branding enterprises to reshape (and homogenize) the skylines of Rio de Janeiro, Guangzhou, Doha, Astana, Taipei, Miami, Lagos, and many other cities seeking "world-class" status by attracting financial partners and tourist dollars. These and other cities compete for the tallest corporate headquarters, the most luxurious hotel, the biggest mall, the largest museum, or the cutting-edge green university campus to solidify their stature as global competitors and guarantee a favorable return on investment. "Capital-A Architecture," designed by "starchitects," has become an important symbolic marker of globalization and networked economies. Reinhold Martin takes the measure of this race to compete when he observes that "architecture and urbanism form one element in a complex network

---

6. One of the most dramatic examples is the town of Ordos, where entire museums and neighborhoods remain empty. For more, see Bill Powell, "Inside China's Runaway Building Boom," *Time* (April 5, 2010), http://tinyurl.com/lxqdbmh. For images, see "Ordos, China: A Modern Ghost Town," *Time*, http://tinyurl.com/nojxbdo.

7. "China's 2014 Economic Growth Misses Target, Hits 24-Year Low," *New York Times* (January 20, 2015), http://tinyurl.com/lp5f8dn.

8. See "Urban China: Chinese Urbanism in Africa," *Go West Project*, http://tinyurl.com/my3ck62.

Aerial view of Doha, Qatar (Credit: WBYA?)

of cultural practices that make financial globalization—and by extension, its crises—not only visible but also imaginable (and therefore possible)."[9]

In this regard, architecture produces an alluring image of a future in which vertiginous feats of engineering in the form of twisted helices and bulbous pinecones signify the future of capitalism. Jumbo shopping malls with miles of storefronts purveying global luxury brands and towering atria that enclose water parks illustrate the future of shopping and entertainment. Top museums compete with one another to erect the most fantastical architectural backdrop for their expanding collections of Old Masters and cutting-edge art in order to symbolize the future of culture. International campuses built by American universities, capitalizing on the rising value of knowledge production worldwide, exemplify the future of education. State-financed mega-facilities for private sporting events, such as FIFA and the Olympics, market the future of leisure. Faux Tuscan villas, built on the urban fringe anywhere from Lagos to Dubai to Mumbai, are ironically advertised as the neo-traditionalist homes of the future. By adapting these global architectural branding strategies and tropes, cities demonstrate that they—along with their nations—are friendly to foreign investors. Such measures to build up and transform their physical inventory also allow cities to tap into cultural and heritage networks, such as the Guggenheim's brand or a UNESCO designation, to leverage visibility and prestige. Invariably, however, the construction of many of these award-winning projects requires the mass recruitment of migrant and unskilled laborers from around the globe. Typically, this migrant workforce labors under exploitative conditions that include withheld pay, poorly regulated labor recruitment practices, lax safety measures, and substandard housing. The process by which these buildings and mega-projects are erected stands in direct contradiction to the values of cultural openness and tolerance these cities and states wish to project to the world.

For the cycle of capital accumulation to generate additional wealth through large-scale building projects, a substantial workforce employed over the course of several years of the construction process is needed. Where the local pool of labor is too small, especially for projects requiring an army of workers thousands strong, private contractors or

9. Reinhold Martin, "Financial Imaginaries," *Grey Room* 42 (Winter 2011), p. 66.

state authorities draft a labor pool from migrant and immigrant populations who live elsewhere.[10] On building sites in places like Saadiyat Island, Abu Dhabi, and Doha, Qatar, for example, workers are being recruited from across South Asia, the Middle East, and Northern Africa. According to Amnesty International, more than 1.35 million foreign nationals are working in Qatar—a country that is home to only 250,000 citizens.[11] The migrant workers have few rights and still fewer avenues to protest their violation, even though many have committed to multi-year labor contracts. Construction workers are casualties of unscrupulous conduct on the part of recruitment firms, subcontractors, and local officials. Persistent problems with the recruitment process can generate exorbitant fees charged by recruitment firms and false representations of the type of work and compensation offered. Employers confiscate passports to prevent flight or deliberately fail to issue proper identification cards that would allow workers to move freely around the city. Migrant workers are also subject to dangerous, at times deadly, conditions on jobsites due to weak regulations and the requirement to build complicated structures without proper training or experience in those construction methods.

The unluckiest workers live in poorly maintained, substandard accommodations located in sprawling "workers' camps" on the outskirts of the city, far from jobsites and amenities.[12] These accommodations result in the segregation of a large population of men outside the civic and economic life of the city they are constructing. This separation prevents workers from integrating into the social and cultural life of the host city and curtails the establishment of migrant-owned businesses that might fuel additional movement of both men and women to a particular city or region. Their isolation and lack of political agency also precludes political reforms that would open the host nations to the development of immigrant communities outside the purview of current and highly restricted employment contracts.

---

10. Harvey, *Rebel Cities*, pp. 5–6.

11. Amnesty International, *The Dark Side of Migration: Spotlight on Qatar's Construction Sector Ahead of the World Cup* (November 17, 2013), p. 17.

12. These conditions have been documented in a number of publications, including Human Rights Watch, *"The Island of Happiness": Exploitation of Migrant Workers on Saadiyat Island, Abu Dhabi* (May 19, 2009) and Human Rights Watch, *The Island of Happiness Revisited* (March 21, 2012).

Because of the jurisdictional differences between the home nation-states and the countries in which migrants work, human rights and international labor organizations have been systematically challenging the legalities of the current recruitment system found in many parts of the world. Local and international law is clearly the primary and critical area in which to intervene and abolish the exploitative dimensions of the current system. However, many of the problems migrant construction workers face are also inherently spatial, urban, and architectural in nature. For example, Amnesty International's 2013 report *The Dark Side of Migration* profiles how UK-based Krantz Engineering mismanaged its workforce on an educational campus project outside of Doha. That case study reveals how the global circuits of the construction supply chain move workers, architects and engineers, capital and debt, building materials, and waste to and from building sites—in very unequal ways.[13]

Disciplinary and professional practices

Globalization's multiplication of actors and points of access has affected how the profession of architecture is practiced. Large-scale architectural projects are created through global business transactions, international real estate deals, complex tax loopholes, and government subsidies that shape the protocols and procedures of practice. If architects are to be trusted with the design and construction of such projects, can they continue to ignore the means through which both materials and human labor are extracted and transported to construction sites?

One outcome of the introduction of new technologies of representation and production to architecture has been to reorganize hierarchies of labor within practice. In his review of the historical transformation of architectural practice from the mid-century to today, Andrew Ross discerns that the most recent incorporation of new technologies into the design and construction process has prompted two divergent reactions from architects. Either they become "proponents of a brave new world of design," buoyantly proclaiming that modernizing the field will fully maximize the

---

13. Amnesty International, *The Dark Side of Migration*, pp. 17–30.

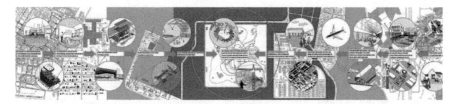

Journey of architects, construction workers, and materials to jobsite (WBYA?). Detail below.

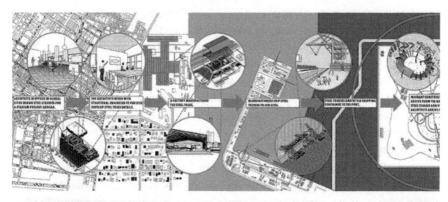

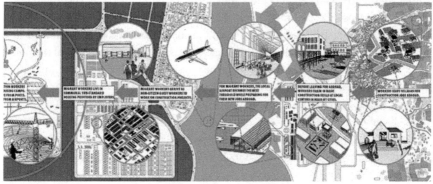

potential of the "hitherto-underutilized cognitive faculties" of the architect; or they become "forecasters," soothsayers of architecture's demise, darkly envisioning "automation as a de-skilling process."[14] One result of the development and proliferation of networked digital technologies is that the architect's design process (labor) has been abstracted from its final object. Those most intimately knowledgeable about the design and engineering of most projects—interns, junior designers, project architects—will likely never set foot on a construction site or interact with the workers for whom they produce the instructions about how to build their designs.

Architects' increasing focus on algorithmically created form-making and digitally simulated renderings of projects—methods that concentrate creative energies on articulating the surface of architecture rather than its material impact—further illustrate how architecture is practiced within a disciplinary cocoon. This quarantine might also be a result of how the profession is dominated, as are many transactions between individuals and institutions, by an aversion to risk and a desire to diminish liability. Contractual obligations and professional liabilities are foremost in determining the types of relationships that get established between all the parties engaged in building architecture. In a typical building project, architects are contractually accountable to the client. The client also enters into a contractual agreement with a contractor, who can allocate segments of the building's construction to other contractors across the building supply chain. One outcome is that risk, along with accountability, is distributed among a legion of contractors in the same manner that securitization distributes risk in the mortgage market. As the implosion of the housing market in 2008 demonstrated, securitization did not eliminate risk, but rather aggregated and spread it—with catastrophic results.

Any possible relationship between architect and construction worker has become so mediated by a variety of factors as to be rendered almost entirely abstract. These factors include legal structures to reduce liability as the number of participants in the building process increases—architects, engineers, contractors, managers, agents,

---

14. Andrew Ross, "Foreword," in Peggy Deamer and Philip Bernstein (eds.), *Building (in) the Future: Recasting Labor in Architecture* (New York and New Haven: Princeton Architectural Press and Yale School of Architecture, 2010), p. 12.

representatives, supervisors, consultants, and more. When Hadid claimed she was not to blame for the plight of the workers in Qatar, she was, legally, correct. But that is less a condition of her position within the design and construction process than of the fact that blame itself is now almost impossible to locate. Culpability has been securitized and dispersed to the extent that no single person or entity holds sufficient legal responsibility to be held accountable. But despite this dissection and atomization of the building process, architects remain intimately linked to the workers who construct their project through the knowledge transfer implicit in the central contract document between architect and client: the construction drawing.

Scrutinizing more closely how architects work, we can see how Building Information Modeling (BIM) software facilitates collaborative exchanges between architects, engineers, and contractors to make the design, consulting, and construction process more efficient. Just as contracting subdivides work within the construction industry, the design process has been parcelized into specialized domains, managed by consultants who specialize in geo-tech engineering, façade design, sustainability, accessibility, food services, and terrorism prevention, to name a few. The BIM modeling platforms help architects to monitor in real time how changes to their design influence a range of factors such as material selection and cost, and to approximate the phasing of construction and the maintenance schedule of the finished building. For all of BIM's up-to-the-nanosecond, down-to-the-millimeter modeling capability, the cost of labor is not yet a factor in the equation.

Given that every aspect of the design and construction process can be accounted for through BIM modeling—from conceptual design through to demolition—perhaps it is this visualization tool that empowers the architect with agency over decisions that in the end directly affect how construction workers operate in the field. What architects specify in architectural details, from the type of material to assembly methods, help determine the time, physical effort, handling of materials, and number of workers at the construction site. New offsite and onsite fabrication processes and innovative component assemblies impact the scope of the work that construction workers undertake onsite and could be used to educate workers on new techniques of construction—invaluable knowledge for securing future work. BIM would then become not just a tool for design efficiency but a means by which knowledge could be shared and the links between architect and builder strengthened. With new technologies of efficiency and building intelligence reshaping every phase of contemporary practice, architects can coordinate the logistics of assembly for each stage of the building process, leaving little outside their purview.

The power of BIM and other technologies of cross-platform and multi-user efficiency is their penetration into the various professions and discourses pertaining to architecture and building, specifically within the realm of academia and the multiple organizations that govern the profession. The American Institute of Architects (AIA) has proven adept at supporting new technologies and methods of working, most strikingly by adopting the language of so-called "sustainability" and environmental concerns as a core principle of contemporary practice. The rise over the past 20 years of Leadership in Energy and Environmental Design (LEED) as a certification system to promote and validate good sustainability practice by architects, clients and contractors demonstrates that good practices can become industry standards if economically incentivized. The extent to which new technologies and benchmarks such as LEED have been adopted by both the profession and its governing institutions speaks to a field that is eager to create an image of architecture that can adapt to and address current global concerns. But at the core, such technologies provide marketing material for clients and the ability for the profession to shave costs by working more seamlessly across fields, and this is what primarily explains their wide adoption.

LEED and the ethic of sustainability have been too easily translated to image, a green gloss that distracts clients and architects from the broader environmental concerns of the building industry. And the logic of BIM and cross-platform working models is framed strictly in terms of business efficiency and cost effectiveness. While the question of labor, and the profession's attitude and responsibility in addressing it, cannot be so easily solved through checklists, plugins, and new building products, a similar system—a Labor LEED—might be developed to recognize and reward good labor practices.

Ultimately, WBYA? contends that responsibility for fair labor does indeed fall under the purview of the professional ethics of architects. Currently, the code of ethics for the AIA contains a one-sentence general statement on human rights: "Members should uphold human rights in all their professional endeavors." Elsewhere in the AIA's code of ethics, the architect's obligation to the environment includes three tenets that uphold sustainable design, development, and practices. Since the value of environmental sustainability is rooted in its significance for human flourishing, should not the human rights section be more emphatic and expansive in setting out the architect's obligation to protect social sustainability?

Addressing these concerns at the ethical level would challenge the AIA, other professional organizations around the world, and the profession at large to find solutions that go beyond and deeper than the language of business and marketing. It would also challenge the profession to stop ignoring and demonstrate relevance on an issue that is central to architectural practice. In these terms, architects should be demanding these discussions to take place, and for the building professions to be well represented within them.

Architects are one part of a solution that will require legal intervention, economic incentives, and grassroots activism from all participants in order to achieve a fair resolution for workers. The problems of labor that have emerged via the development of a globally networked construction industry are not limited to high-profile architectural projects underway in Doha or Shanghai, but can be as readily found at building sites in New York City or Charlotte, North Carolina. As a matter of social justice, we believe that the problem should be approached with the same vigor and urgency with which the profession has addressed environmental concerns through the development of sustainability practices and protocols over the past four decades. By doing so, it will be possible to expand the language and definition of what sustainable building is, to include the global environment, the lives of those who inhabit it, and those who build it.

Why Gulf Labor? Statements of Intent

Walid Raad, Naeem Mohaiemen, Hans Haacke, Ayreen Anastas,
Rene Gabri, and Doris Bittar

Walid Raad

During the past decade or so, I've been hearing more and more about Arab artists, contemporary Arab art, Islamic art, and Middle Eastern art, along with its makers, sponsors, consumers, genres, and histories. I've also been fascinated by the growing number of festivals, workshops, museums, galleries, residencies, exhibitions, prizes, foundations, schools, and journals emerging in Arab areas such as Beirut, Doha, Cairo, Alexandria, Marrakech, Tangiers, Ramallah, Sharjah, and especially the United Arab Emirates, fronted by the cultural developments on Saadiyat Island. Suffice it to say that all of this, for me as an artist, an Arab, or even as an American, is truly fascinating. How long have we been waiting for an Arab government to spend its wealth on art, education, healthcare, and culture? It is happening today. Not just in Abu Dhabi, but also in Qatar, Saudi Arabia, and Kuwait. Why are these sheikhs and sheikhas in the Gulf suddenly so interested in the arts? Why have they started spending all this money on culture? Every time you ask these questions, you should also be ready to hear, in response, the two dominant and weighty caricatures that have emerged to make sense of all this.

The first caricature is that the new pattern of investment represents a cynical move on the part of autocrats seeking to shift their economies away from petrochemical dependence and toward tourism, all the while veiling their stay-in-power-longer, get-even-richer schemes under the "civilizing" cloak of culture. Emirati sheikhs' sudden passion for the arts aims, moreover, to curry favor with restless and suspicious foreign powers such as France, the UK, and the US—powers whose protection will surely be needed should things get out of hand with a nuclear-armed Iran. In other words, the royals in the UAE and Qatar don't give a damn about the arts; they care only about more power and more money. But if, in the midst of their negotiations with the French government for Mirage fighter jets and military bases, they need to throw in the purchase of a Louvre franchise, then so be it. What's a billion dollars for the museum's name? This sum, by the way, is what the Abu Dhabi government agreed to pay the French government to license the Louvre brand for 30 years. A billion dollars is a small fraction of the interest earned by Abu Dhabi's sovereign wealth fund annually. It's Emirati pocket change.

The second caricature insists that this new interest in the arts and culture is the sign of an Arab renaissance, driven by young new rulers seeking to assert the complexity and diversity of Arab, Islamic, and Emirati values, especially in the wake of 9/11. We are told that this renaissance is led by Western-bred visionaries who are tired of the old ways, and who are wholeheartedly trying to first democratize the taste of their subjects via the arts, and then democratize all aspects of civil and political life in their intellectually thirsty but socially conservative lands. Yes, they may be licensing Western brands such as the Louvre and the Guggenheim, but let's give these leaders a break; these are the same people, after all, who only a few years ago would have spent their petro-dollars buying more Ferraris and Bentleys than they could drive, and more high-end properties in New York, London, Tokyo, and Paris than they could possibly live in. Not so long ago they would have been spending most if not all of their wealth overseas, but today they are investing at home, in healthcare and education as well as in culture. Besides, they are only trying to do in 10 or 20 years in the 21st century what it took their Western counterparts 100 years to put in place in the 19th and 20th centuries. Who established the Metropolitan Museum of Art after all? Were the robber barons not the American sheikhs of their day who established the nation's great art museums more than 100 years ago, and who helped shift the center of modern art from Paris to New York 50 years later? Why can't Arab sheikhs do the same for Arab culture? They may not be relocating the center of the contemporary artworld to the East, but they will certainly establish an outpost for it there.

I must say that I don't care to sort through these caricatures, and I don't care to find out whether the sheikhs and sheikhas in Abu Dhabi and Qatar are enlightened,

Walid Raad, "Views from Inner to Outer Compartments" (2012). Exhibition view Thyssen-Bornemisza Art Contemporary, Vienna (Jakob Polacsek)

sincere, or cynical. I assume they are complex people, indeed, that they may be sincere, cynical, and enlightened at one and the same time. But I don't know. In fact, I am quite sure that I will never know.

There is one thing about which I am absolutely certain. At the opening of the Guggenheim Museum in Abu Dhabi, or another museum in Qatar, or elsewhere in the Gulf, sometime between 2017 and 2024, a proud local resident approaches the entrance only to find that he is unable to proceed. Why can't he proceed? Why doesn't he go in?

Is it because he is dressed in jeans and a black t-shirt and sneakers, and this is a black-tie affair? He feels underdressed. Is this why he does not go in? No.

It must be the thugs who are shielding the ruling dynasty, a ruling class that is attending the event *en masse* to showcase its benevolence and refined sensibilities, pubescent future rulers in tow. Do the thugs prevent his access? No.

He simply feels that if he walked in, he would certainly "hit a wall." That he would literally hit a wall.

On the spot, he turns to face the onrushing crowd and screams: "Stop. Don't go in. Be careful!"

Within seconds, the security services arrive. They beat him severely, handcuff him, and send him to a psychiatric facility.

The very next day, I open the newspaper, turn to page six, and look at the bottom right-hand corner. I read the following headline: "Demented Man Disturbs Opening: Claims World Is Flat."

This event has already happened. This headline has already been written. About this, I am absolutely certain.

Naeem Mohaiemen

Air Arabia is a low-cost carrier that has been eating into Emirates and Etihad's dominance of the high volume South Asia–Middle East route. The overwhelming majority of passengers on these flights are migrant laborers. Many are recruited from rural areas of South Asia, for whom this commute will be their first flight out of the home country. Knowing their liminal status, airline staff and airport security have little incentive to be humane, let alone kind, to these passengers, and they are not. On an

Air Arabia flight a few years back, I noticed something unusual. Instead of struggling to carry heavy bags filled with gifts, many passengers were empty-handed and wearing sandals (this was a winter flight). The absence of luggage meant the boarding was "smooth" for all, as there was no prolonged struggle to fit hexagonal, twine-bound packages into rectangular overhead compartments (usually this process is another opportunity for the aforementioned bullying).

When immigration forms were handed out, the migrant workers asked the literate passengers to help fill out forms. I started filling out one for the man in the aisle seat next to me. As I went through his papers, I noticed that, instead of a passport, he had a form from the Bangladeshi Embassy that was a *"Replacement for Lost Passport."* Nestled within that form, the "last place of domicile" was listed as "Abu Dhabi jail."

I started inquiring down the row, and everyone had the same paper. It emerged, through intermittent conversations, that there were more than a hundred deportees on this flight. They had all been working on one construction site. When it was shuttered, they were immediately fired instead of being relocated. As soon as a worker is fired, he is "out of status" or illegal. But most choose not to return home, since a family, and even a portion of a village, is depending on their income. Instead, they find another work-site that will hire undocumented workers—for a fraction of the already minuscule legal pay. The calculation is simple: *stay in the country and continue to work, knowing that you will eventually get caught.*

When they do get apprehended, in fairly quotidian situations (one deportee was arrested when he stepped outside the site for a cigarette break), they are sent to prison and eventually deported, with no chance of recovering their possessions and savings. Faced with the possibility of deportation, most workers send back any income as fast as possible before they get arrested—either through formal channels, or through the informal *hundi* system.[1]

After the arrests, the process of expulsion begins, usually after a jail period of at least three months. This is where the low-cost carrier comes in as the cheapest option for deportation, at the migrants' own expense. Beyond providing a rudi-

---

1. AKM Ahsan Ullah and Pranab Kumar Panday, "Remitting Money to Bangladesh: What Do Migrants Prefer?" *Asian and Pacific Migration Journal* 16.1 (2007), pp. 121–37.

mentary certificate, the local embassies do not carry out any advocacy for safety and rights of the detainees. Bangladeshi embassies in the Middle East rarely if ever stand up to the host governments. There is too much cynical concern, at the embassy and the government level, about killing the remittance flow. Maintaining the reputation of Bangladeshi workers as easygoing, docile workers is crucial for this process.

There were no docile workers on the Air Arabia flight, however. They all knew that once they had been deported from Abu Dhabi there was no going back, and that knowledge seemed to have liberated them. Stories of employer abuse flowed freely, along with angry observations about the hypocrisy of the idea of "Islamic" virtue in a Middle East where migrant labor was so routinely abused.

In Yasmine Kabir's film, *My Migrant Soul*, the narrative makes use of the diary of a Bangladeshi worker who died while in custody in Malaysia. In one of his last messages to his mother, he implores her to tell all family members and friends never to send any of their sons to Malaysia. Worker dissent seems to explode at the point of expulsion, or, as in Kabir's case study, at the point of death.

Recent wildcat strikes demanding unpaid wages by Arabtec workers in Dubai and Abu Dhabi point to much more dissent simmering under the surface. Similarly, when Doug Ashford and I visited a Sharjah barbershop during the 2012 Sharjah Biennial, the Bangladeshi men there talked about cases of resistance that go unreported in the press. Typically, in such occurrences, a group of workers get identified as "ringleaders" and are arrested, beaten, and deported *en masse*. In the wake of Arabtec strikes in May 2013, Pakistani workers were brought in to replace Bangladeshi "troublemakers," leading to a high-profile, pitched battle later that summer in the Saadiyat Accommodation Village. When the Gulf Labor Coalition went on one of several investigative trips to Abu Dhabi, centralized and in our opinion deeply dehumanizing "workers' villages" were touted as a solution to "security concerns" from both the strikes and the ongoing Arab Spring.

Events to date hint at much more that is kept under tight control, through extensive surveillance and harsh policing. The threat of arrests, punishment, and deportation keeps this huge, itinerant workforce under control, for now at least. In an environment where disciplining mechanisms are so strong, external voices of solidarity, including those of cultural workers, have become essential. Although artists are contained by capital in their own way, their labor is policed far less directly and punitively. It is urgent that artists use this relative freedom to speak up on behalf of those whose labor makes the global distribution of our work possible.

Hans Haacke

Immanuel Kant characterized beauty as offering "disinterested pleasure." More than 2,000 years earlier, Plato spoke of "The Good, the True and the Beautiful." Traditionally, art has been associated with both concepts. Even though they are rarely heard in contemporary discussions, they tacitly pervade attitudes toward art and the practices and institutions of the artworld today.

What has this to do with the Guggenheim Museum, the Louvre, the British Museum, New York University (NYU), and the Tourism Development & Investment Company (TDIC), the agency of Abu Dhabi's Tourism and Culture Authority developing "a natural island a 10-minute drive from downtown Abu Dhabi featuring luxury resorts, championship beachfront golf courses, sophisticated residential communities, retail destinations, and cultural institutions"? The aura of art, science, and the humanities has made the four Western institutions and their peers a magnet for corporate sponsors, real estate developers, entertainment moguls, and tourists and oligarchs of various stripes.

It is therefore not surprising that they also inspired the rulers of the oil-rich United Arab Emirates and Qatar to make their kingdoms attractive for the seekers of "disinterested pleasure." The museums and universities gladly collaborate by building spectacular franchises in the sands of the Gulf States—for a contribution. Henri de Loyrette, president and director of the Louvre, has been quoted as saying: "It's a fair fee for the concession of the name. This tutelary role deserves reward. It's normal."

And, as Gulf Labor's allies have asked, "who builds your architecture," as allies of the Gulf Labor Coalition ask? Most notably, they are Frank Gehry, Jean Nouvel, Norman Foster, Rafael Viñoli, and Zaha Hadid. These architects, of course, don't do the building with their own hands. Contractors in the UAE, working under the auspices of TDIC, have imported many thousands of laborers from South Asian countries to do that work, in tropical temperatures.

The migrant laborers are paid notoriously low wages. They work many months or even years to pay off recruitment and travel fees for which they went into debt at home, just to get to the site of hard labor. The employers in the UAE often "safe-keep" their passports. The workers cannot change their employer, they cannot bargain over wages, and it is illegal for them to form unions and go on strike. If they do, they risk being deported. All this for the greater Good, the True, and the Beautiful!

Human Rights Watch has published several scathing reports on the exploitative living and working conditions of the laborers building these showcases for the enjoyment of beauty on Abu Dhabi's Saadiyat Island. The UN's International Labor Organization (ILO) has also been investigating working conditions on the 27 billion USD construction site.

Zaha Hadid, one of the architects with a stake on the sandy "Island of Happiness" in the Emirate, responded to a question by the *Guardian* about the welfare of workers on one of her construction sites in the Gulf, after a number of them died in the heat: "I have nothing to do with the workers. I think that's an issue the government—if there's a problem—should pick up."

The Guggenheim Museum and NYU insist they have done and are doing everything to improve the lot of the imported Indians, Pakistanis, Bangladeshis, Nepalese, and laborers from other poverty-stricken regions of the world. They understand that, if their name is associated with human rights violations, it could tarnish their image (brand) and alienate current or future donors—and the clients of UBS, a major sponsor of the Guggenheim Museum.

UBS, the Swiss bank with a major presence in South Asia and the financial power behind Art Basel, Art Basel Miami, and Art Basel Hong Kong, is one of the Guggenheim Museum's lead sponsors of contemporary art from Asia. It therefore has a particular interest in Abu Dhabi's role as the expected fulcrum between East and West.

At the behest of the directors of the three museums and the president of NYU, backed by their respective boards of trustees, the public relations machines of these institutions jump into high gear every time a critical article appears in the *New York*

Times, the *Guardian,* or another media outlet with a readership that could be relevant to their futures.

It is therefore all the more embarrassing to gather from the most recent (2014) report by PricewaterhouseCoopers (PwC)—the company that Abu Dhabi's TDIC hired to monitor compliance with its Employment Practices Policy—that, contrary to TDIC rules, 93% of the workers interviewed, in one sample, had not been reimbursed for their recruitment fees, and 7% had only received partial payment.

Over the years, learning how "disinterested pleasure," a basic concept of Kant's *Critique of Judgement,* is, in fact, experienced, it dawned on me that it may not exist. Kant might have gotten it wrong. In 2010, I co-signed a call to boycott the 800 million USD Guggenheim Abu Dhabi.

Ayreen Anastas

Did you join Gulf Labor because it spoke directly to the politics of your art practice?
Neither.

Why do you think support for GLC was not always forthcoming from certain sectors of the artworld?

Some have simply just not understood and that is all. And if they were given the chance they would support this struggle. In rare cases, there are those who are just on the same plane as the ruling elite and some may even benefit from exploitation of workers in their own studios, museums, and galleries. Some cannot bear any contradictions, their senses are dulled by the weight of a world that reduces everyone to a cash machine and thus their deeds have to be commensurate with their stream of desires for more money, fame, and applause. Congratulations.

Has GLC made the best use of boycott tactics?

No, it could have gone further and more radical.

What criteria would you use to gauge the success of GLC (so far)?

Sometimes there are visible and sometimes invisible gauges of success. I am sure others have mentioned the visible ones; as for the invisible, they are the ones that one can never attribute directly to GLC, yet they are connected to it in some way. And the most interesting manifestations are still to come. We are just starting.

Is GLC's stand on worker rights a reflection of renewed attention of cultural workers to labor in general?

Yes.

What operational challenges are involved in mobilizing such a large group of artists and writers to common ends?

I have a problem with the notion of mobilization. I would prefer to be part of some kind of a movement with no beginning nor end. A movement closer to life in its widest sense. A movement from and toward the common(s). A movement that sees through the divisions, separations, and apartheids, and understands what lies underneath and beneath them.

In your mind, is GLC a specific goal-oriented campaign or more of an open-ended initiative with long-term applications?

The latter.

What do you think?

I think therefore I am thinking that this I does not make much sense nor does the be on its own. I am we are I are we am. They are we are they are. Are they. I am a worker we are artists they are prisoners and so on. No I am a prisoner we are workers they are artists.

What is this life that we-they-I live?

I am thinking of what may be happening in detentions and prisons in Egypt now, while lucrative "business opportunities" are picking up there, such as Tony Blair advising President Sisi in Sinai. I am thinking of all the "undocumented" refugees in Europe and the idea of a market fundamentalism. Ms. Merkel versus Ariadne. The thread is definitely lost. And what about feminism where.

A western world forward and backward: development, colonialism, materialism, capitalism, and so forth.

Development is haunting everyone everywhere. Development in this sense is destruction in every sense. The discourse on development is what they use today, for what used to be the discourse on the savage, the backward, or the primitive.

We have to break Karl into pieces, cut his pages, rewrite everything he wrote one more time. Class consciousness is lacking for sure, and yet we need to rethink this obsession in production and labor as separate from all other realms of life. Work has seeped into every aspect of our everyday and our alienation has many masks.

Brinjal (eggplant) in preparation, Musaffah labor camp, Abu Dhabi (Credit: Gulf Labor)

We are not we and the workers are not themselves. On one level we can bring something that will change the conditions that someone or a group of people are subjected to including exploitative labor conditions. But the struggle should be much bigger. And requires us to ask different kind of questions.

But maybe it is in vain what I am trying to say here. The specialist is everywhere near and speech is charged with feelings.

Rene Gabri

What do you think?

I think there is no "I" that can think this thought. Because the thought is so big, so immense that the "I" cannot contain it or hold it together.

It comes and goes, with time, sometimes it is incredibly concrete, like a hillside, with countless terraces and peasants who stream across, below, to the side, above, on intersecting paths, some moving up, down, with other animals, with dung heaps for compost, seeds, water, dreams, balancing acts, bird songs, with time, against time, and without a choice, sometimes.

The claim is made of a civilizational choice, at some point, toward increased forms of subjugation, contradiction, and of antagonism.

But this is a thought without a choice. I have no choice in this thought. I have no choice but to think with this thought. I have nothing without this thought.

It is a thought that undoes me and any other who tries to think it.

It is a thought that resists time, the productive time, time as money and circulation, fruited time, dried time, the pulps of expropriation, infinity replaced by endlessness, an endless accumulation, investment, the time in between worn down, *a nulla*, a gain is realized, again realization: nothing is gained.

It is a thought that does not need to resist, it is what every resistance realizes. On the other side of this chain-link fence of equivalences is a communism with neither a system nor a party nor any claim for power. A *commun* without its "*ism*".

It's a holding pattern, only the hold has been lost. It's a gripless hold. The pattern is familiar. It awaits the precise moment, *kairos*. *"And when it comes, then what?"* We have no choice here, we have to go, the swell is sweeping us away, the floods, torrents, the trees toppled, coupons, registers, black ash, nightmares, one after the other, a dam, the damned, disappeared also, the land never was ours, the land belonged to itself, it was never ours.

That inevitable moment when power looks itself in the mirror hoping to find, maybe a king, festooned with riches, glory, but finding only this incessant drive to continue. *"One must continue,"* but why?

We live in parodic times. In a parody, the violence always stays muted in laughter.

Where memory could disrupt this reconciled image of having done what one could do, the mirror shatters into stadiums, towers erected to perpetuate clouds, a race for the hammer which will finally shatter the time that stands between the speculated and its return, between the lives between.

"To smother each and every thing living, ha, ha, ha, ha."

It's a drive, a race, a wager, a bet, I bet!, I bet a thought (a thought that counts is no thought at all).

They are thinking thoughtless thoughts.

But I have a thought that is not mine, that undoes me. I have it exactly because it is not to be had. It is a plaything, a very serious thing that plays with me, as it will others to come.

It is a contagious thought and that's why all efforts will be made to destroy it. Even the words that have tried to name it have been sullied, driven to madness, extreme opposites, driven to confessions through unheard-of tortures and acts that cannot be called acts, inside places, times, that only the scars can hide, they scarred until the words seemed to not make sense, and that thought just seemed to vanish.

But it returns again. And somewhere else it settles, but it is restless, in one place one moment, then another, sometimes for those who follow it, it is hard to see the relations between these separate moments, worlds really, constellations, galaxies.

There is war here, there is loss here, deserts bloom into forests of concrete steel, and jet fuel pours from the skies as a kind of witch hazel, a cure-all, fueling, keeping happening again and we, forced, *forced?*

No one here has been forced if not everyone. But by who?

So many lives just wasted, life wasted, but what would be its opposite? A life enjoyed?

He says that some will benefit and others will only be a burden or their lives worth less.

"We did what we could. The rest was reality. Things were not better for them there, where they were."

It is a thought that writes countless letters, revisions, returns. Can you provide this as guarantee? The response comes, there is no guarantee, except the ledger sheet that says we are owed and we have families to feed.

"Don't hide behind poetry, there are matters here worth taking into account."

We will be exploited, we will exploit, we deserve this, we stand accused, all that we have and we what, we what, should be grateful for it. We should be grateful and even more, more, more, *what?*

It is a thought that cannot bear the weight anymore alone. Or, situated so that it is seen or heard or thought in isolation. It is a thought that can only overwhelm and lose, loosen the ties.

It is a thought that returns, maybe it is the thought as return. Return to what has been said is lost.

"They would like to see it as one thing when in fact it is everything."

It cannot be fixed in one place. It cannot be built on anything other than the dispossession which displaced it.

It is a thought that wants to laugh at itself. But it is always someone else who laughs. At them, with them, against them.

And when they bring their hands together, there is food that can remind them all of something else, sometime else.

It's a destabilizing thought. It's a thought that cannot rest, it is sleepless, it is a thought that wakes up the tyrants even. But sometimes also, this thought is slumbering with the ones who kneel, stealing rest away from those that continue to steal time.

It's not a timeless thought, it is constantly thinking of time, all the time that it has taken to arrive here, where we all are.

This thought is more than this, and more than that. It is a this that expands into *that* and *that*, to *those*, and from *those* to *them*, *them* to *us*, and *us* to *everyone, everyone* to . . . no single one could hold it all together. Thus, sometimes there are explosions.

Insurrections, unexplained and uncertain, but full of sense. They crush us, they crush us to bits. We fought for it, and it showed in the grimaces they wore on their masks of holiday smoke. Fragments of this thought recompose again.

It is a thought that winds through those who have thought, maybe once, or twice, or more, each day. More and more each day, it would seem to be getting more. The labels that keep falling, and they, having to pick them up, paste them on the walls to remind us that there are leaders, chiefs, directors, executives, presidents and servants, followers, employees, slaves, cleaners, there in the simplest gestures of picking up after.

A thought that can only be, thus, thought with others, picked up by others. Those others unthought of. I am thinking of a thought that others long before me have thought and those long after will follow to think. The thought I am thinking is thus not mine. It cannot be. Maybe all thought has this character of undoing the one who thinks it. I am thinking of a thought that I cannot recognize as anyone's, but it grounds every thought, even the most petty, the most insincere, the most duplicitous, the most counter to this thought.

It is a common thought, but it is by no means commonplace or even what they refer to as *common sense*. It has even lost sense, because not only its sense, but sense itself is lost if it is not common.

Struggles are awakened in this thought and they have their sense, they get their sense, only in the light or shadow of this thought.

Doris Bittar

Though I signed the Gulf Labor boycott petition early, I hesitated joining the core committee and discussed my apprehension about doing so with Greg Sholette and Walid Raad. "You have fame, and you're in New York. You send missives out every six months, and have no idea how disconnected and fearful we may be." My fear reawakened memories from my former role as a labor organizer, for five years in the 1980s, at Yale University's Library. Management, then as now, isolated weaker workers from the stronger ones. I had learned I would be safer being part of the pack that stood its ground. As an artist I have much in common with other artists, especially those who share Gulf Labor's social justice and conceptual leanings, but, as a worker in the

1980s, I had little in common with fellow employees. The unglamorous job I did at the library alongside others consumed most of our waking lives, yet because we organized, our friendships became among the most enduring and significant in our lives.

In 2013, I and some other Southern California colleagues began to recruit regional and international artists from Milan to Vancouver on behalf of Gulf Labor's *52 Weeks* project. Through our networks we soon had 40 artists committed to the collective pieces: boteh/paisley-shaped installations to honor the icons and culture of workers in India, Nepal, and Pakistan. Early on, we linked the Arabian/Persian Gulf to our own proximal pool of salty water, the Gulf of Mexico. The symbol of the boteh/paisley became more potent when we learned that it was also how illiterate workers in India once signed documents. Fists, saturated with ink, were stamped onto pay documents creating the shape of a boteh/paisley. A scroll of stamped fists was subsequently incorporated into *Labor Migrant Gulf*, our traveling exhibit.

Artists are migrant workers of sorts—perhaps a rung or two above the traditional kind, and with trendsetting clothes, but *de facto* migrant workers nonetheless, moving from venue to venue as "independent contractors" with only ephemeral links to institutions that show our work. This simple realization should spur us to connect to the labor movement, influence legislation that concerns artists, set compensation standards with museums, and leverage them to support the communities that artists create.

I became an artist in order to be free to direct myself, and not be manipulated by a system. Yet I am repeatedly asked to donate art for nothing, exhibit without any support for materials, pay application fees, and speak only when spoken to. Museums, elites, bureaucrats, and nation-states build their cultural standing by associating with artists. Entrepreneurial networks have learned to take advantage of artists' presence to gentrify urban neighborhoods. Both sectors predictably and routinely spit out the artists when we are no longer useful. Artists live within this normalcy, and cannot fail to realize that it is oppressive and limiting. Gulf Labor helped to draw attention to that pattern of exploitation by elegantly unseating everyone from their *de facto* powerful/powerless roles.

In my view, Gulf Labor emerged from two main wellheads: Occupy and the Arab Spring. The widening income gap and ever more powerful financial oligarchies gave birth to the Occupy Movement with its bramble of grievances, encompassing social, economic, and environmental justice, and more. Occupy showed us how to work in tandem and decisively connect the dots. As for the Arab Spring, this long-overdue questioning of authority emerged from the broadest mobilization of the population across North Africa and the Middle East.

Do the initiatives represented by Gulf Labor disappear when the workers in the Arabian/Persian Gulf get some form of justice? I think not, because we have developed a global network with artists, writers, architects, universities, museums, unions, and their support structures. My personal endeavor focuses on the development of Gulf Labor West, formed to emphasize North and Latin American migrant issues, to shepherd the traveling exhibit, *Labor Migrant Gulf*, and to forge ties with organized labor. We have developed a working relationship with the Interfaith Center for Worker Justice (ICWJ) based in Southern California. It links us to regional, national, and international unions, and promises to help us reach a wider audience through joint initiatives. Gulf Labor West now has a voice at the table with big labor. For Gulf Labor's project to end, the Internet would have to be dismantled, and our collective memories erased. Gulf Labor is an umbrella. Its affiliates such as Gulf Labor West find strength through the expansion of like-minded networks. In the long run, our work will strengthen artists and cultural entities to become more independent of the elites that seem to entrap us into untenable circumstances. Our open process combines friendship with organization—an antidote to isolation and an opportunity to be a part of labor's evolving shape. I try to keep my activism and artmaking separate, because they may be weakened by proximity. I do not want an issue forced into an aesthetic mold. Nor do I want to waste an aesthetic pursuit—a laboratory kind of inquiry, a formal investigation—by conforming it to an issue. I can work on the "issues" without them governing my art. However, through my activism with Gulf Labor, I found a way to create art where the two impulses worked together organically. Gulf Labor gave me a new awareness of how that intersection may be nurtured.

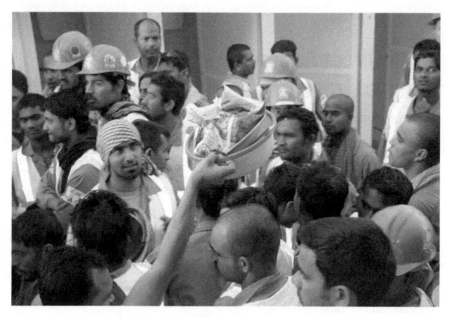

Food coming through, Musaffah, Abu Dhabi (Credit: Gulf Labor)

On Direct Action: An Address to Cultural Workers

Global Ultra Luxury Faction—G.U.L.F.

What time is it on the clock of the world? —Grace Lee Boggs

We amplify a cry reverberating across the globe. From Istanbul and Sydney to New York and São Paulo, the proliferation of direct actions is disrupting business as usual at elite cultural institutions: Black Lives Matter at the Museum of Natural History, climate protests at Tate Modern and the Metropolitan Museum of Art, collective pressure for boycott at Haifa's Technion, and worker solidarity disruptions at the Guggenheim Museum NYC, to name only a few.

We see that actions are employing a diversity of tactics. At times, uninvited assemblies inside museums are announced. At other times the unexpected occurs, unheralded. Actions take aim at a range of targets: labor exploitation, white supremacy, the capture of public space, climate injustice, gentrification, police violence, Israeli apartheid, rape and sexual assault, and more. They are beautifully disruptive within their own arenas of concern. But these concerns are also connected.

We know that by hacking the media machine our actions can have deeply transformative potential or they can reinforce existing norms and power relations. They can accept the limits of a given context—and implicitly affirm them—or they can change the nature of that context altogether. Let our actions be an opportunity to test, to unlearn, and to train in the practice of freedom.

*

We are the Global Ultra Luxury Faction (G.U.L.F.). Our name aggressively reflects back to the actually existing artworld its true nature: a spectacular subsystem of global capitalism revolving around the display, consumption, and financialization of cultural objects for the benefit of a tiny fraction of humanity—the 1%. But we believe that a shift is beginning to occur. We strike the global ultra luxury economy in the interest of making a new space of imagination, one that builds power with people and facilitates the rearrangement of our own desires in the struggle for justice and freedom.

We are cultural workers. We are students, teachers, thinkers, makers, painters, writers, musicians, and more. We recognize and use our privilege to speak out but must always be wary of reproducing the privilege of our location. We work with the imagination and the senses, with hearts and minds, with bodies and voices. We recognize that our work, our creativity, and our potential are channeled into the operations and legitimization of the system. We work—often precariously—as both exploiters and exploited, but we do not cynically resign ourselves to this morbid *status quo*. We will not allow our songs to become ashes, or our dreams to become nightmares. We see our proximity to the system as an opportunity to strike it with precision, recognizing that the stakes in general far exceed the discourses and institutions of art as we know them.

We are living, working, and creating in an expanded field of empire. This field is marked by mortal crises—crises of finance resulting in gaping inequality, of climate, of dispossession and displacement, of poverty and neocolonialism, of state violence and creeping fascism, and always of patriarchy. But this field is also traversed by freedom struggles, from striking workers in Abu Dhabi and Dubai to insurgents in Palestine, Ferguson, Athens, and beyond. G.U.L.F. itself emerged, in part, from the occupation of Wall Street. There, inspired by uprisings in Tunisia, Egypt, Greece, and Spain, we bypassed the institutions of a corrupted representative democracy. We put our bodies directly on the line at the symbolic doorstep of global capital. Wall Street is an abstract space, everywhere and nowhere at once. By de-occupying it, we created space for collective powers to surge forth and for struggles to connect. Walking together, we have asked questions. How do we live? What is freedom? What does solidarity look like? What role can art play?

We target global systems and local conditions at once. G.U.L.F. names an overarching system, but it also evokes a specific location that exemplifies that system in its most spectacular form: the oil sheikdoms of the Persian Gulf. These states aspire to be a prime recreational playground for the global 1 percent. Artistic and educational institutions from New York to Paris have eagerly contributed their brands to the development of the *de luxe* cityscapes of the Emirates. We see monuments to "culture" woven into a monstrous assemblage of fossil fuels, financial power, and imperial geopolitics. Holding up the pyramid—bearing the weight of the entire edifice—are the legions of workers from Bangladesh, India, Pakistan, Nepal, Philippines, Sri Lanka, and, most recently, Cameroon, Uganda, and Nigeria, who seek dignity and a better future for their families. They are drawn to the Gulf by economic precarity in their home countries, and typically end up bonded to their work through debt. Many of these workers have been at the forefront of struggles for wages and labor reforms that challenge the very terms of Gulf petro-capitalism, which is itself embedded in flows of capital and labor. The global cultural brands setting up in Abu Dhabi—Guggenheim, Louvre, British Museum, NYU—claim zero responsibility. They insist that the problems of the workers should be addressed to the government, to the subcontractors, to the middlemen, to the "sending country," but never to the disinterested heights of art institutions themselves who possess a leverage they refuse to acknowledge.

We combine analysis, art, and action. What can be done? Our partners in the Gulf Labor Coalition first brought these conditions of life, work, and debt to public attention. They called for an artists boycott of the Guggenheim Abu Dhabi in particular, demanding that certain conditions on the Island of Happiness be met. Trips have been taken to labor camps and construction zones in Abu Dhabi and Dubai. Reports have been written. Extensive meetings have been convened. G.U.L.F. brought a new element to this arsenal: artistic direct actions targeting the flagship museum in New York, and its Venice branch, designed to incite solidarity, rather than benevolence. We have made unsolicited alterations to the building, to the spectator environment, and to the internal protocols of the museum itself, making it into a temporary zone of the marvelous while drawing connections between the speculative real estate booms and busts from Manhattan to Abu Dhabi. Banners were dropped, propaganda flung like confetti from the heights of the famous spiral, dissenting voices thundered and echoed throughout the rotunda. Police were called in to secure the museum as it shut down. We have disfigured its corporate brand and magnified the pressure on the museum's trustees to accept responsibility for the human suffering at the bottom of the subcontracting chain.

We realize solidarity is a verb. When we act in New York—the capital of the global artworld and global media alike—we perform on an outsize stage, and can amplify many voices, especially those that go unheard on Saadiyat Island. How do we understand that the struggles of the UAE's migrant workers are connected to our own, and are a precondition to our own liberation? We do this not by imagining the worker as a victim to be saved, but rather as a fellow human whose freedom is bound up with our own. We have connected with their plight because our own dignity depends on it. Our liberation is either collective or it is nonexistent, and so we assail the Guggenheim in New York because it is our gateway into a larger struggle. When we proclaim solidarity, we do not ignore very real differentials of condition, temporality, experience, power, and privilege. We hold on to the specificities of struggle because we understand that history is more awesome than good will. We will not be solidarity tourists. Spectacular actions are necessary yet insufficient on their own, but how do we *sustain* solidarity?

We imagine escalation—at the Guggenheim and beyond. The Guggenheim has been for us an urgent target in its own right. But it has also been a testing ground, a laboratory of learning, a training in the practice of freedom with ramifications far beyond the museum itself. Even if the Guggenheim Foundation trustees accede to the demands of the Gulf Labor Coalition and take independent action to protect the rights of workers and abolish their debts, our work will not be over. Saadiyat Island will still be there as a challenge and a target, along with every other cultural stockpile designed to embellish the lives of ultra-luxury elite at the expense of the lives of a great majority—especially the lives of black and brown people who are systemically devalued and rendered disposable under carceral neoliberalism. The workings of the artworld have long been bound up in the fine art of gentrification—the by-now formulaic intertwining of culture-driven development, realty speculation, and enclave policing that disciplines and displaces poor peoples from urban neighborhoods. On Saadiyat Island, we see these components in a slightly different, but fundamentally related, combination—brown and black bodies in accommodations that resemble detention camps, toiling under debt bondage and brutal law enforcement to build a real estate paradise for a light-skinned overclass.

We who believe in freedom cannot rest. The ultra-luxury economy is deeply racialized, locally and globally. In the Gulf, Americans and Europeans doing business are called "expats," whereas people constructing and maintaining these surreal cities in the desert are "bachelor migrant workers." Actions within and against this economy must make the struggle against racism and white supremacy an essential part of their drive. This extends to the occupation, exploitation, and ethnic cleansing characteristic of Israeli policy—indeed, a global cultural boycott of institutions connected to Israeli Apartheid is well within our sights. Boycotts, strikes, pickets, die-ins, occupations, web-hacks, media hijacks. . . . Whatever the combination of tactics, our actions are at once oppositional and abundantly creative. As we disrupt and refuse the role that art is now playing in the normal functioning of this global system that propagates racism and inequality in its shadows, we make space for something new to come into the world that would have otherwise seemed impossible. The heart of this new culture is solidarity and human dignity. We who believe in freedom cannot rest . . . until it is won.

Six Occupations of a Museum (and an Alternative Plan)

Global Ultra Luxury Faction—G.U.L.F.

This dossier includes images from five actions taken inside the Guggenheim Museum, New York by Global Ultra Luxury Faction (G.U.L.F.). The actions took place on February 22, 2014; March 25–29, 2014; May 24, 2014; November 5–6, 2014; and May 1, 2015. In a sixth action, on May 8, 2015, the Peggy Guggenheim Collection in Venice was occupied.

G.U.L.F. was formed in February 2014 amid growing frustration at the lack of progress in the Gulf Labor Coalition (GLC)'s formal dialogue with the museum.

While each action was aimed at mounting a spectacular performance for the public, we also produced artwork—much of it destroyed by guards within the museum—that was designed to synchronize with the aesthetics of the exhibition on display. Materials explaining the actions to museum-goers and to security guards were also distributed. Participant numbers ranged from 20 to more than 100.

The fifth action, on May Day, represented an escalation of the pressure tactics. It commemorated five years of inaction on the part of the museum authorities, and resulted in a five-hour occupation and a shut-down of the entire museum. The occupiers drafted and released the following declaration.

Declaration from the Occupation of the Guggenheim (May Day, 2015)
Today we successfully occupied the museum with bodies and voices, inside and out. The Guggenheim authorities would rather shut down the museum for the day than talk to their critics. We didn't come to shut the museum—we came to ask to attend a meeting with the Board of Trustees, and we hope that meeting happens soon.

Today is International Workers' Day. When workers in Abu Dhabi—who are not allowed to organize—go on strike, they may be arrested, beaten, and deported. We repeat the demands for a living wage, a debt jubilee, and the right to organize. We appreciate all the workers we spent time with. On this May Day, we also stand in solidarity with the struggles of workers everywhere, including the museum guards who make $11 an hour, and the groundskeepers who make $9 an hour, which is not a living wage in New York City. The art we brought with us was shared by all but then violently destroyed by the museum.

We thank SASI (South Asian Solidarity Initiative), DRUM (Desis Rising Up and Moving), the Taxi Workers Alliance, the Guerrilla Girls, Mahina Movement, and our allies in the South Asian community who rallied in support outside.

This is part of an ongoing campaign, with 52 weeks of actions to come. The museum's disdain for the public and criticism will mean that this movement only grows.

One week later, in its first activity as an official participant in the Venice Biennale, Gulf Labor collaborated with G.U.L.F. and S.a.L.E.-Docks (a Venetian arts collective) in a waterborne action at the Peggy Guggenheim Collection on the Grand Canal. Enacting a scene from the GLC's Biennale banner—which re-purposed a Whistler sketch of a boat approaching Venice—the museum was occupied for several hours, and the request to meet with board trustees received a positive response.

In March 2014, G.U.L.F. sent out a press release in the Guggenheim's name announcing a redesign of its Abu Dhabi museum along more ethical lines, incorporating fuller attention to labor and environmental components. By September, the spoof had morphed into a more serious endeavor with the launch of The Next Helsinki (www .nexthelsinki.org), an alternative design competition for the proposed Guggenheim Helsinki. The Next Helsinki, which called for a fusion of arts and urbanism, and an end to the squandering of public monies on private starchitect-designed blockbusters, attracted 220 entries from more than 42 countries. The winning entries, which were offered to local organizations for development into practicable projects, may have more chance of being realized than the winner of the official museum competition.

Guggenheim petro-dollars rain down (March 2014) (Credit: G.U.L.F.)

The dirty currency of artworld speculation (March 2014) (Credit: Noah Fischer)

What does a sustainable cutting-edge museum look like?

Submit your designs and concepts for Guggenheim Abu Dhabi here.

#futureguggenheim

"Guggenheim" announces sustainable design competition for Abu Dhabi branch (March 28, 2014)

G.U.L.F. pamphlet for NYU and Guggenheim actions, (February 2015) (credit Noah Fischer)

Launch of design competition as alternative to Guggenheim Helsinki (September 2014)

Italian Futurist agit-prop on the walls of the museum (May 2014)

Agit-prop G.U.L.F. artwork (May 2014) (Credit: Noah Fischer)

Eat Up! Speak Up!, *Guggenheim's annual fund-raising gala (November 5, 2014) (Csaba Nemes)*

Meet Workers Demands Now, the parachute banner in position (May Day 2015) (Credit: G.U.L.F.)

Solidarity pickets outside the museum (May Day 2015) (Credit: G.U.L.F.)

May Day in Seven Languages (Credit: G.U.L.F.)

Win! The end of the May Day occupation (Credit: G.U.L.F.)

Gulf Labor's official banner at the 56th Venice Biennale

Dramatization of banner through the naval occupation of the Peggy Guggenheim Collection, Venice (May 8, 2015) (Credit: Gulf Labor)

Messaging on the Grand Canal (May 8, 2015) (Credit: Marco Secchi)

Competing signage at the Venice occupation (May 8, 2015) (Credit: Gulf Labor)

Celebrating the Venice occupation (May 8, 2015) (Credit: Gulf Labor)

Observations and Recommendations After Visiting Saadiyat Island and Related Sites (March 14–21, 2014)

Gulf Labor

Members of Gulf Labor visited the worker accommodations on Saadiyat Island on March 17, and the Louvre and the Guggenheim sites on March 20, 2014. This chapter outlines the group's main observations, concerns, and suggestions. These are also based on: a) visits to related off-island sites in Abu Dhabi, Dubai, and Sharjah; b) interviews with workers both in the UAE and in their home countries; c) discussions with informed local sources; and d) previous visits by members of Gulf Labor. Our recommendations for TDIC Abu Dhabi and the Guggenheim Foundation are made with the sincere intention of cooperating with these institutions on their implementation.

Gulf Labor was invited by TDIC (Saadiyat Island's master planner and developer) to visit the sites and accommodations on Saadiyat Island. We acknowledge TDIC's willingness to engage with Gulf Labor and the issue of workers' welfare seriously and in an open way. Our discussions with TDIC were held in the spirit of honest, straightforward debate and exchange of views. The representatives we met were TDIC's Public Relations staff. Unfortunately, we did not meet or interact with anyone at TDIC whose principal role was investigating and monitoring labor conditions, or promoting workers' welfare.

Our visits to the sites were accompanied by TDIC representatives and, in the case of the Saadiyat Accommodation Village (SAV), by employees of Brookfield Multiplex (BM), a private company in charge of those facilities. Visits to the SAV and construction sites lasted about four hours in total, but were preceded by lengthy discussions held in the TDIC office in Abu Dhabi, which we feel were productive in setting up a framework for dialogue. The visits were documented on photo and video by both

A view of the Saadiyat Accommodation Village from the approach road (Credit: Gulf Labor)

Gulf Labor and TDIC. We have mutually agreed to publish any or all of this documentation, except where (as requested by TDIC and members of Gulf Labor) it directly identifies workers or representatives.

For ease of reading, this document is divided into the following sections:

1.   Main observations
2.   Recommendations
3.   Detailed Findings

    A.   Workers in the SAV
    B.   Living conditions in the SAV
    C.   Wages and companies in the SAV
    D.   Recruitment fees
    E.   Louvre and Guggenheim sites
    F.   Concerns beyond the SAV, including NYUAD
    G.   Overview of camp conditions in the UAE

Main Observations

The official name for the labor accommodation site (SAV) on Saadiyat Island is "village," rather than the more commonly used "camp." Village life is often what is left behind in the great migrations for work all over the world, and this name seems to invoke a re-creation of community. Actually generating a sense of community and well-being for thousands of migrant workers is a challenging task, and any effort to do so is up against prevailing conditions in the UAE. In many respects the SAV is similar to other labor camps; it consists of temporary housing tied to a construction project, hosting temporary workers while they are employed on Saadiyat Island projects, where onsite supervisors are still addressed as "camp bosses" and a broader national-level context of indebted migrant labor remains in place.

The road leading to the SAV travels for a dusty two kilometers beyond a checkpoint, beyond which casual visitors and members of the public are not permitted. The Saadiyat construction site itself acts as a giant buffer between the SAV and public roads and services. The thousands of workers in the SAV are thus isolated, and it was our impression that this inaccessibility contained and produced other forms of seclusion that are psychological, economic, legal, and gendered in nature. The SAV is 99.99 percent male in its population. It is designed to last for 20-odd years, the build-out period for TDIC's Saadiyat Island projects. It is not, and will not be, integrated socially with the city or even the island areas it serves. For these reasons, we do not believe that the SAV should be considered a model for workers' housing in the region or elsewhere.

Nevertheless, there are concrete benefits that the SAV offers to workers on Saadiyat. Among these are proximity to worksites (avoiding 1–3 hour commutes that are common elsewhere) and generally modern and clean facilities conforming to minimum international standards. There are television rooms, a well-manicured cricket pitch, a gymnasium, a library, pool tables, and other amenities rarely seen in accommodation for migrant workers. Gulf Labor's principal concern is that such components of progress and comfort be directly linked to workers' welfare and well-being. Our visits allowed us a small window to evaluate some of these concerns, and to talk to workers about them. Our conversations in the SAV were limited in time and scope, but we list below some of the chief concerns that emerged from them.

Wages on Saadiyat Island remain very low. Workers we met, including those contracted to the Louvre Abu Dhabi, Saadiyat Villas, and other TDIC projects, were earning basic salaries in the range of 650–900 AED (177 USD to 245 USD) a month. In Musaffah, an area of Abu Dhabi that hosts many labor camps, employees who had worked on NYU's Saadiyat campus cited figures as low as 572 AED a month. With overtime, this could add up to between 1,000 and 1,200 AED a month, for 10–12 hours of work, six days a week. Overall, wages inside the SAV were not better than those for comparable employment in construction elsewhere in the UAE. It was also reported to us that a much-publicized 20 percent pay raise, announced by the large manpower firm Arabtec after strikes by its workers in May 2013 (including many in the SAV working on the Louvre), has not materialized. Low pay was the single largest complaint we encountered in talking to workers throughout our visits.

All the 20 or so workers we spoke to at the SAV had paid recruitment fees. No one had yet been reimbursed these fees as required by TDIC's current Employment Practices Policy (EPP). As a result, for example, a Bangladeshi worker who had been in the

UAE for three years, and had been working on Saadiyat for two of those years, had still not paid off his original debt. Workers in the SAV and on off-island sites described the average time needed to pay off their recruitment debt as two years, which is also the term of the work visa. This combination of high initial debt and low wages, along with dependency on a sponsor for renewing the two-year visa, generates intense pressure on workers, especially in the first few years after leaving their home countries.

The complaints redressal system at the SAV was not perceived to be functioning well. Workers claimed that when they call the hotline, there is no immediate feedback, and they do not see responsive action taking place swiftly. Widespread problems were reported with the quality of the SAV food, and with sewage leaking from the upper bathrooms onto those below. The latter was quite a serious matter, since a number of workers said they were unable to take clean baths.

Facilities management said that the problem of leakage was being dealt with, but that similar problems arose from time to time due to corrosion, specifically from the type of construction of these temporary buildings. The food issue was something they described as "complex" and related to different tastes of the workers. Both TDIC and BM seemed sincere in trying to fix infrastructural problems on the SAV site, but the complaints process may need to be thought of differently, beyond merely reporting to the facilities managers.

There are no organized workers' groups to speak to, and any representative system of worker coordination is not permitted. While it seemed to us that efforts are being made to address housing standards and general well-being in the SAV, communication with the workers seemed to be quite poor. In the absence of any formal worker representatives or workers' councils, it will remain difficult to evaluate problems and to gauge properly if employee needs are being fulfilled.

On our visit to the Louvre site, an engineer described to us the painstaking detail (to the millimeter) involved in the execution of the building's complex structural plan, and assured us that lavish resources were allocated to meeting any and all technical challenges involved. Similarly, considerable money and resources are spent on select features of the SAV, for example on maintaining the cricket pitch in a green and trimmed condition. Indeed, companies housing their workers in the SAV pay TDIC on average more per worker than that worker is paid in wages.

Little fiscal or human attention seems to have been devoted to direct benefits to employees, such as recruitment debt relief or raised compensation levels. Committing resources to workers' priorities should be on a par with realizing the complexity of the museums' architectural plans.

Recommendations

What follows below are recommendations that were discussed or put forward by us in our meetings with TDIC. Others have been considered and discussed among ourselves since the visits. Gulf Labor is proposing to collaborate with all parties involved to find solutions, and to contribute its own resources wherever possible to achieve positive results.

1.   In order to deal with the recruitment debt issue as a historical and ongoing problem, we propose that workers relocating to Saadiyat to build the Guggenheim should be paid a one-time Relocation Fee. This would cover workers who have been in the country for many years, as well as those newly arriving. It would be an upfront payment to compensate for the average amount of recruitment fee, visa, and flight costs that are almost universally known to have been paid by workers, which as per our current information would be about 2,000 USD. This would help relieve workers of the immediate burden of debt, a condition (sometimes described by informed commentators as bonded labor) that underpins their extreme vulnerability. Workers building the region's most luxurious and large-scale developments should be able to offer their labor without this extreme pressure of indebtedness.

2.   We understand that the above recommendation is no panacea for the issue of recruitment fees in general. To ensure that such a move does not have a negative effect on future recruiting or fees in home countries, we have three immediate suggestions:

    A.   Contractors responding to the Guggenheim and other museum tenders should describe their recruiting processes in detail (as per their own EPP).

Guggenheim contractors should set an example for how information on the recruitment chain (i.e., which recruiters they are employing and which sub-contractors the recruiters are using) should be shared with recommended groups in home countries to ensure that recruitment abuse is minimized.

B. An authoritative survey should be undertaken of the recruitment and relocation histories of all workers at SAV immediately, so that this process can be mapped and made graspable for the first time. This would reveal patterns and concentrations of abuse, as well as throw up opportunities for further mitigations, not least by helping us implement the Relocation Fee reimbursement/payment recommendation above. This research should be enhanced by the inclusion of a main contractor on Saadiyat, such as Arabtec, engaging in or enabling the same research.

C. In common with other major contractors in the UAE (Al Nabooda and ATA Escon, to name two) the EPP should include a requirement that main contractors establish their own recruitment agencies in the country of origin for their incoming workforce. This is not a perfect solution but it does dramatically reduce the scale of potential exploitation and increase the transparency of the process.

Taken together, these offer a way for the transnational problem of recruitment fees to be addressed positively, in cooperation with organizations in home countries and international bodies, such as the ILO, with a shared interest in preventing the abuse of workers. Gulf Labor has already been in touch with organizations that are willing and able to undertake further studies for developing appropriate approaches and remedies. A list of these groups and organizations, in Nepal, India, Pakistan, Bangladesh, and other relevant countries, were made available, to TDIC by May 15th 2015.

3. TDIC should encourage the formation of workers' councils within the SAV. Workers themselves are well equipped to assess their welfare needs and how they might be best addressed. These councils, operating without fear of recrimination, should be trusted to represent workers' concerns and grievances and to look out

for their general welfare. The current grievance redressal system is too top-down, and appears to have generated little trust within the SAV. Furthermore, Gulf Labor would like to be in contact with a TDIC official who is directly responsible for workers' welfare. In our view, neither Brookfield Multiplex nor TDIC's Public Relations team currently performs this role. We have been informed that there are TDIC employees who are doing research on workers' welfare and recruitment, and that studies have been conducted on how conditions can be improved. We would like to see these studies, and be in contact with the employees who conduct them.

4.   Given our finding that not all workers engaged on TDIC projects are even living in the SAV, PricewaterhouseCoopers (PwC)—TDIC's commissioned compliance monitor—should be encouraged to amend its auditing methodologies. Interviews conducted only in the SAV and in contractors' offices (both heavily surveilled locations) will not garner the fullest or the most qualitatively useful information. Nor will this kind of data-gathering capture the testimony of workers housed on off-island labor camps.

5.   In all our interviews, the topmost grievance expressed by workers concerned their depressed wages. Accordingly, we recommend that TDIC establish a Saadiyat Island living wage. A living wage is distinct from the minimum wage, which in most locations is estimated at the threshold of mere subsistence. Hundreds of municipalities and other smaller institutions (universities, airports) have adopted living wages as the standard by which employees can maintain a safe, decent standard of living within the cost horizon of a given community. At this point in time, the methods for calculating living wages are quite mature, and have been developed by labor economists on a comparative international framework. Among other things, a living wage would give Saadiyat workers a basic mobility and independence over how and where they choose to live in the UAE.

6.   We encourage the participation of the International Labor Organization (ILO). We recommend that the Guggenheim Foundation and TDIC work with the UAE Ministry of Labor to invite the ILO into a multi-stakeholder process with the goal of designing and implementing these and other recommendations.

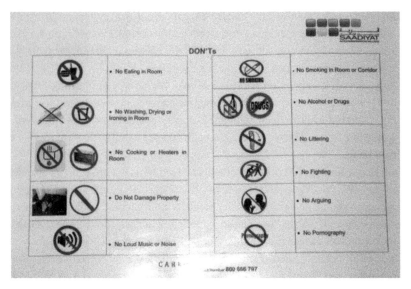

A list of Don'ts inside the Saadiyat Accommodation Village (Credit: Gulf Labor)

A panoramic view of ICAD, a model workers "city" in Musaffah, Abu Dhabi (Credit: Gulf Labor)

Exterior of ICAD (with surveillance tower) (Credit: Gulf Labor)

Some of the structural challenges to the well-being of migrant workers require long-term, and nation-scale, solutions. These include the need for collective bargaining rights, guarantees of freedom of movement, and reforms of the sponsorship relationship. Similarly, the challenge of integrating worker housing into the social and physical fabric of host cities needs to be addressed seriously. Nonetheless, we believe that the proposals above can mitigate some of the immediate problems we encountered on and off Saadiyat Island, and that they are relatively easy to implement.

TDIC has a unique opportunity to set a model example for employee relations in the region. If it follows such a path now, we can envisage how, in the fullness of time, Saadiyat Island might be judged not just for the virtuosity of its urban and building designs but also for the humane conditions afforded its workforce.

Detailed Findings

3.A Workers in the SAV

According to Brookfield Multiplex, there were at the time of our visit about 6,000 workers living in the SAV, building the Louvre and other Saadiyat projects and infrastructure. Of these just two were women, working in services onsite.

The very first group of workers we spoke to in the SAV was a group watching television in an otherwise largely empty recreation facility. These men had been moved to the SAV from Mafraq the night before our visit, and had been told about the move at 3 pm that day. After a mostly sleepless night setting up in new rooms at the SAV, these 125 workers had been taken in the morning to their usual Saadiyat Villas worksite, and had been sent home early in the afternoon.

TDIC informed us that such movements were common at the SAV because different contractors bring in employees for short-term work. However, in this case at least, a group of more than a hundred people who were moved that day appear to have been working on a TDIC project (the Saadiyat Villas) while living in Al Jaber company's accommodations in Mafraq Workers' City, about 50 kilometers away. This information was at odds with TDIC's steadfast claim that everyone working on TDIC projects on Saadiyat is housed in the SAV.

At an off-island labor camp we met three employees of Robodh Construction, a sub-contractor working on the St. Regis Hotel, the Louvre, and NYUAD. These workers had spent 33 days, two months and six months in the SAV respectively. Two of them reported being "promoted" out of the SAV by being made supervisors, without an increase in pay, so they could be moved from the SAV into cheaper and more distant housing. They were housed first in Musaffah (45 minutes away) and then Al Ain (more than two hours away) while still working on Saadiyat Island.

The vast majority of the workers we spoke to during our brief visit to the SAV had been there for a few months, rather than years. It therefore appears that the SAV is more a short-term venue for those who are working on part of a project—on the Louvre's foundations, for example—than long-term housing for a community of workers. In some cases, as with Al Jaber's and Robodh's workers above, even this temporary stay in the SAV while working on a TDIC project does not seem to be guaranteed.

At the same time, the SAV operates at less than half its 20,000 capacity. According to TDIC there have never been more than 14,000 workers there at any one time. This is not because there are only that many workers actively engaged on Saadiyat. It is because companies do not always heed TDIC's requirement ("obliged" is the term in the EPP) to house their workers there. Those companies not contracted by TDIC often prefer to avoid the higher accommodations rates at SAV, even though they are working on Saadiyat and are encouraged to use the facility for its proximity to the jobsites. (More detail on the possible reasons for this is in the wages section below.)

3.B Living conditions in the SAV

The first impression upon approaching the SAV by road is of its isolation from the rest of the city and from public roads. The SAV is two kilometers inland from a checkpoint that marks the edge of the construction site, rendering any casual or unannounced approach impossible. According to TDIC and BM, there are hourly buses going to and from the checkpoint, which are the only way for workers to travel to the main road and connect to the city bus services outside of traveling to work.

There are two principal kinds of accommodation in the SAV. Laborers' accommodation is six to a room, while foremen and supervisors are housed two to a room.

A six-person room we were shown in the SAV (Credit: Gulf Labor)

The six-people rooms can be compared favorably in size to rooms in other camps we have seen. There are three twin bunk beds and lockers, but no other furniture. A prominent list reminding residents of what is not permitted in the room includes eating, cooking, washing and drying, drinking alcohol, and pornography.

All meals in the SAV are provided by the central kitchen, as there is no cooking allowed elsewhere. The kitchen, like the other central facilities such as the gym, computer room, and television rooms, is well-equipped. However, during our visit we heard many complaints from workers about food. Indeed, in the SAV this was the first thing many workers wanted to talk about. Complaints ranged from objections to its taste to allegations that something in the food made workers drowsy, as a result of which they ate very little. There was no way for Gulf Labor to verify these claims or sample the food itself, but we brought them to the notice of TDIC and BM officials. They noted that the food was subject to a complex negotiation at the SAV, as would be expected of different nationalities and varied cultural diets, but that they are working to improve the food quality overall.

Pakistani and Bangladeshi workers were "segregated" across the SAV. In the wake of strikes by Arabtec workers in May 2013 (the most prominent and well-reported among the "many" strikes that TDIC acknowledges have affected the facility), workers recounted that many Bangladeshi men were sent home and replaced by Pakistani workers. According to them, this was among the factors that resulted in clashes between the two national groups, which turned violent in August 2013. After these events, Pakistani and Bangladeshi workers were kept separate, a policy that remains in place in the SAV today.

During our visit, a group of workers returned from the Louvre site to the SAV. They had been working from 7 am to 6 pm, with a one-hour lunch break. A standard work day is 10 hours, including two hours of overtime. One day a week is off, usually Friday. These workers and others we met in front of the buildings had specific complaints about leaking sewage water in several lower-level bathrooms. According to one worker, "The vast majority of us are Muslims. Because of the sewage from above we cannot have a clean bath even before prayers." BM reported that some recurring problems were related to corrosion and construction flaws in these temporary buildings, and that they were currently fixing the leakage problems.

3.C Wages and Companies in the SAV

In our interactions inside the SAV, we recorded some of the base monthly salaries as reported by workers:

- Carpenter, working on Saadiyat Villas: 650 AED (177 USD)
- Louvre worker: 750 AED (205 USD)
- Louvre infrastructure worker: 800 AED (218 USD)
- Three-year veteran of SAV, worked on infrastructure projects: 850 AED (231 USD)

TDIC did not allow us to distribute questionnaires to workers, and we do not have more detailed data on wages in the SAV. But such statements, combined with those from more detailed off-island interviews with men who had worked recently on NYU Abu Dhabi, the St. Regis hotel, and the Saadiyat Villas (the last two being TDIC projects), led us to conclude that base salaries range from 550 AED to about 900 AED for general building trades. Combined with overtime, which on Saadiyat projects is highly controlled and seems to be mandatory, the net salary of the vast majority of workers is between 1100 and 1200 AED (300 to 320 USD) a month. Salaries are paid electronically, and, these days, generally on time.

Only after clearing their debts and deducting phone, hygiene, and other personal costs are workers able to send money back to their home countries. Sample remittances to Bangladesh were about 15,000 Taka and to Pakistan a similar amount in Rupees, which is less than USD 200 per month. In many home countries, skilled construction workers could earn at least that much while employed in urban areas. But evidently there are still many who come to the UAE for the sliver of advantage in savings it permits them to eke out. Not having many expenses of their own, combined with the savings from living in a camp without family, becomes an additional advantage for some. Many migrant workers are paid far less than they were promised by recruitment agencies.

Notwithstanding conditions elsewhere, this does not qualify as a living wage in Abu Dhabi, the richest and most expensive of the Emirates, where per capita GDP of citizens is estimated at more than 100,000 USD a year.

According to an EPP compliance officer we interviewed, companies housing their workers in the SAV have to pay TDIC 42 AED per day per ordinary worker, and 66 AED per day per foreman-level worker. These would be the respective tariffs for six-bed or two-bed rooms. It is striking that, as noted above, this amount comes to more than the average wages paid to a worker. Thus, TDIC is asking companies such as Al Jaber, Al Futtaim Carrilion, Arabtec, and their many smaller labor suppliers who are active on Saadiyat Island to pay more for these facilities than they pay the workers. Given the choice, contractors on non-TDIC projects, notably NYUAD, prefer to house workers elsewhere, and these other camps are located as far away as Dubai and Al Ain—a minimum two-hour one-way commute. This reality—that the flagship housing project at SAV is at best only half-full—needs serious thought from TDIC and the companies that are working on Saadiyat Island.

3.D Recruitment fees

Every worker we met in the SAV and at off-island sites had paid recruitment fees to come to the UAE. Bangladeshi workers on the NYUAD sites reported paying between 1 lakh 20 thousand, and 3 lakhs in fees (1,545 USD to 3,864 USD). In the SAV, a worker who had come from Rajasthan in India three months ago had paid 65,000 Indian rupees (1,078 USD) to an agent, on top of his visa and travel costs. Pakistani workers in Musaffah reported paying between 80,000 and 200,000 each (820 USD to 2,050 USD). There is no difference between workers currently in the SAV and workers outside in terms of recruitment fees. A TDIC official who did not wish to be named observed, "If there is a worker who said they have not paid a recruitment fee, I would not believe him."

Six Bangladeshi workers whom we met in the SAV while they were playing *carrom* all said that they had taken loans with family land as collateral three to five years ago in order to pay recruiters. One of them who had arrived in the UAE three years ago categorically said that he had not yet been able to pay his loan back yet and would lose his land. According to an off-island interview with two Nepalese workers who had worked on NYUAD, three or four out of 10 workers lose their land as they are unable to pay the debt back in time.

Recruitment debt is a pervasive and ongoing problem that is recognized by all parties in this situation. Yet it seems to be an integral component of the migrant worker system. Who would work for such low wages for two years, unless to pay off a debt that had entrapped the lands and livelihoods of their families?

3.E The Louvre and Guggenheim sites

On March 20, 2014, Gulf Labor members were taken to visit the Louvre and Guggenheim construction sites. The visit demonstrated the scale of the engineering challenges that TDIC was encountering while constructing these buildings.

This visit also showed us that, contrary to the Guggenheim Foundation's persistent claim that "the museum is not being built at the moment," a good deal of work has already gone into its foundation pilings and the massive surrounding infrastructure without which the building will not stand. The Foundation's statements also belie the fact that as tenders for the Guggenheim Abu Dhabi were floated in October 2014, workers are expected to be hired by the appointed contractors by this summer. The conditions of work and housing on the museum sites are being determined right now.

3.F Related sites and issues beyond the SAV, including NYUAD

Members of Gulf Labor also visited other work and housing sites around Abu Dhabi, Dubai, and Sharjah. We were able to record a number of interviews with workers. Some of these workers had been engaged on TDIC's Saadiyat projects but had not always lived in the SAV. Clearly, TDIC is not getting fully accurate information on where workers are being housed. Since PwC (TDIC's compliance monitor) only interviews workers in the SAV and at their employer's Saadiyat offices, its audits are failing to capture the full scope of the workforce, and the potential EPP violations that occur in off-island sites.

This section of the report focuses on NYUAD workers, because many of our off-island interviewees had been engaged in building the university's new Saadiyat campus. NYUAD is not a TDIC project, and so its workers are not required to be housed in the SAV. Its Statement of Labor Values was established prior to TDIC's EPP, and in some respects is stronger. Accordingly, there are good reasons to expect that many of the concerns we documented from these interviews with those who worked on the Saadiyat campus also apply to workers on the TDIC projects.

NYUAD is being delivered under the auspices of Tamkeen, on behalf of Abu Dhabi's Executive Affairs Authority. Mubadala, an investment vehicle of the government,

Pilings and earthwork at the Guggenheim site (Credit: Gulf Labor)

is the developer responsible for design implementation and construction. Our understanding is that workers are all supposed to be housed in Operatives Villages 1, 2, and 4 located on Yas Island or in the ICAD Residential City located in Musaffah, Abu Dhabi. However, we found workers housed in substandard facilities elsewhere, as have other independent investigators from Human Rights Watch and the foreign press.

In contrast to the compliance reports that PwC has delivered to TDIC, the reports of NYUAD's labor monitors, overseen by Mott MacDonald, have recorded very few violations of NYUAD's labor standards. Among the conflicts of interest associated with Mott MacDonald's appointment as monitor, it is worth noting the 27 billion USD contract awarded to the firm by the Abu Dhabi Water and Electricity Authority to oversee the development of water and electricity systems on Saadiyat Island. Mott MacDonald mentions visits to the Yas Island and ICAD facilities in its reports, and we assume that the auditors have not ventured beyond these camps. In the course of our spot visits to a camp in Al Quoz in Dubai and to the BK Gulf camp in Musaffah, we found and spoke to workers who had been, or were still, engaged on the NYUAD project. In the course of our interviews with these workers and with other local sources we recorded the following violations of NYUAD's Labor Standards:

1.   No worker was in possession of his passport.
2.   Some workers did not have a written contract regarding hours and wages.
3.   Overtime (amounting to 11- or 12-hour work days, and sometimes longer) was described as mandatory, not voluntary.
4.   Sub-contractors (such as Robodh and Al Reyami) had failed to pay wages in a timely fashion, and were in arrears by several months.
5.   Employers had not paid recruitment fees.
6.   Some workers were housed in substandard camps, and some had endured long work commutes (up to three hours).
7.   Many of the employees engaged in work stoppages (a four-hour strike by Al Reyami workers in June, and a larger two-day strike in August by BK Gulf workers housed in Yas Island and Jebel Ali) were terminated and deported without due process. These summary actions appear to violate NYUAD's Statement of Labor

Values that "no worker shall be subject to harassment, intimidation or retaliation in their efforts to resolve work disputes."

8. _ While food allowances had been slightly increased in response to the August strike, subcontractors' promises of salary increases had not been kept.

3.G Overview of camp conditions in the UAE

Throughout our visits, we heard from workers a consistent set of grievances: low-pay; heavy recruitment fee debts; long working and commuting hours; abuses relating to relocation and vacation costs including air tickets which companies are supposed to pay but which in practice fall on workers; late pay; poor and expensive f food when included in salaries or benefits; isolation and exclusion from society and lack of access to public spaces; difficulties in pursuing legitimate grievances (including length of process, requirement for physical presence and payment for translations into Arabic), and a culture of buck-passing amongst contracting employers. Such conditions were encountered in all the labor camps we visited in Sharjah, Dubai and Abu Dhabi, hosting men from Pakistan, India, Nepal and Bangladesh who had either arrived in recent weeks or had been working there for up to 10 or 15 years.

Al Sajaa (Sharjah) was the most isolated industrial area and labor camps district we visited. It is surrounded by an impressive, newly-built infrastructure of roads and utilities serving the nearby airport and connecting to Fujairah on the eastern coast, but otherwise feels derelict and abandoned, located as it is some 30 kilometers from the city. The dozens of camps here border the desert and most interior roads are unpaved. Despite the geographic isolation, men can socialize publicly in cafeterias and small shops, cook and sell food, and walk to public transport in ways that are impossible in the high-security containment of the SAV.

Al Quoz (Dubai) and Musaffah (Abu Dhabi) are both large industrial areas with labor camps interspersing anonymous industrial blocks. There are supermarkets and cafeterias/restaurants nearby, where we were able to meet with workers. The edges of large arterial roads dividing the camps appeared to be the only public spaces available, other than mosques, for workers to congregate and socialize; i.e., to be part of a society broader than their own camp. "Workers City" is the preferred nomenclature in

Workers return to their camps in Al Sajaa on Friday, a holiday (Credit: Gulf Labor)

A view of the compound in Musaffah camp where NYUAD workers live (Credit: Gulf Labor)

Musaffah, but these new urban-scale housing projects are nevertheless far from and have very little to do with the actual city of Abu Dhabi.

We could not access the interiors of the accommodations at Mafraq Workers City nos. 1 and 2 (Abu Dhabi), but were able to take a guided walk through this "city" itself, which is to say, within its secured perimeters. Immediately outside the guarded gates was a large supermarket and gym. Inside the camp was a large mosque, and more evidence of efforts to create a quasi-urban feel: wide streets, dotted with occasional retail outlets and some spaces for gatherings amid the gridded layout with its pavements and street lighting. While the potential capacity of Mafraq Workers City and the SAV is, in both cases, more than 20,000 men, the former uses far less temporary building materials and occupies a larger area on the ground.

Jebel Ali Industrial Area 1 (Dubai) hosts about 50 labor camps of varying sizes and an aggregate population larger than the SAV or Mafraq. Here again the camps occupy a section of Jebel Ali's industrial quarters and are isolated from any other urban connection. However, within the camp area there are several supermarkets, *masjids*, and cafes/restaurants, in addition to recreational space outside the loosely contained camp areas—though not much more. Although it is a dusty, grimy place, its inhabitants are free to come and go beyond their immediate camp-blocks and can be seen gathering in groups or sitting alone at dusk throughout the camps. Overall this felt like a more benign, sociable environment in spite of its neglected appearance, and its residents' freedom of movement contrasted starkly with the excessive focus on "security" in some of the more heavily fenced-in and remote locations, like the SAV or Jebel Ali's larger labor camps. Particularly evident in such places was the existence of street life in the sociable "owned" spaces of cafes and restaurants as well as in the informal, or "hidden," corners of the smaller camps. The advantages of the latter must be weighed against the cleaner accommodation and green lawns at SAV.

We visited a newly-built labor camp in Jebel Ali where a construction company, along with some architects, is attempting to improve conditions in its new workers housing building with larger rooms, higher ceilings, and natural as well as machine ventilation in rooms arranged around central ventilation shafts. These kinds of improvements need to be combined with efforts to create "people-friendly" environments, allowing for more light and air, and the preservation of informal social spaces and access to the public realm.

One way to work toward that goal at Saadiyat itself would be to include, in the long term, more permanent schemes of workers housing, not centralized but rather scattered throughout the 27 square kilometer area. This could be a bridge toward a more healthy and just society to come, in which construction and maintenance workers might live among communities of more permanent residents, either in state-provided social housing or in rented or other accommodation of their choosing.

Overall, what is crucially necessary to address is the removal from view and understanding of the men who are building the UAE from its citizenry and its visitors. Currently segregated in invisible and unacknowledged circumstances, workers are imperceptible to those populations whose infrastructural needs they are serving. If we withhold from suggesting that Emirati homes, tower blocks, and museums should be built in the midst of workers' cities (although that may be the one way to achieve a properly mixed, healthy society), we must at least insist that migrant workers be recognized as full participants of the broader society in which they live and work.

52 Weeks, and Engaging by Disengaging

Mariam Ghani with Haig Aivazian

Most people know of Gulf Labor from our cultural boycott of the Guggenheim Abu Dhabi, which is now entering its fourth year. But others first learned about us through the 2013–14 campaign *52 Weeks,* which marked an important tactical shift for the group. Every week for an entire year, Gulf Labor published one or more artist's projects calling attention to some aspect of workers' conditions on Saadiyat Island, the political context of their plight, and the problematic compact between the Western cultural institutions and their Abu Dhabi partners. Gulf Labor used this campaign to apply regular and constant pressure on these institutions to seek uniform and enforceable human rights protections for all workers on their construction sites.

While Gulf Labor's position may appear from the outside to be a straightforward staging of refusal, the overall campaign has unfolded as a series of engagements, disengagements, and reengagements. By this we mean that the group has used refusal strategically, in order to open negotiations that previously seemed impossible, to change the tenor of those negotiations when they began to seem untenable or insincere, and to try to negotiate real changes and concessions. The group has also attempted a strategy that we might call *engaging by disengaging*: that is, to use the cultural boycott to open a parallel space for a different kind of engagement of ideas and issues behind and around the boycott itself.

The *52 Weeks* campaign presents the clearest example of this tactic. Since each week of the campaign was produced by a different artist, *52 Weeks* allowed Gulf Labor's central call—to boycott the Guggenheim Abu Dhabi—to be connected to and amplified by multiple voices, each with things to say about related issues and struggles, not only on Saadiyat Island and in the UAE, but also in the Gulf, in the workers' home countries, and across the world. These additional layers of detail, meaning, byplay, and analysis accumulated over its year-long duration. By the end of the year, *52 Weeks* had not only succeeded as a pressure tactic, but also provoked Gulf Labor organizers like ourselves to reconsider how art-driven campaigns could be used most productively and deliberately to boost public attention, as a supplement to other, more introverted and administrative forms of organizing.

Like those of most long-term boycotts, our campaign strategy has shifted over time, as we came to deploy different tactics. At certain moments, the group has engaged in intensive behind-the-scenes dialogue with both the Guggenheim and their partners in Abu Dhabi, even making recommendations to them with regards to resolving their own employment policies. We have read, dissected, and responded to monitoring reports by PwC, as well as Human Rights Watch reports. We have conducted our own monitoring missions on Saadiyat as well as in other labor camps, and have, in consultation with rights groups, journalists, activists, and United Nations agencies like the International Labor Organization, drafted reports setting out our own assessments of working conditions, along with recommendations for remedying the situation on Saadiyat and elsewhere. In order to formulate these recommendations, we have had to conduct research and look to other case studies while thinking creatively about finding solutions to complex problems, not least of which is the particularly complicated issue of recruitment fees. Besides our public statements, articles written by our members, and some interviews granted here and there, the bulk of our work has been conducted out of the public eye, and produced little that could be addressed to a public that may be mildly interested but not invested enough to decode the tedious legalese of monitor reports and legislative reforms.

The launch of *52 Weeks* in the fall of 2013 represented a distinct shift in strategy for Gulf Labor. From the outset, the boycott was premised on using artworks strategically, either by withholding them from the Guggenheim's acquisition plans, or by imposing conditions on particular sales, commissions, and exhibitions. *52 Weeks* inverted the tactic by producing and circulating artworks that directly addressed or enacted the ideas behind the boycott, while bypassing the museum and market systems altogether.

52 Weeks was able to maintain a prolonged (if somewhat one-sided) conversation in public with the Guggenheim, its chief Emirati partner TDIC (Tourism Development

& Investment Company), and the other Western institutions active on Saadiyat. But *52 Weeks* also allowed Gulf Labor to connect our efforts vis-à-vis Saadiyat Island to relevant issues and parallel activist projects—from the construction of stadiums for the World Cup in Qatar, to the globalization and aggressive corporatization of university campuses, to the struggles of migrant tomato pickers in Florida—through the projects produced by a diverse group of artists and writers from outside the core working group. In addition, *52 Weeks* created an occasion for direct actions to be performed as part of the campaign, giving birth to the Gulf Labor spinoff Global Ultra Luxury Faction (G.U.L.F.), which assailed the Guggenheim Museum officials and trustees in a more confrontational way.

While some contributions to the *52 Weeks* project created space for direct action, others took more laconic, analytical, or abstracted approaches to highlighting the ironies and contradictions of the grand project of Saadiyat Island. Examples include: Week 15 (by WBYA?), which proposed new architectural standards to be added to the AIA Code of Ethics and Professional Conduct; the launch, through Week 34, of an activist Twitterbot programmed to alert prolific tweeters about the Guggenheim and Louvre Abu Dhabi's disregard for human rights; Week 18's reflection on the absence of migrant labor encyclopedias from the sunset of the British Empire; and Week 11's presentation of an entry on 50° Celsius for a new Emirati encyclopedia, reflecting on the dangers of working in extreme temperatures. These examples illustrate the projects' tonal range, from playful to elegiac, from meditative to sardonic.

Overall, the *52 Weeks* campaign, with its many brilliant contributors, helped to reimagine what a group like Gulf Labor can be and do, moving us beyond the declaration and maintenance of the boycott, and the more tactical and bureaucratic aspects of pressuring our target institutions. *52 Weeks*, which succeeded in bringing labor to the very center of artworld discourse, was a reminder that a boycott can and should be the beginning of a larger conversation, rather than a means to shut down dialogue around an issue. The organizers of a cultural boycott in particular have the leeway to highlight practices like unfair labor, or apartheid, as objects for debate, not simply as candidates for taboo.

In "My Guggenheim Dilemma," the text published for the second week of *52 Weeks*, Thomas Hirschhorn asserts that the real dilemma of a cultural boycott lies in the contradiction between the "politics of 'good intentions' that guides 'the engagement of the artist' . . . and my belief and conviction that Art, as Art, has to keep completely out of any daily political cause in order to maintain its power, its artistic power, its real political power." If, in Hirschhorn's formulation, the real political power of art lies in maintaining a space that can resist the simplifications of political idealism and realism, then why use art to enact real-world politics? One response is that when culture is deployed for overtly political purposes—as it often is by autocratic regimes who want to cloak that autocracy with performances of freedom—the weave between aesthetics and politics becomes so complex that the space of art is required to pick it apart.

The conversation around cultural boycotts in the artworld and in academia appears to be approaching a critical threshold. This development owes, in part, to a resurgence of a particular kind of institutional critique, or to be more precise, a growing interest by artists in questioning the conditions under which they produce, exhibit, and circulate art. Artists engaged in this critique are most often not producing works about the institutional conditions of art, but rather have mobilized into activist entities that directly intervene in the realities on the ground, confronting tedious technicalities that often exceed their professional expertise. While there is a long history of such collective mobilizations and their alignments with experts in the fields on which they touch, the most recent examples address issues ranging from the working conditions of art handlers who hang artworks in art fairs and auction houses and the endemic exploitation of interns in the gallery system to censorship and other improper institutional conduct, just to name a few examples.

But more often than not, when artists are moved to action by injustice in the artworld, their activism quickly exceeds both the confines of the artworld and the confines of their own art practices. Renewed media attention around Gulf Labor's boycott followed the *52 Weeks* launch, but it was also buoyed by G.U.L.F.'s occupations of the Guggenheim Museum and by front-page *New York Times* revelations about labor abuse in the construction of NYU's Abu Dhabi campus. The carefully negotiated artist withdrawals from the Sydney Biennale in protest of main sponsor Transfield's involvement with widely criticized migrant detention camps resulted in the withdrawal of Transfield's chairman from the Biennale board and the return of the boycotting artists to the show. The most recent edition of *Manifesta* was also the target of a call to boycott, due to its Saint Petersburg location and the manifold challenges to free expression in the current political and cultural climate of Russia, including the so-called "homosexual propaganda" laws. Accordingly, the public program of *Manifesta* included self-reflective discussions on the distinctions between "making art politically" and "making political art."

The Boycott, Divestment, and Sanctions (BDS) campaign against Israeli companies and institutions complicit in the violation of Palestinian rights received a fresh jolt of publicity when the American Studies Association voted to endorse it in the fall of 2013, and American politicians seized the opportunity to denounce professors who dare to take public and professional stands against Israeli policies. Shortly prior to the opening of the 2014 São Paulo Biennial, a group of 61 participating artists published a collective letter outlining the grave risks that the prominent Israeli funding of the event posed for Arab artists. Threatening to withdraw from the biennial, the signatories of the letter asked for the Biennial's foundation to return the Israeli funding. Instead, a strategic compromise was reached, whereby all materials made very clear that Israeli funding was being used exclusively to support works of those artists not opposed to such an association, as opposed to crediting Israel as a general sponsor of the entire event.

When the Creative Time exhibition *Living as Form*—a survey of socially engaged art practices—was being toured by Independent Curators International, it traveled to Israeli venues that are deeply embedded in the country's military-industrial-settlement complex without prior notification of participating artists, some of whom are BDS signatories. Creative Time and ICI have both announced that they do not participate in any cultural boycotts, because they believe it is more important to engage—to try to shift the limits and possibilities of the discourse by participating in it—than to disengage—to try to shift the discourse entirely by withdrawing from it.

Notwithstanding the limited definition of boycott implied by this formulation, the question raised by Creative Time is a strategic dilemma at the heart of every boycott. Can a given predicament be changed more by engaging, or by disengaging? The answer is certainly different for every person, for every government, for every institution, and for every situation. For some, "boycott" will always be a dirty word—whether because of a reflexive stance against blanket prohibitions, or because of harsh experience at the wrong end of economic sanctions. For others, the boycott is just another bit in the activist toolkit, or really, just an ordinary fact of life: part of the endless, everyday struggle to negotiate our personal ethics.

Thomas Hirschhorn raised another pressing question in the last line of his *52 Weeks* text, when he declared that "my signature for the boycott of Guggenheim Abu Dhabi will make sense if I have to pay a price for it." Since his text was originally a letter sent from Hirschhorn to Guggenheim deputy director and chief curator Nancy Spector and director Richard Armstrong about a proposed exhibition of his at the Guggenheim Bilbao, the allusion to paying a price was quite apposite. Yet the reality of paying a real, personal price for participation in a cultural boycott is not often acknowledged. It is more typical for us to join what Hirschhorn himself calls a "fancy artists' boycott," either as an all-but-routine gesture of solidarity—just another e-signature on a petition—or, for the organizers, as some sort of esoteric career move. But for a boycott to make a maximal impact, there ought to be a real price—lost income, frayed relationships, a certain reputation for troublemaking—and signing on must mean that you are willing to accept that price. Garnering a lesser number of signatories who have seriously weighed what it means to sign is more valuable than collecting a greater number who sign without having to bear any real consequences.

Ultimately, our experience in Gulf Labor has brought us to the following conclusions. A boycott (like a strike) should be a tactic of last, rather than first, resort. Public boycotts should be called only when negotiation proves either impossible or fruitless. Moreover, a boycott should be launched only when it is likely to produce results: that is to say, a cultural boycott will work only if the creative work being withheld has significant and immediate value to the institution or government being boycotted. If that government or institution does not in fact need cultural products for a specific purpose in that specific moment, then cultural workers have no leverage with them, and so the boycott is unlikely to succeed. Likewise, if the boycott does not include a significant portion of the most visible cultural workers necessary to the immediate purpose or project of the government or institution, then it is also likely to fail. A public boycott should not be called until enough organizing has been done to ensure a minimum of consensus around the goal and necessity of the boycott in the community most important to its success. If the demand behind a boycott is vague or diffuse, it is also unlikely to work. In a long-term boycott, however, it is possible that goals may develop over time as the situation and relationships change, from one central demand into a series of more specific or interrelated demands.

Thus far, the Gulf Labor experience suggests that the boycott dilemma, as formulated by Creative Time, is something of a false dichotomy. Describing participation in a cultural boycott as disengagement, and refusal to participate in a boycott as engagement, can be a misleading oversimplification. A long-term boycott like ours involves a good deal of dialogue with the targeted institution about the conditions under which a boycott can be lifted. So, too, many people in the coalition became involved with Gulf Labor after first producing art in the region, including long-term research-based projects. As a result, artists initiating such projects were already directly engaging with, and thus becoming implicated in, the ethical dilemmas at hand. But most of all, the dilemma of engagement versus disengagement is a false one because of the potential for a cultural boycott that, while enacting physical or economic withdrawal from a particular institution, simultaneously opens a parallel space for critical engagement with the issues motivating the boycott, as well as dialogue with all the players involved. This is precisely what *52 Weeks* achieved.

Gulf autocrats' massive investment in cultural projects does hold out a sort of promise, both to artists across the Middle East who need more support and exposure for their work, and to inhabitants of Gulf countries who might imagine that freedom of expression granted to artists within museum walls could eventually lead to greater freedom of expression in other sectors of life. But if this promise is to be more than a desert mirage, or a whitewash of dubious human rights practices, the institutions charged with realizing these cultural projects must be constructed in a truly equitable way, and held to high standards. Gulf Labor has said that it is not enough for a satellite museum, or a college campus, to function as a zone of exception, where the prohibitory norms and rules are bent for certain actors to operate within a sequestered, showpiece site. Gulf Labor thinks these institutions can be more, and should do more. By being held accountable for their openly expansionist agendas, they can be turned into levers to generate wider change across the whole region.

Saadiyat has become a particular flash point for at least two reasons. First, because the western institutions loaning their names and institutional cachet to Abu Dhabi's new "culture zone" have brands to protect, and reputations that project images entirely incompatible with the unsavory image of the labor camp. These institutions have significant leverage, and Gulf Labor, along with groups like Human Rights Watch, has argued that they are refusing to use it. Consequently, Gulf Labor has had no alternative but to apply its own leverage to force these institutions to confront their responsibilities in illiberal countries where they choose to operate. Second, Abu Dhabi's sovereign wealth fund is among the largest in the world. The annual interest income from the fund alone nets the Emirate an average of 43.47 billion USD per year. Clearly Abu Dhabi does not lack the funds to resolve the problems identified by Gulf Labor, along with countless investigative journalists, rights groups, and even the state's own appointed labor monitor (PwC) on Saadiyat Island. What it lacks is the will to put its resources to this particular use. To put it even more clearly: the Abu Dhabi authorities could easily improve the living and working standards of these workers, but they visibly do not want to do so. The distinction is crucial, because it points to the global importance of this local struggle. The rulers of Abu Dhabi do not want to require better conditions for their migrant workforce because doing so would set a precedent that would spread to other countries.

Gulf Labor believes we should not be asked to overlook how our museums are being built simply out of gratitude that they are being "provided" in the first place. We don't think art has to enter the portals of the museum before the museum can become an agent of change; we think change should be demanded from the moment the museum is first imagined. We think it is just to ask more of these institutions, not because we think so little of them, but rather because we value their function and potential more highly than perhaps even their executive officers do. We are boycotting, perhaps in a funny way, out of our love and care for these institutions, because we want them to be their best possible selves.

Gulf Labor fully recognizes that the predicament of migrant workers is not limited to the Guggenheim/Louvre Abu Dhabi, to Saadiyat Island, the Emirates, or even to the Gulf region. While it is engaged in what is undoubtedly a worldwide struggle, the group has chosen to focus its energies on this particular battle because we believe

End of the shift, Musaffah, Abu Dhabi (Credit: Gulf Labor)

it is winnable. We are asking the Guggenheim, the Louvre, and the British Museum to either halt on the brink, or, in the case of NYU, commit their resources to bettering the human rights environment in which global outposts are established in locations like the Gulf. When corporations made the same move into globalized production and distribution, the anti-sweatshop movement emerged to hold them accountable for their deliberate negligence overseas. But Nike and the Gap were not claiming to be protectors of our culture or standard-bearers for our educational methods; they were clearly seeking to maximize their profits while expanding their global presence. When museums and universities go offshore, but hold on to their claims about their cultural standing, this struggle takes on a new importance. More than any dispute over which objects end up on the walls or plinths and which names are included in the curricula, the questions of where and how museums and universities choose to expand, and which compromises they are willing to make along the way, will determine how culture is preserved, distributed, and extended. If we are to have any say in this debate, the workers who provide the currency for this sector of cultural trade and services must hold our institutions accountable, and we must begin now.

52
Weeks

WEEK 1

52

WEEKS OF...

art
action
discomfort
anticipation
disagreement
expectation
persuasion

suggestion
dissensus
demands
trouble
poetry

shame

Workers are also
artists
and artists are also
workers
We stand together
in solidarity
in our dignity
in our rights
in our strikes

GULF LABOR
in support of

One year of interventions for workers and their rights
in the construction of the Guggenheim, Louvre, and
other institutions in Abu Dhabi

gulflabor.org

WEEK 2

PART ONE

Banners, Thomas Hirschhorn, 2009
Made at the occasion of the exhibition "Contemplating the Void: Interventions in the Guggenheim Museum," Solomon R. Guggenheim Museum New York, 2010

Beyond my project-participation, *Banners* is for me an opportunity to give form to what I think Art can do.

1. Art—because it's art—is resistance. Art resists facts. Art resists political, aesthetical and cultural habits. Art, in its resistance, is movement, positiveness, intensity, belief.
2. Art—because it's art—has the power of transformation, the power to transform each human being.
3. Art—because it's art—can create the conditions of implication—beyond everything else.
4. Art—because it's art—is autonomous. Autonomy is what gives the artwork its beauty and its absoluteness.
5. Art—because it's art—is universal. Universality means: Justice, Equality, the Other, the Truth, the One world.
6. Art—because it's art—can provoke a dialogue or a confrontation from one to one.

PART TWO

Letter to Nancy and Richard (My Guggenheim Dilemma), Thomas Hirschhorn, 2011

Text written and read at the occasion of the panel-discussion for the exhibition 'The Luminous Interval: The D. Daskalopoulos Collection' at Guggenheim Bilbao, 2011. Thomas Hirschhorn's work "Cavemanman" (2002) was part of the exhibition.

Dear Nancy, Dear Richard,

As you know, I am one of those who signed the petition for the boycott of the Guggenheim in Abu Dhabi, to put pressure on the museum to do everything it can in order to remedy the labor exploitation on Saadiyat Island, to treat the workers as they deserve to be treated, and to protect their rights as workers. I am happy and willing to do everything I can do in order to achieve this; that's why I signed the petition for a boycott.

Nevertheless, there is a dilemma. The dilemma—my dilemma—is not about exhibiting, here and now, my work "Cavemanman" in the Guggenheim Bilbao, while at the same time boycotting the Guggenheim in Abu Dhabi. That is not my dilemma, and the dilemma is not about some other contradiction observers might point out either.

The dilemma, my dilemma, the real dilemma, is the contradiction between the politics of "good intentions," "the good conscience," "the engagement of the artist"—that I should in fact call "pseudo-politics" or "making politics," for it implies narcissism and selfishness, but which I signed the letter for—and my belief and conviction that Art, as Art, has to keep completely out of any daily political cause in order to maintain its power, its artistic power, its real political power.

By signing the petition for this boycott, I am facing this dilemma, my dilemma. It's a problem without a solution; it's a dead-end. On the one side, I really want to do what I can, what I think is in my power, to fight for equality, universality, and justice. But I also know that it is easy to add my signature to this fancy artists' boycott. Too easy, because I know that when signing a boycott, I have to pay the price for the boycott—myself first—so that the outcome can be a real success.

Art—because it's art—resists a simplified idealism and a simplified realism, because it refuses aesthetic and political idealism and aesthetic and political realism. And Art—because it's Art—is never neutral, but Art cannot be neutralized by doing politics. I want to admit that this is the "dead-end" I am in. I have to face it. I have to confront this dilemma and furthermore—as an artist—I even have to assert it as my dilemma.

My hope is that something that makes sense remains.
— My signature for the boycott will make sense if it does change the conditions of the workers for Guggenheim Abu Dhabi.
— My signature for the boycott will make sense if the dilemma, the trap, and the temptation of politics allow me to confront the hard core of reality, which is the limit of such a boycott.
— And my signature for the boycott of Guggenheim Abu Dhabi will make sense if I have to pay a price for it.

Thank you,
Thomas Hirschhorn, April 2011

WEEK 3

location/dis-location(s): contingent promises (installation excerpt), Jayce Salloum, 2012

I remember installing an exhibition in the UAE. The workers transformed this massive hanger-like conference hall into separate galleries for each artist. For lunch break the workers would lay down the drywall/gypsum board onto the ground and sleep for a bit, curled up on top of it after eating from their tiffins. In the evenings outside their living quarters thousands of men milled about, shopping and socializing, absent were women and children, their families not able to accompany them. It was as if two-thirds of the demographic had suddenly disappeared.

Michael Ruiz, San Diego/Tijuana, cofounder of Gulf Labor West
Migrant/Al Milagro 2013, erased photograph

WEEK 4

Guggenheim Abu Dhabi Labor Camp for Guest Workers, Sam Durant, 2013
Poster

GUGGENHEIM ABU DHABI
LABOR CAMP FOR GUEST WORKERS

Gulf Labor est une coalition d'artistes et d'activistes qui travaillent depuis 2011 pour mettre en évidence le recrutement forcé et les conditions déplorables dans lesquelles vivent et travaillent les ouvriers migrants dans l'île de Saadiyat et du Bonheur à Abu Dhabi. Notre campagne se concentre sur les travailleurs qui construisent le Guggenheim Abu Dhabi, le Louvre Abu Dhabi, une Musée national Sheikh Zayed (en collaboration avec le British Museum) "52 weeks" est une campagne qui va durer un an, à partir d'Octobre 2013. Artistes, écrivains et activistes de différents pays seront invités à contribuer un oeuvre, un texte, ou une action chaque semaine, pour dénoncer ou éclaire l'injustice des conditions de vie et travail des ouvriers migrants qui bâtissent ces institutions culturelles à Abu Dhabi.

Pour en savoir plus: www.gulflabor.org   Pour infos supplémentaires: contact@gulflabor.org

WEEK 5

"I paid ...," Hans Haacke, 2013
Poster

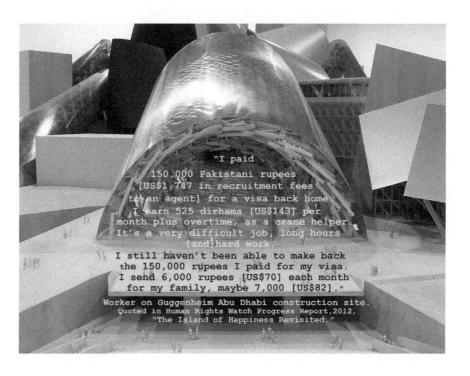

"I paid
150,000 Pakistani rupees
[US$1,747 in recruitment fees
to an agent] for a visa back home.
I earn 525 dirhams [US$143] per
month plus overtime, as a crane helper.
It's a very difficult job, long hours
[and] hard work.

I still haven't been able to make back
the 150,000 rupees I paid for my visa.
I send 6,000 rupees [US$70] each month
for my family, maybe 7,000 [US$82]."

Worker on Guggenheim Abu Dhabi construction site.
Quoted in Human Rights Watch Progress Report, 2012,
"The Island of Happiness Revisited."

WEEK 6

Me, we, the, be/coming migrant, Guy Mannes-Abbott, 2013
Poster

me, we,
the, be/
coming
migrant

WEEK 7

Saadiyat Island Workers Quarters Collectable, Matt Greco & Greg Sholette, 2013
3-D Prints "Shop-Dropped" at the Solomon R. Guggenheim Museum, printed label, plastic boxes: unlimited edition.

Photo Credits: Karin Cintron

SOLOMON R. GUGGENHEIM MUSEUM
SAADIYAT ISLAND WORKERS QUARTERS COLLECTABLE

 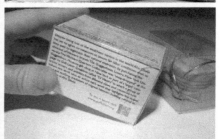

WEEK 8

Refuse Complicity, Mieke Bal & Michelle Williams Gamaker (Cinema Suitcase), 2013
Poster

CONDONING IS
DOING REFUSE
COMPLICITY
EXPLOITATION
BRINGS YOU
DOWN

WEEK 9

If FIFA did..., Farid Sarroukh and Maha Traboulsi in collaboration with Walid Raad, 2013
Poster

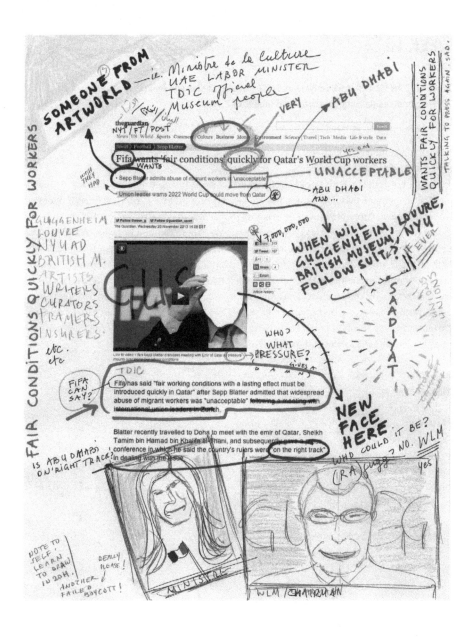

WEEK 10

NO DEBT IS AN ISLAND, Andrew Ross and MTL (Nitasha Dhillon and Amin Husain), 2013
Triptych; multimedia components and a printable PDF

Launch of a solidarity initiative, December 2013:

A high school graduate with an offer from a prestigious art institute dreams of artworld renown and takes out loans that will burden her for decades. Her brother is enrolled at NYU, national leader in student debt—the university is a growth machine, feeding off tuition and cheap credit to expand at home and overseas. In Bangladesh, the eldest son of a heavily indebted family dreams of Gulf riches, and borrows money to pay his recruitment and transit fees for passage to the UAE. There, on the "Island of Happiness," Abu Dhabi's showpiece real estate venture, his bonded labor is now linked to the "indenture" of the American students. Their respective financial obligations are connected to, and amplified by, Abu Dhabi's over-leveraged boom economy, which rests on an ever-growing carbon debt. *No Debt Is An Island* traces the chain of debt that sustains the fortunes of the international art market, the global aspirations of Anglophone higher education, and the ascent of the Gulf petroleum states.

BREAK THE CHAINS
Make the links
Follow the money
Do the research
Walk the talk
Pressure the brands
Raise the bar
Break the chain
(and keep the oil in the soil)

From NYU to the Guggenheim, February 17–21st

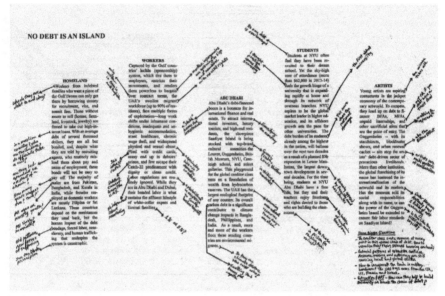

DETAIL ON NEXT PAGE

NO DEBT IS AN ISLAND

HOMELAND

Workers from indebted families who want a piece of the Gulf Dream can only get there by borrowing money for recruitment, visa, and transit fees. Those without assets to sell (homes, farmland, livestock, jewelry) are forced to take out high-interest loans. With an average debt of several thousand dollars, they are all but bonded, and, despite what they are told by recruiting agents, who routinely mislead them about pay and terms of employment, these bonds will not be easy to pay off. The majority of males are from Pakistan, Bangladesh, and Kerala in India, while females employed as domestic workers are mostly Filipina or Sri Lankans. These countries depend on the remittances they send back, but the human impact of the debt bondage, forced labor, near-slavery, and human trafficking that underpins the system is catastrophic.

WORKERS

Captured by the Gulf countries' kafala (sponsorship) system, which ties them to employers, restricts their movements, and renders them powerless to bargain over contract terms, the UAE's swollen migrant workforce (up to 90% of residents), face multiple forms of exploitation—long work shifts under inhumane conditions, inadequate and unhygienic accommodation, scant healthcare, chronic wage theft, and widespread physical and sexual abuse. Plied with credit cards, many end up in debtors' prison, and few escape their Catch-22 predicament with dignity or clean credit. Labor regulations are routinely ignored. While they are in Abu Dhabi and Dubai, their bonded labor is what sustains the affluent lifestyle of white-collar expats and Emirati families.

ABU

Abu Dhabi
boom is a
ternational
estate. To
tional inv
tourists, an
dents, th
Saadiyat I
stocked w
cultural
Louvre, Gu
ish Museum
leigh scho
galleries. T
for the glob
rests on a
wealth fron
reserves. Th
largest ecol
of any coun
carbon debt
contributor
change imp
desh, Phil
India. As
and more
from these
tries are env
grants.

Handwritten annotations:

who do they owe debt to and why?

only written in Arabic and English

workers insurgencies are growing in size and number with no civil rights

in a muslim country? who are the lenders? do officials take a cut?

are they indentured or part of a chain?

How many years wages? one? two?

All ages or mostly youth?

All single? married?

Old patterns, new forms of suffering

see the Dhebt principles

a stable home for investments?

36% interest rates

Debtors cannot leave the UAE

No independent labor monitoring

especially true in domestic contexts

established in response to Gulf labor boycott

1% or 5%?

STUDENTS

Students at NYU often feel they have been recruited to their dream school. Yet the sky-high cost of attendance (more than $62,000 in 2013-14) fuels the growth binge of a university that is expanding rapidly at home and through its network of overseas branches. NYU aspires to be the global market leader in higher education, and its offshore growth sets the pace for other universities. The debt burden of its students, already among the highest in the nation, will balloon over the next two decades as a result of a planned $5b expansion in Lower Manhattan, the largest downtown development in several decades. For the time being, students at NYU Abu Dhabi have a free ride, but they and their teachers enjoy freedoms and rights denied to those who are building the classrooms.

ABU DHABI

[...]habi's debt-financed [...] is a bonanza for in[-] [...]nal finance and real [...] To attract interna[-] [...] investors, luxury [...], and high-end resi[-] [...] the showpiece [...] Island is being [...] with top-brand [...] amenities–the [...], Guggenheim, Brit[-] [...]seum, NYU, Cran[-] [...]school, and select [...]s. This playground [...] global creditor class [...]n a foundation of [...] from hydrocarbon [...]s. The UAE has the [...] ecological footprint [...] country. Its overall [...] debt is a significant [...]utor to climate [...] impacts in Bangla[-] [...] Philippines, and [...] As a result, more [...]ore of the workers [...]hese sending coun[-] [...]e environmental mi[-]

ARTISTS

Young artists are aspiring contestants in the jackpot economy of the contemporary artworld. To compete, they load up on debt to finance BFAs, MFAs, unpaid internships, and other sacrificial stints that are the price of entry. The Guggenheim -- with its starchitects, blockbuster shows, and urban renewal cachet -- sits atop the artists' debt-driven sector of precarious livelihoods. More than other institution, the global franchising of its name has hastened the internationalization of the artworld and its markets. Has the museum sold its social responsibilities along with its name, or can the power of the Guggenheim brand be extended to ensure fair labor standards on Saadiyat Island?

Some Bigger Questions

- The creditor class sucks revenue at every point in this global chain of debt. How to visualize this? Flying squeegees hovering overhead?
- Colonial patterns of extraction continue. Resource mining and autocracy are still serving local and global elites.
- How to incorporate the trade in military hardware? The UAE buys arms from the UK, U.S., France and Israel.
- Education & ART - How can they help to build solidarity or break the chain of debt?

[handwritten annotations around the page:]

Its own debt is overleveraged

I thought prestige comes from scarcity

the first global university

he winner takes all

not ok if you don't have a trust fund

working for exposure

aka the Bilbao Effect

artists are model workers of neoliberalism

diversifying the economy

Gucci produces Louis Vuitton in striking contrast

Consuming more natural resources than any other

40% more than the national average

frankly opposed by faculty and residents

the bubble of academic freedom

and to those in prison for raising their voices

Guest Museum Authority buys 1 billion of art annually

Is this like the NIKE sweatshop boycott?

So they are climate debtors who owes who? Emitting 36.6 tonnes per capita

WEEK 11

50° Celsius, Lynn Love and Ann Sappenfield, 2011
Page layout from *2010 Supplement to the New Emirati Britannica, Third Edition*

The *2010 Supplement* focuses on science, technology and natural history and was commissioned by the Sharjah Art Foundation, UAE for the Tenth Sharjah Biennial, 2011.

dozens were admitted to hospitals. "Every day we receive between 30 to 50 workers suffering heat exhaustion and stroke," one hospital official reported.

Up to 60 percent of companies openly ignore the Mid-Day Break rule, which does not hinge on a specific temperature being reached, but rather a duration of heat higher than 38°C typical during summer months. The UAE has a history of not fining companies for violating the Mid-Day Break law. The ILO's 50°C standard is simply the upper limit by which the UAE government attempts to enforce the law. After three consecutive days of 50°C, night construction shifts are mandatory. In recent summers and despite global warming, the temperature has, according to local weather reports, hovered in the high-40s for weeks on end.

Heat stroke occurs when the body is unable to regulate its temperature. The body's temperature rises rapidly, the sweating mechanism fails, and the body is no longer able to cool down. Body temperature may rise to 41°C or higher within 10 to 15 minutes. Heat stroke can cause death or permanent disability if emergency treatment is not provided. As a point of comparison, chocolate typically melts at 32°C, candle wax melts starting at 55°C, and the body's tissues are damaged when body temperature reaches 43°C.

Due to intense criticism and negative reports from international monitoring groups like Human Rights Watch, a few companies have hired safety managers who monitor workers' well being while keeping the project on track. Now, a pair of Australian scientists is helping those managers become more objective in their worker safety monitoring. The researchers have launched a study to observe and document the effects of thermal stress. Using an assessment tool called the Thermal Work Limit (TWL), they have determined that most healthy people can labor under very hot conditions if they stay well hydrated and modify their pace of work according to their level of fatigue. The study, admittedly small, suggests that men of varying fitness levels and ages work harder when they arrive at the site, and remain, well-hydrated throughout the day. Despite differences in strength and endurance, well-hydrated workers maintained similar and consistent heart rates while exerting themselves in hot conditions and did not experience a rise in core body temperature. Workers most at risk were those who did not drink or had limited access to water. Workers who had inadequate sleep the night or nights before were also at risk for heat-related illness.

Next summer's heat related challenges may intensify. Construction workers laid off during Dubai's economic downturn in 2008 are increasingly desperate. Despite being homeless with little access to proper food and water, most are working odd jobs outdoors during the day and trying to get back on a construction site. They are stranded in the Emirates with no money to pay their way home, and still separated from the passports that brought them in to the country.

Contractors, whose increasing knowledge about how to keep workers healthy and productive in hot weather by providing water on the job site, must avoid exploiting a labor force that has little left to lose.

50°C Dangerously hot, especially when coupled with humidity of 80 percent or more, as is often the case in the UAE from May to September. This temperature is the equivalent of 122°F and the basis of the International Labor Organization's (ILO) standard that outdoor work halt and alternative shifts are offered. The UAE is a member of the ILO and as such, agrees to its labor standards. In addition to adhering to the ILO's guidelines, the UAE adopted its own "Mid-Day Break" rule for workers in contracting and construction in 2005. The rule, applicable in summer months, means that between the hours of 12:30 and 3 p.m., outdoor work is prohibited in order to protect against heat exhaustion.

The labor force for construction in the UAE is vast, due to the pace of development. It is a workforce largely comprised of foreign-born laborers—from India, Bangladesh, Nepal, Sri Lanka and Pakistan—who are paid low wages, offered no benefits, and live in crowded, camp-like conditions. They often have long commutes to their workplace and limited access to food. Employers hold their passports, which is illegal, but discourages workers from filing grievances.

Before the Mid-Day Break rule was established, as many as 5000 construction workers per month were brought to the accident and emergency department of Rashid Hospital in Dubai during July and August. During summer power outages in Sharjah in 2010, a 27-year-old Indian laborer died of heatstroke shortly after being brought to an emergency ward. Heatstroke cases quadrupled and

WEEK 12

And Justice For All, Rasha Salti, 2014

… And Justice for All
Rasha Salti

Who remembers Al Pacino's Academy Award nominated rendition of
the driven-to-the-edge defense attorney, Arthur Kirkland, in
Norman Jewison's 1979 courtroom drama, *… And Justice for All*?
It's probably a generation thing, for those 'not of age', it's
definitely worth looking up on YouTube. Most likely on YouTube,
is a rebroadcast—or capture—of Pacino's unforgettable scene
when he erupts screaming: *"You're out of order! You're out of
order! The whole trial is out of order! They're out of order!"* As
the year 2013 nears its conclusion, the scene has mysteriously
resurrected from the folds of my memory and played over and over
and over… For the words I have lost and struggle to string to
make sentences that make sense of the world and of this year, Al
Pacino's fit incarnates, all too often, the release I contain, day
after day, Facebook browse after browse, news broadcast after
broadcast, for fear of being taxed with emotional or pyscholog-
ical instability… When it plays in my head, the identification
is so immediate, it instigates a sedating effect and I learn to
live with images of starving, freezing Syrian refugees, tweets
announcing more detentions in Egypt or car bombs in Beirut.

Yet, in my heart of hearts, I refuse to surrender to despair.
When I am asked to opine on the "sorry" or "awry" state of the
Arab spring, I smile wryly and insist, I do think it's a spring,
not a winter, nor a summer, and certainly not an autumn. The
reason is simple, I hold a uniquely privilged position. By virtue

of my profession as a visual arts curator and film programmer, I have the privilege of apprehending the world, our present, our everyday and our tomorrow, our elderly and youth, our country-sides and cities, our farmers, workers, public servants and unemployed, our men and women, our icons and forgotten, our living and our dead, through the fabrications of artists, film-makers, novelists, poets, musicians and dancers. With Arab media outlets tongue-tied at the service of their trustees, courts and judiciary bodies cowered to power, dissidents jailed and tortured, more than ever since decades, an ever growing number of Arab artists have been fearless, tireless, enchanting and inspiring. Security forces think they can execute with impunity and eliminate hard (forensic) evidence of their murders, but their crimes are recorded in poems, novels, paintings, pho-tographs and films. Rulers think they can lacerate our social fabric with sectarian, ethnic or cultural strife, turn us against one another, but our civility and solidarity are recorded in poems, novels, paintings, photographs and films. In our films, photographs, paintings, novels and poems, artists have given our martyrs dignified burials and consoled their beloved, kept traces of the missing, safeguarded our aspirations, reclaimed our rights.

What we have demonstrated, what we have showed, was unimag-inable to them: men and women, from across classes and genera-tions, standing peacefully side by side, sharing food, song and dance, shaping their destiny and taking their dignity, knowing they have the moral highground. The inalienable outcome of the Arab spring is the dissipation of the prohibitions we had in-ternalized and the demons that bucked creative expression from within. It is the decisive rupture, and the fuel propelling the captivating flourishing in artistic production. The inalienable animus of the Arab spring are desire and necessity, essential constituents to the creative expression. In 2013, our rulers robbed our rights, governed us with injustice, denied our aspirations. In 2013, our artists —those not at the service of power— gave us poetic justice. It's a metaphor that cannot quench thirst, quell hunger, or repel despair, but it's an empowering representation of a becoming, the herald of a future for us, nearer than suspected. In 2013, an ever growing number of Arab artists has not only rescued me from surrendering to despair, but given me the strength to imagine that the future is mine, ours, and not to those who rule us and their policemen "out of order". Nearer than suspected… and with justice for all.

WEEK 13

Life is as beautiful as..., Office for Anti-Propagada, Marina Naprushkina, 2013
Poster

WEEK 14

Of Saadiyat's Rectangles & Curves, or Santiago Sierra's One Sheikh, Two Museum Directors, Three Curators, One University President, Two Architects, and One Artist Remunerated to Sleep for 30 Days in 13 x 14 foot Windowless Room with Shared Bathroom and No Door, Pedro Lasch, 2013

Of Saadiyat's Rectangles & Curves, or Santiago Sierra's *One Sheikh, Two Museum Directors, Three Curators, One University President, Two Architects, and One Artist to Sleep for 30 Days in 13 x 14 foot Windowless Room with Shared Bathroom and No Door* (2013). From ART BIENNIALS & OTHER GLOBAL DISASTERS by Pedro Lasch.

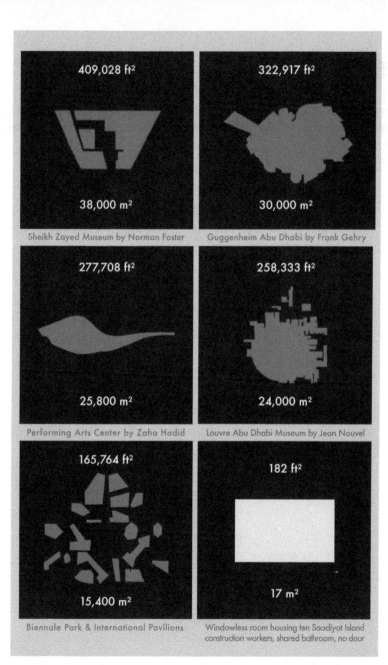

409,028 ft²

38,000 m²

Sheikh Zayed Museum by Norman Foster

322,917 ft²

30,000 m²

Guggenheim Abu Dhabi by Frank Gehry

277,708 ft²

25,800 m²

Performing Arts Center by Zaha Hadid

258,333 ft²

24,000 m²

Louvre Abu Dhabi Museum by Jean Nouvel

165,764 ft²

15,400 m²

Biennale Park & International Pavilions

182 ft²

17 m²

Windowless room housing ten Saadiyat Island
construction workers, shared bathroom, no door

WEEK 15

WBYA? proposes new standards be added to the AIA Code of Ethics and Professional Conduct in order to fulfill our professional and ethical obligation to those who build our architecture, Who Builds Your Architecture?, 2014
Printable PDF

THE AMERICAN
INSTITUTE
OF ARCHITECTS

2007 Code of Ethics
& Professional Conduct

**WBYA? proposes expanding standards for
Human Rights and Obligation to the
Workers who Build Our Architecture**

How can architects:

E.S. 1.4   Uphold human rights at job sites where migrant
workers are being employed?

E.S. 1.5   Perform design work that is socially responsible
and advocate for sustainable building practices
that improve the lives of workers?

E.S. 1.6   Perform professional services that advocates for the
design, construction and operation of job sites that
sustain the human lives those who build our
architecture?

CANON I
General Obligations

E.S. 1.7   Use humane and sustainable practices in all facets
within their firms and on job sites, and encourage
their clients to do the same?

**expand
HUMAN RIGHTS**

E.S. 1.4 Human Rights:
Members should uphold human
rights in all their professional
endeavors.

CANON VI

Obligations to the Environment

Members should promote sustainable
design and development principles in their
professional activities.

E.S. 6.1 Sustainable Design:
In performing design work,
Members should be environmentally responsible and
advocate sustainable building
and site design.

E.S. 6.2 Sustainable Development:
In performing professional
services, Members should
advocate the design,
construction, and operation
of sustainable buildings and
communities.

E.S. 6.3 Sustainable Practices:
Members should use sustainable
practices within their firm and
professional organization, and
they should encourage their
clients to do the same.

ENVIRONMENT

WWW.WHOBUILDS.ORG

DETAIL ON NEXT PAGE

THE AMERICAN INSTITUTE OF ARCHITECTS

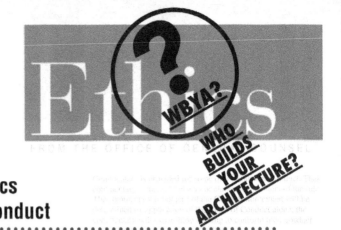

2007 Code of Ethics & Professional Conduct

WBYA? proposes expanding standards for Human Rights and Obligation to the Workers who Build Our Architecture

How can architects:

E.S. 1.4 Uphold human rights at job sites where migrant workers are being employed?

E.S. 1.5 Perform design work that is socially responsible and advocate for sustainable building practices that improve the lives of workers?

E.S. 1.6 Perform professional services that advocates for the design, construction and operation of job sites that sustain the human lives those who build our architecture?

CANON I
General Obligations

E.S. 1.7 Use humane and sustainable practices in all facets within their firms and on job sites, and encourage their clients to do the same?

expand HUMAN RIGHTS

E.S. 1.4 Human Rights: Members should uphold human rights in all their professional endeavors.

CANON VI

Obligations to the Environment

Members should promote sustainable design and development principles in their professional activities.

E.S. 6.1 Sustainable Design:
In performing design work, Members should be environmentally responsible and advocate sustainable building and site design.

E.S. 6.2 Sustainable Development:
In performing professional services, Members should advocate the design, construction, and operation of sustainable buildings and communities.

E.S. 6.3 Sustainable Practices:
Members should use sustainable practices within their firms and professional organizations, and they should encourage their clients to do the same.

WWW.WHOBUILDS.ORG

WEEK 16

Akima and Arif, Jim Goldberg, 2007
Bangladesh

We drove all day and into the night to reach this village in the north of Bangladesh. The village could not sustain itself, as it was no longer farmable. The trees had been cut down, the streams poisoned, and the floods had gotten worse.

There were plenty of children, grandfathers, and grandmothers, but few mothers, fathers, and teenagers. Everyone who was of age and able had left to seek work in Dhaka, or paid away their savings to a middleman who arranged for them to be sent to the Middle East.

Akuma had only seen her father once, seven years before, when he returned to the village and Arif was conceived.

Three fathers from the village had disappeared that year alone.

WE HAVE ONLY
SEEN FATHER
ONCE IN LIFE

AKITTA AND
↓
12

ARIF
↓
6

WEEK 17

Cultural (En)richment, Charles Gaines and Ashley Hunt, 2014
Poster

IN A WORLD WHOSE IMAGINATION OF WEALTH IS ROOTED IN
THE FREE LABOR OF OTHERS, WHERE CULTURE AND THE
GOOD LIFE ARE ENABLED BY COUNTLESS SERVANTS AND
WORKERS WITH NO CHOICE BUT TO ACCEPT THAT JOB AT
THAT PAY, IN A SOCIETY WHOSE WEALTH IS THE BLOOD OF
MIGRANT WORKERS AND PEOPLE DISPLACED FROM THEIR
LAND, IT WILL SEEM LIKE NOTHING TO ENSLAVE A PEOPLE,
TO ROB A PEOPLE OF THEIR NARRATIVE AND SUPPLY THEM
A NEW ONE AS BUILDERS OF SOMEBODY ELSE'S TEMPLES.

IT'S JUST ANOTHER DAY'S WORK,
BUILDING CULTURE ON THE BACKS OF THE VULNERABLE,
BUILDING THE HIGHER THINGS UPON THE SUBORDINATED.

WHOSE HANDS ARE THESE?
WHOSE BODIES ARE THESE?
WHOSE LABOR IS THIS?

FOR
A WORK CAMP IS A WORK CAMP,
AND A SLAVE IS A PERSON, A PERSON MADE A SLAVE,
A SLAVE WAGE IS A WAGE SLAVE,
IS A SLAVE IS A SLAVE BY WHATEVER NAME YOU CALL IT,
A PERSON REDUCED TO THE ENRICHMENT OF ANOTHER.

WEEK 18

Migrant, John Pitman Weber, 2013
Woodcut

WEEK 19

Migrant Labor did not exist in the Wonderland of Knowledge Encyclopedia, 1938, Anna Stump, 2013
Gouache and Collage on Paper

MID'SHIPMAN. See Rank.

MIGNONETTE, *min yun et'.* The mignonette, or "little darling," is a luxury in any flower garden. "Its sweetness wins all hearts." Everyone should grow a small patch of it. In the improvement of the mignonette, the flowers in some cases have been greatly increased in size, but the colossal blooms are almost without fragrance. Both the fragrant and the improved sorts should be grown, as each is of interest in its own way.

The mignonette belongs to the *Reseda,* the name of which pease. The Romans us treat bruises.

BEATEN SKY-PATHS
Migrating bobolinks fly the same route twice each year.

...ND MILES A YEAR
the northland plover flies,
moving climates. Ocean flights from
... to Brazil are made entirely non-stop.

MIGRATION OF ANIMALS AND BIRDS. Like early people, many animals are nomads, wandering from place to place in large groups in search of better food supplies and living conditions. Such wanderings, whether occurring regularly each fall or spring, or irregularly, are called migrations, and may affect any animal.

Food is the primary reason for any migration. For instance, deer, bear, and other animals will live in one region for years as long as food is plentiful and danger from other animals is not too severe. But, should a forest fire sweep the area, or a town be built, or the streams of the region run dry, these animals will move somewhere else in order to find a place where food is more plentiful and danger less constant.

WEEK 20

Protest action inside the Guggenheim Museum, New York City, Saturday, February 22, 2014, Global Ultra Luxury Faction (G.U.L.F.), 2014

G.U.L.F. took direct action against the Guggenheim Museum in New York as part of a solidarity initiative with South Asian migrant workers on Saadiyat Island. The following statement has been released by G.U.L.F. in response to a series of statements made by the Guggenheim Foundation this week:

Each time the Guggenheim speaks, its approach to migrant labor issues on Saadiyat Island sounds more like that of a global corporation than that of an educational or art institution. We would like to remind the Guggenheim that it's a museum, with a mission to "explore ideas across cultures through dynamic curatorial and educational initiatives." Museums should help the public come to a greater understanding of the global complexities we all face.

Each day the Guggenheim hides behind the excuse that "construction has not yet started on our building" is another day of evading decisions and actions which could prevent a future migrant worker's servitude. Right now, the Guggenheim Abu Dhabi's infrastructure is being constructed. That infrastructure includes roads, sewage, water, electric, net pipes, etc., leading to the museum. But other components of the work are also under way. We can only assume that money has been transferred to the Guggenheim here in New York in order to hire the curators and administrators of Guggenheim Abu Dhabi. We know that events off-site have already been organized. Works of art have certainly been bought, insured, and stored. Last but not least, Saadiyat Island is being sold to investors on the basis of the Guggenheim's name, along with those of the Louvre, the British Museum and others. How can the Guggenheim claim that construction has not begun?

Even if we were to take at face value the claim that construction of the Guggenheim Abu Dhabi has not begun, we would say the following: NOW thousands of workers who will build your museum are taking on the massive debt that will take them years to repay; NOW workers are being recruited with promises that will not be fulfilled, for jobs that will pay less than they expected; NOW workers are applying for the passports that may be confiscated as soon as they land in the UAE; and, surely, NOW is the time to do something about all of this.

It is unfortunate but not surprising that the Guggenheim refuses to open its doors to a serious public dialogue about the migrant labor issues in Abu Dhabi. A museum of its stature must foster public education about the conditions under which art is viewed. The Guggenheim is stepping back from this social responsibility as it focuses on expanding into new global markets.

As for the underpaid Guggenheim guards' wages in New York, passing off culpability to a subcontractor is no longer an acceptable practice, even in the corporate world. The Guggenheim should pay all employees at least a living wage, even if they are on a contractor's payroll.

Sadly, the Guggenheim's latest response confirms our expectation. It has tried to hide behind technicalities and PR spin as it waits for news cycles to die down. We know the composition of their board and it does not surprise us. A 1% Global Museum with a 1% Board that cares very little about its lowest-paid employees and the example it is setting to the world.

We will be back.

G.U.L.F.
(Global Ultra Luxury Faction)

WEEK 21

~~they~~ built for eternity, Maryam Monalisa Gharavi, 2014
Acrylic and inkjet

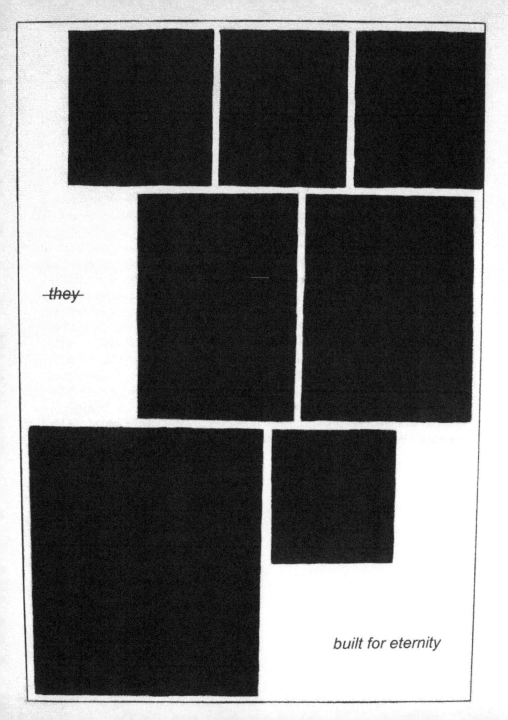

WEEK 22

Labor-Migrant-Gulf, an Exhibit at Southwestern College, San Diego, March 13 to April 10, 2014, curated by Doris Bittar, 2014
Mixed media

Labor/Migrant/Gulf explores migrant workers struggles throughout the world with pointed emphasis on workers from Central and Southeast Asia who work in the Arabian/Persian Gulf, Mexican workers on the US–Mexican border, and California's migrant history. The exhibit at Southwestern College, a few miles away from the US–Mexican border joins artists from around the world to bring awareness to the human struggles of the world's poorest laborers. Many of the artists in the exhibit that have shown in the United Arab Emirates (Dubai, Abu Dhabi, Sharjah) first became aware of the conditions at the Sharjah Biennial in 2009 and began a petition to push the Guggenheim Museum to be mindful of the harsh and unsafe working conditions. A sub-theme is the artist's identification with migrant laborers. Perhaps artists are one or two rungs above the world's poorest labor pools? This exhibit attempts to break down hierarchies between established artist and other artists, therefore children and young adults are included. Labor/Migrant/Gulf at Southwestern College will be organized in two parts: One part is a traditional group exhibit of about a dozen artists. The other part is collective pieces made up of art from about 90 artists to form the shape of large boteh or paisley designs. The boteh/paisley is a significant ornamental design that has religious, historical, colonial, counter culture, and labor meaning and inferences. The boteh/paisley designs honor the Asian migrants that inspired this art exhibit.

WEEK 23

Fist of the Day, Hend Al Mansour, 2014
Silk screen print

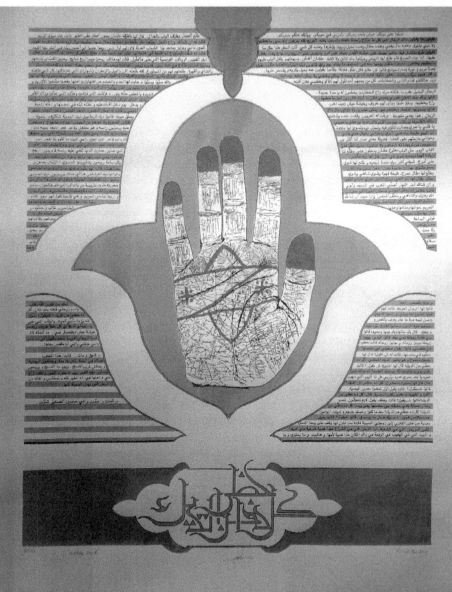

WEEK 24

Rebranding the Guggenheim for Exploiting Migrant Workers in Abu Dhabi, The Illuminator and Global Ultra Luxury Faction (G.U.L.F.), 2014

At 10:00 pm on March 24, 2014, members of Gulf Ultra Luxury Faction (G.U.L.F.) joined by the OWS Illuminator occupied the facade of Guggenheim Museum in Uptown Manhattan for over 40 minutes. G.U.L.F. rebranded the Guggenheim's flagship museum in protest of complicity at the ill-treatment and economic exploitation of migrant workers in Abu Dhabi who are beginning to build the new Frank Gehry-designed Guggenheim on Saadiyat (aka 'Island of Happiness'. G.U.L.F.'s act of messaging solidarity follows recent reports from Human Rights Watch, as well as investigative findings from members of the Gulf Labor Coalition (some of whom overlap with G.U.L.F.) who have just returned from a fact-finding mission in Abu Dhabi where they visited several worker camps and spoke with workers. They confirmed a reality that is the opposite of happy: multiple labor violations, generated by a system built on human suffering and debt bondage.

Last night, G.U.L.F. renewed the call on the Guggenheim to own up to its responsibility as a leading cultural, educational and art institution, and not take economic advantage of the workers seeking the 'Gulf Dream'. Workers should not be caught in a debt spiral where they must work for years on building the museum only to pay the fees that brought them to Abu Dhabi in the first place. Guggenheim has a choice here. It must refuse to lend its cultural capital to build the 'Island of Happiness' where art and luxury mask and maintain a racialized exploitative labor regime, while using its PR department and those of its partners to hide the facts and mislead the public. Unless the Guggenheim changes course with the new museum in Abu Dhabi, G.U.L.F. will continue to remind the Guggenheim that their brand is: "1% Global Museum."

1% Museums means 1% Art.
Art built on Oppression Loses Meaning.
There are other possible Futures of Art.

WEEK 25

CARNIVAL, Rawi Hage, 2012
Poster

The text is an excerpt from the novel CARNIVAL by Rawi Hage (2012). The author is grateful to the following people for their contribution to the design, and to the translations from English into the various languages. Jennifer de Freitas at Associés Libres Design, Foreign language typesetting: Resolvis.ca, Anita Badami and Rahul Varma (Hindi), Rita Boustany (Arabic), Asoke Chakravarty (Bengali), Dominique Fortier (French), Murtaza Haider (Urdu). Also a special thanks to Madhav Badami, Rana Bose and Azza Tawil.

The text reads:

Otto looked revolted and said, Culture? Let me tell you about culture. I walk through the museums and I look at the monuments, those celebrations of theft and oppression, and all I can think of is the suffering of the slaves and the starving workers who shaped those massive stones and carried them on their backs. You know what culture I believe in? I believe in the slave revolt of Eunus against the savagery of the Roman Empire; I believe in Haiti's emancipation from the colonial French, and when they gave it to Napoleon the Third up the ass. Violence and resistance are the only answer. Empire has to feel pain or it will never stop devouring you. It is only when a gun is put in a person's face that anything changes. All empires are hungry cannibals...

[illegible]

तमाशा

रानी ग्रांव (अनुवाद: अनीता वाजपेयी और राहुल वर्मा) ओटोने घृणित होकर कहा, "संस्कृती? मैं बताता हूँ आपको उस संस्कृती के बारे में। जब मैं उन संस्कृति के संग्रहालयों और स्मारकों को देखता हूँ जो चोरी और शोषण के जश्न मना रहे हैं, तो मुझे उन गुलामों और कामगारों की याद आती है जिन्होंने उन भारी-भारी चट्टानों को ढोया और नक्काशी की। आप जानना चाहते हैं मैं किस संस्कृती में विश्वास करता हूँ? मैं रोम साम्राज्य के विरुद्ध गुलाम यूनुस की बगावत में मानता हूँ। मैं हैटी की स्वतंत्रता में विश्वास करता हूँ जिसने फ्रांसीसी उपनिवेशवादियों से मुक्ति के लिये नेपोलियन की गुदा छिला कर रख दी। परिवर्तन का एकमात्र उपाय है क्रान्तिकारी, हिंसा और विद्रोह। अगर शासक साम्राज्य को पीड़ा अनुभव न हुआ तो वह नरभक्षक का आनन्द लेता रहेगा। शासक साम्राज्य नरभक्षी है - जब तक उसके सर पर बंदूक न तानी जाय वह नहीं बदलेगा।

آٹو غصے میں دکھائی دے رہا تھا۔ ثقافت۔ میں تمہیں ثقافت کے بارے میں بتاتا ہوں - میں جب عجائب گھروں میں پڑے نوادرات کو دیکھتا ہوں، وہی نوادرات جو سرقہ اور بربریت کی علامت ہیں، تو میں ان بھوکے مزدوروں اور غلاموں کی صعوبتوں کے بارے میں سوچتا ہوں کہ جنہوں نے ان بھاری بھرکم پتھروں کو تراشا اور پھر اپنی پیٹھ پر لاد کر بلندیوں تک پہنچایا - تمہیں معلوم ہے میں کس ثقافت میں یقین رکھتا ہوں؟ میں اونس کے غلاموں کی سلطنت روم کے ظلم و جبر کے خلاف بغاوت میں یقین رکھتا ہوں۔ میں ہیٹی کی نو آبادیاتی فرانس سے آزادی میں یقین رکھتا ہوں، اور جب انہوں نے نپولین سوم کو ناکوں کے چنے چبوا دئے تھے - عسکریت اور مزاحمت ہی واحد راستہ ہیں - ان سلطنتوں کو جب تک تکلیف نا پہنچائی جائے یہ ظلم سے باز نہیں آئیں گی - جب تک پستول کی نالی کسی کے چہرے پر نہ تانی جائے کچھ تبدیل نہیں ہوتا۔ تمام سلطنتیں بھوکی آدم خور ہوتیں ہیں

Otto a eu l'air dégoûté et il a rétorqué
La culture? Laisse-moi te parler de culture. Je parcours les musées et je regarde les monuments, ces célébrations de vol et d'oppression, et je ne peux penser à rien d'autre qu'aux esclaves et aux travailleurs affamés qui ont façonné ces immenses pierres et les ont transportées sur leurs dos. Tu sais en quelle culture je crois? Je crois dans la révolte des esclaves d'Eunus contre la sauvagerie de l'Empire romain, je crois dans l'émancipation d'Haïti du joug des colons français, et quand ils ont botté le cul de Napoléon troisième. La violence et la résistance sont les seules réponses. L'Empire doit éprouver de la douleur sans quoi il ne cessera jamais de vous dévorer. Ce n'est que lorsqu'on met un revolver au visage de quelqu'un que les choses changes. Tous les empires sont des cannibales affamés.

Otto looked revolted and said, Culture?
Let me tell you about culture. I walk through the museums and I look at the monuments, those celebrations of theft and oppression, and all I can think of is the suffering of the slaves and the starving workers who shaped those massive stones and carried them on their backs. You know what culture I believe in? I believe in the slave revolt of Eunus against the savagery of the Roman Empire; I believe in Haiti's emancipation from the colonial French, and when they gave it to Napoleon the Third up the ass. Violence and resistance are the only answer. Empire has to feel pain or it will never stop devouring you. It is only when a gun is put in a person's face that anything changes. All empires are hungry cannibals

لم يكن أوتو في منزله، فعدت إلى البار حيث رأيته يجلس ويتحدث إلى رجلٍ أنيق بحماس. اقتربتُ منهما، فوجدتُ نفسي وسط جدال محتدم. كان الرجل يتكلم بلكنة فرنسية غليظة ذكّرتني بالسيدة الملتحية. لم سمعتُ أوتو يقول إن الإمبراطورية الفرنسية وثقافتها قد اضمحلّتا، وأن الأمر له ما يبرّره. في حين كان يتحدث الرجل عن مساهمة متواصلة فيالثقافة العالمية. قال أوتو بعد أن استفزه كلام الرجل: أي ثقافة؟ دعني أخبرك عن الثقافة. عندما أمشي في أروقة المتاحف، وأنظر إلى التماثيل والنصب المعروضة هناك، تلك الأمجاد المبنية على السرقة والقهر، فكل ما يمكنني أن أفكر فيه هو معاناة المستعبدين، والعمالالمحرومين، الذين نحتوا تلك الحجارة الثقيلة وحملوها على أكتافهم. هل تعرف أي ثقافة أؤمن بها؟ أؤمن بثورة يونس على همجية الإمبراطورية الرومانية، أؤمن بتحرر الهايتيين من الاستعمار الفرنسي، وبمبالغتهم في الثورة على نابوليون الثالث. أؤمن بالعنف والمقاومةفقط لا غير. على كل إمبراطورية أن تعاني الألم، وإلا فلن توقف انقضاضها عليك. طالما أنك لم تضع المسدس في وجه الآخر، فهذا يعني أن الأمور ستبقى على حالها. إن جميع الإمبراطوريات آكلةٌ جائعةٌ للحوم البشر.

WEEK 26

'SIGNING WITH LIGHT,' G.H. Rabbath, 2014
Still from a GIF animation

'SIGNING WITH LIGHT' is an ongoing performative photography project by G.H. Rabbath taking place at the 392RMEIL393 art project spaces, in Beirut. People coming into the gallery space are told about the Gulf Labor project, and the ones who accept are photographed while reading posts from gulflabor.org or signing the petition.

WEEK 27

Crystal C / planting, Pioneer Works, JAŠA, 2014
New York

As a concluding action of Crystal C project, I planted a tree, a Weeping Willow, that was part of the installation. In many situations of artist's labor, the conditions and value are misunderstood in the market and money driven contexts; therefore I strongly believe that we need to fight for a true understanding of work and the motivations that fuel it. Bare survival is a reality of many; poets as workers. We need to redefine the idea of success, see it as a fist of clay that has to be molded by many hands into a new shape. Togetherness is not only a word, it should be the world.

WEEK 28

A Paradox on Citizenry and Creativity, Alien Abduction Collective (AAC), 2014
Poster

A PARADOX ON CITIZENRY AND CREATIVITY.

FOR A WHILE WE HAVE BEEN TOLD THAT WE LIVE IN A POST-INDUSTRIAL ERA. THIS IS A SITUATION WHERE
THE SERVICE SECTOR GENERATES MORE WEALTH THAN THE MANUFACTURING SECTOR OF THE ECONOMY. WE
HAVE ALSO BEEN TOLD THAT ART, ARTISTIC PRACTICE ENTERED A POST-MEDIUM CONDITION, SOME TIME AGO
AND THAT IT IS THREATENED BY DE-SKILLING (DEMISE OF A FINE ART OF PAINTING AND PURE PAINTING).
THE COMMON DENOMINATOR FOR BOTH STORIES SEEMS TO BE LABOR, LABOR THAT ALLEGEDLY SEEMS TO BE
BECOMING EXTINCT OR MORE TO THE POINT, GETTING RAREFIED IN OUR POST-WHATEVER WORLD.

ON THE OTHER HAND WE KNOW THAT EVERY CITIZEN NEEDS TIME FOR THE DEVELOPMENT OF CREATIVITY AND
FOR ACTIVE PARTICIPATION IN POLITICS. IF THIS IS THE CASE, WHY THEN WOULD EVERYONE BE SO CONCERNED
BEYOND ANY REASONABLE DOUBT ABOUT LABOR EXTINCTION? IS THIS PERHAPS BECAUSE ALL THESE DIFFERENT
POSTS OR RATHER POST-LABOR NARRATIVES ARE MADE POSSIBLE PRECISELY BY A PRESSING PRESENCE OF A
LARGE POPULATION OF WORLD CITIZENS, LABORERS STILL BEING TREATED TO WAGE-SLAVERY?

COULD IT BE THAT VARIOUS RHETORIC OF POSTS ARE YET ANOTHER WAY TO NATURALIZE THE FACT THAT WORLD
CITIZENS ARE TREATED EVEN TODAY AS A MARGINAL MINORITY... IN OUR POST-IDEOLOGICAL SOCIETY...?

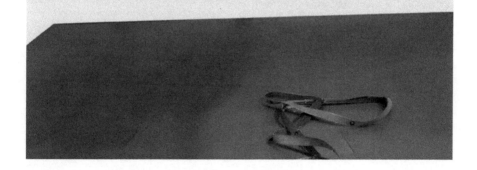

WEEK 29

And we wondered, Mariam Ghani, 2014
Poster

Text based in part on interviews given to the Swedish press by former Gulf Air flight attendants. The text reads:

> We would see them at certain gates in certain airports—Dhaka, Delhi, Kathmandu—groups of young men in bright T-shirts, emblazoned with the names of Gulf construction companies. They would be nervously excited, joking with each other, already set apart from the rest of us—not simply travelers but migrant workers. We wondered, always, if they knew yet the devil's bargain they had made when they accepted the tickets and the T-shirts—how long it would take to repay the recruiters, how many ten-hour shifts, how many two-hour trips from camp to city in the invisible hours of late night and early morning, how many times they would snatch at sleep in unlikely places in the tiny intervals of rest. Certainly they were unaware as they waited to board their flights to Doha, Dubai, or Abu Dhabi, coffins were being offloaded at these same gates, from the cargo holds of those same planes, returning the bodies of men who had made the same trip scant, or several, or many years before. And we wondered, always, if they knew, would it make any difference?
>
> (or would we all just continue on, accumulating compromises, because after all, somehow, some way, we all have to eat?)

We would see them at certain gates in certain airports - Dhaka, Delhi, Kathmandu - groups of young men in bright T-shirts, emblazoned with the names of Gulf construction companies. They would be nervously excited, joking with each other, already set apart from the rest of us - not simply travelers but migrant workers. We wondered, always, if they knew yet the devil's bargain they had made when they accepted the tickets and T-shirts - how long it would take to repay the recruiters, how many ten-hour shifts, how many two-hour trips from camp to city in the invisible hours of late night and early morning, how many times they would snatch at sleep in unlikely places in the tiny intervals of rest. Certainly they were unaware that as they waited to board their flights to Doha, Dubai or Abu Dhabi, coffins were being offloaded at those same gates, from the cargo holds of those same planes, returning the bod ies of men who had made the same trip scant, or several, or many years before. And we wondered, always, if they knew, would it make any diffe rence?

[Or would we all just continue on, accumulating compromises, because after all, somehow, some way, we all have to eat?]

WEEK 30

Blue Skies, White Walls, Brown Bodies, Jaret Vadera, 2014
Poster

BLUE
SKIES
WHITE
WALLS
BROWN
BODIES

WEEK 31

Commentary on the Universal Museum Project in Dubai, which can be easily transferred to Saadiyat Island, Creischer, Siekmann, 2009
Poster

"Culture-nation" lends corporations and clans the shape of a state. It is not a population that legitimizes this state, but this empty space. The things in this space exist in and for themselves, without dedication and history. That makes them logical and aesthetically true for the purpose of the power that annihilates the history of things and the violence with which they were produced. "Culture nation" is the expertise of the national state that lends its own social crimes a shape.

WEEK 32

30 Untitled Men, John Suleiman Jurayj, 2007-2011/2014
Digital archival print on vellum with burn holes, 30 images, 2007-2011
Poster, 2014

Images are courtesy of the Trustees of the British Museum

WEEK 33

MOBILE IRONY VALVE. On the Pearl Interpolation (PERP) in a Monument to Bad Memory, Emily Verla
Bovino, 2014
Screenshot of project in various media (PDF chapbook, blog post scroll montage, 3D Animation,
Youtube ethnography elliptical edit and thermoplastic printed object)

To see how to add a perp to the herp to the lerp and the berp already present in the library of
things, download the chapbook and watch scroll montage here:
http://peddlers-and-bandits.blogspot.com/2014/05/blog-post.html

WEEK 34

Organizing tool kit, Sarah Farahat and Aaron Hughes, 2014
Twitterbot

Artists Sarah Farahat and Aaron Hughes offer a downloadable organizing tool kit complete with posters, postcards, and suggestions for solidarity actions and organizing in your community.

In collaboration with an anonymous programmer, they launched a twitterbot campaign on June 3rd to alert high profile tweeters across the globe about NYU, Louvre and Guggenheims' disregard for human rights. #GulfLaborAction

WEEK 35

Dangerous Lexicon, Silvia Kolbowski, 2014
Detail

DANGEROUS LEXICON

Denial (disavowal) A mode of defense that consists in the subject's refusing to recognize the reality of a traumatic perception...

Phantasy Imaginary scene in which the subject is a protagonist, representing the fulfillment of a wish (in the last analysis, an unconscious wish) in a manner that is distorted to a greater or lesser extent by defensive processes.

Projection The operation whereby qualities, feelings, wishes or even "objects," which the subject refuses to recognize or rejects in himself, are expelled from the self and located in another person or thing. Projection so understood is a defense of very primitive origin, which may be seen at work especially in paranoia, but also in 'normal' modes of thought.

Trauma An event in the subject's life defined by its intensity, by the subject's incapacity to respond adequately to it, and by the upheaval and long-

WEEK 36

"At the very least...," Pablo Helguera, 2010
From the series *"Artoons"*

"At the very least there has to be a Guggenheim nearby."

WEEK 37

Farmworker Justice, Mazatl, 2014
Poster

Created in solidarity with the Coalition of Immokalee Workers (CIW) based in Florida, Santiago Mazatl's poster connects struggles for migrant worker rights in Abu Dhabi to movements for farmworker justice in the United States. To learn more about the CIW's work to combat modern-day slavery and other labor abuses common in agriculture, visit http://ciw-online.org/about/.

WEEK 38

KA (JCB, JCB), Nida Sinnokrot, 2009

To view additional images of the production process in a labor camp outside of Dubai, visit:
http://gulflabor.org/images/#prettyPhoto[375]/36/

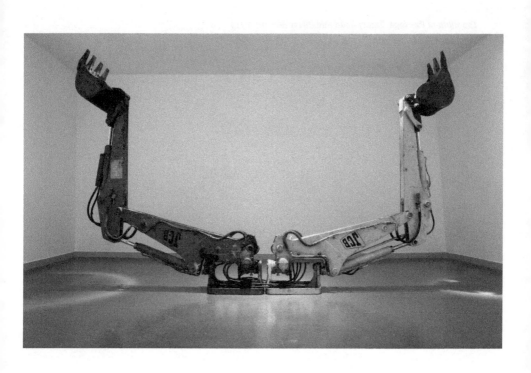

WEEK 39

The Right of Passage, Zanny Begg and Oliver Ressler, 2013
Still from HD film, 19 min

WEEK 40

Digital Catalogue, Jenny Polak, 2014

Captains of Culture
why pay more?

1: Penalized Labor Camp   2: 'Iconicity' Labor Camp   7: 'Promenade' Labor Camp

Modern Labor Camp Typologies
from the US to the UAE
Now Affordable - Available Online
(details within)

4: مصكر قطر العمل   6: Camp De Travail Modèle de l'Europe   [Three] [Labor] Camp

Limited Time! Discounts on Orders Over 1000

Captive Workforce Optional Extra!

8: Camp De Travail L'Arbie Saoudite   3: Tent City Labor Camp   9: 'Perspective' Labor Camp

WEEK 41

Sheikh Mc Abed had a Museum, Mounira Al Solh, 2014
Videoclip still

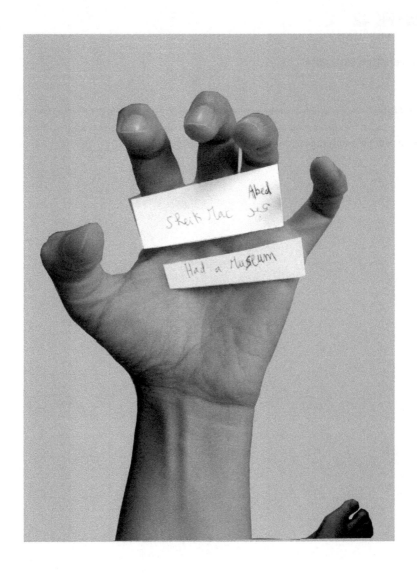

WEEK 42

QR code, Doris Bittar, 2014

Gulf Labor West launches its new website. We draw a direct line from the Arabian/Persian Gulf to the Gulf of Mexico—two pools of migrant laborers whose rights, safety and dignity we seek. Scan your phone over the QR code and read more about us.

gulf labor west.org

WEEK 43

Live / Work, SITU Research, 2014
Poster

LIVE / WORK

WEEK 44

How Long has it Been?, CAMP, 2014
Poster

So when was the last time you left the camp on Saadiyat Island, Sharif?

If you mean other than the bus to work, I haven't left since I came here, eight months ago.

By August 2014 it is clear that the vast majority of workers who have lived in the Saadiyat Accomodation Village since 2010, or will live here in the near future, have as a "best practice", zero contact with the city they are surrounded by, or indeed the one they are building.

Sharif* from West Bengal currently works on ultra-luxury homes called Saadiyat Villas, a stone's throw from the Louvre and Guggenheim museum sites, for a salary including allowances of 720 AED or 196 USD a month.

*yes, name changed

WEEK 45

132 €, Andrea Fraser, 2014

Published as an advertisement in *Frankfurter Allgemeine Sonntagszeitung*, Sunday, August 17, 2014

Who's building the Guggenheim Abu Dhabi?

Guggenheim Abu Dhabi acquisition budget	"potentially unlimited"
Saadiyat Island museum complex estimated construction cost	$27,000,000,000
Former Guggenheim Director Thomas Krens' severance bonus	$2,000,000
Current Guggenheim Director Richard Armstrong's salary	$750,000
Abu Dhabi GDP per capita (2014 S&P estimate)	$103,000
Monthly wage of Guggenheim Abu Dhabi construction worker	$177

Read the reports & sign the petition: gulflabor.org

Sherko Fatah letzte Woche im Kunstquartier Bethanien in Berlin-Kreuzberg

Der Westen ist weich, der Osten fast ohne Hoffnung

Über den großen deutschen Erzähler Sherko Fatah. Und über den Crash der Kulturen: in seinem Kopf, seinem Roman. Und im Nordirak

132 €

ANDREA FRASER

VOLKER WEIDERMANN

ANDREA FRASER

Wer baut das Guggenheim Abu Dhabi?

Ankaufsbudget des Guggenheim Abu Dhabi	"potentiell unbeschränkt"
Geschätzte Baukosten für den Saadiyat Island Museumskomplex	€ 20.000.000.000
Abfindungsbonus des ehemaligen Direktors Thomas Krens	€ 1.500.000
Jahresgehalt des derzeitigen Guggenheim Direktors Richard Armstrong	€ 560.000
Bruttoinlandsprodukt Abu Dhabis pro Einwohner (Schätzung S&P, 2014)	€ 77.000
Monatliches Gehalt eines Bauarbeiters des Guggenheim Abu Dhabi	€ 132

Lesen Sie die Berichte & unterzeichnen Sie die Petition: gulflabor.org

WEEK 46

I have seen everything that is done under the sun, and behold, all is vanity and a striving after wind,
Paul Graham, 2013
9 Color Photographs in Grid

WEEK 47

2015: Grand Opening of the Louvre Abu Dhabi, Janet Koenig, 2014
Digital collage

LOUVRE ABU DHABI

In the spirit of *liberté, égalité, fraternité,*
in which the Louvre first opened in 1793
and in recognition of those whose labor made
the Louvre Abu Dhabi possible today, the
museum is pleased to feature in its inaugural
exhibition an installation and ongoing
performance by the workers themselves.

WEEK 48

Points of View, Carole Condé and Karl Beveridge, 2014
Staged photograph

Documentary image: *Burj Dubai construction workers,* June 4, 2007, Imre Solt (GFDL)

WEEK 49

Your Elite Status is Guaranteed, Dread Scott, 2014
Poster

WEEK 50

Guests, Pat McElnea, 2007-14
SD Video (still)

Guests consists of footage shot in Dubai and Abu Dhabi from 2007.

WEEK 51

Guggenheim Appetizer, Suha Traboulsi, 2014
Newspaper cut-out

Inside Art

Guggenheim Abu Dhabi Will Serve an Appetizer

A Gallery's Western Outpost

Odyssey of a Slave Portrait

WEEK 52

Untitled (Profit comes from exploitation), Claire Fontaine, 2014
Digital print, dimensions: (29 ½" x 41 ¾") (106 x 75cm)

GETTING THE BEST DEAL

Not everyone has the same approach to negotiations – in fact, there are five main styles that people use subconsciously. Understand your own approach and learn to recognize other people's, so you get the best results for all parties in your negotiations.

61 Treat the other party's interests with the respect you give your own.

▲ MAKING A DEAL
Find a way to work toward the best results through bargaining, so that all parties will be pleased with the result.

UNDERSTANDING STYLES

Learn to recognize negotiation styles in yourself and others. A compromise style splits the difference, although both parties could have achieved more. A coercive style relies on being dominant regardless of consequences. Emotional negotiation assumes that appealing to feelings will get the best results, while rational negotiation supposes arguing a point of view will change people's minds. A bargaining style, however, is the most beneficial, because it finds the trade-offs that get the best value for all.

RECOGNIZING NEGOTIATING STYLES

NEGOTIATION STYLE	DISCUSSION
COMPROMISE	"We need a fair deal." "Maybe we can agree to split the difference."
COERCION	"Can we negotiate that?" "No, when we make demands, you should jump."
EMOTION	"Will you extend our credit terms?" "That would cause difficulties for me."
RATIONAL	"Do you see that if we can agree now...?" "But it is sensible to finalize the schedules first."
BARGAINING	"If you can deliver next week, we agree." "We will deliver next week, if you sign the deal now."

DEVELOPING THE SKILLS

Recognize occasions that could be negotiation situations. Before a negotiation, be clear on your outcomes and your bottom line. Make sure you plan and research carefully beforehand, and think through what your best alternative to a negotiated agreement is. This might be to go elsewhere. During the negotiation, maintain a steady emotional state: if you find this difficult, take a deep breath and change the focus of your thinking. Every move should get you closer to a win-win deal or the realization that no deal is the best option.

62 Know you are only as strong as your weakest moves.

63 Work to achieve a good deal for both parties.

THINGS TO DO

1. Before a negotiation, try to imagine the other party's possible sticking points.
2. Gather any useful information on them.
3. Mentally rehearse the parts of the negotiation that you anticipate will be difficult.

BENEFITING THE BUSINESS

Expand your negotiating skills and reap the future rewards in your own performance. Remember that, if a party is unhappy with the results of a deal, long-term relationships may be damaged. Review every negotiation with the benefit of hindsight and look at what you could do differently in the future. Practice in your imagination and make it a goal to improve relationships with every deal. Also, take stakeholders into account with each negotiation, so that your business thrives in the long term. This is win-win-win thinking.

NEGOTIATING ▶ SUCCESSFULLY
In this example, a major organization used negotiation with their suppliers to position themselves as a market leader in environmentally friendly furnishing. Excellence in negotiation allowed them to put together deals that their competition could not match.

CASE STUDY

42

43

DETAIL ON NEXT PAGE

GETTING THE BEST DEAL

Not everyone has the same approach to negotiations — in fact, there are five main styles that people use subconsciously. Understand your own approach and learn to recognize other people's, so you get the best results for all parties in your negotiations.

61 Treat the other party's interests with the respect you give your own.

▲ **MAKING A DEAL**
Find a way to work toward the best results through bargaining, so that all parties will be pleased with the result.

UNDERSTANDING STYLES

Learn to recognize negotiation styles in yourself and others. A compromise style splits the difference, although both parties could have achieved more. A coercive style relies on being dominant regardless of consequences. Emotional negotiation assumes that appealing to feelings will get the best results, while rational negotiation supposes arguing a point of view will change people's minds. A bargaining style, however, is the most beneficial, because it finds the trade-offs that get the best value for all.

RECOGNIZING NEGOTIATING STYLES

NEGOTIATION STYLE	DISCUSSION
COMPROMISE	"We need a fair deal." "Maybe we can agree to split the difference."
COERCION	"Can we negotiate that?" "No, when we make demands, you should jump."
EMOTION	"Will you extend our credit terms?" "That would cause difficulties for me."
RATIONAL	"Do you see that if we can agree now...?" "But it is sensible to finalize the schedules first."
BARGAINING	"If you can deliver next week, we agree." "We will deliver next week, if you sign the deal now."

DEVELOPING THE SKILLS

Recognize occasions that could be negotiation situations. Before a negotiation, be clear on your outcomes and your bottom line. Make sure you plan and research carefully beforehand, and think through what your best alternative to a negotiated agreement is. This might be to go elsewhere. During the negotiation, maintain a steady emotional state if you find this difficult, take a deep breath and change the focus of your thinking. Every move should get you closer to a win-win deal or the realization that no deal is the best option.

THINGS TO DO

1. Before a negotiation, try to imagine the other party's possible sticking points.

2. Gather any useful information on them.

3. Mentally rehearse the parts of the negotiation that you anticipate will be difficult.

62 Know you are only as strong as your weakest moves.

63 Work to achieve a good deal for both parties.

BENEFITING THE BUSINESS

Expand your negotiating skills and reap the future rewards in your own performance. Remember that, if a party is unhappy with the results of a deal, long-term relationships may be damaged. Review every negotiation with the benefit of hindsight and look at what you could do differently in the future. Practice in your imagination and make it a goal to improve relationships with every deal. Also take stakeholders into account with each negotiation, so that your business thrives in the long term. This is win-win-win thinking.

NEGOTIATING ▶ SUCCESSFULLY

In this example, a major organization used negotiation with their suppliers to position themselves as a market leader in environmentally friendly furnishing. Excellence in negotiation allowed them to put together deals that their competition could not match.

CASE STUDY

A leading furniture retailer decided to treat increasing concerns about the environment as an opportunity rather than a problem. Initially their suppliers were resistant to making environmentally friendly changes. The retailer negotiated improvements with each supplier in order to create alternative processes that reduced environmental damage. The suppliers in turn had to renegotiate with their supply chain. This was not an overnight process. Additionally, the retailer decided not to advertise this policy, but to let people hear of it through word of mouth. This method had higher credibility and saved on advertising. The policy was a win-win-win move since customers received sustainable quality products at good prices; the organization grew rapidly because of its reputation, and the environment benefited from reduced waste.

Selling the Saadiyat Dream (Credit: Gulf Labor)

"For Security Reasons" A Gulf Labor Report

(July 2015)

Saadiyat Snapshot

Five years after the Gulf Labor Coalition began its work, we are publishing our second field report. In the last several months, we have seen increased activity on each of Saadiyat's high cultural projects. The Guggenheim Abu Dhabi has issued tenders for its main construction contract, the British Museum is loaning its historic artifacts to the Sheikh Zayed National Museum,[1] and the Nardello report into compliance violations incurred in the construction of the NYU Abu Dhabi campus revealed that a full third of the workforce was excluded from the university's labor protections.[2] On June 8, 2015, an unnamed Pakistani employee died inside the Louvre Abu Dhabi, as workers laboriously mounted the final "star" on its Jean Nouvel–designed dome.[3] He was not the first, and will likely not be the last, fatality on Saadiyat Island; the authorities only acknowledged his death after we brought it to light, in a public letter sent to the Louvre's directors and government overseers.[4]

So, too, in the last several months, members of the coalition were barred from entering the United Arab Emirates. Now, as scrutiny of worker conditions in the UAE intensifies, we call upon the arts community to broaden our campaign and its support base.

---

1. Chris Green, "British Museum Criticised for Loaning Artefacts to Abu Dhabi Organisation Accused of Abusing Rights of Workers," *The Independent* (June 2, 2015), http://tinyurl.com/p3tca7b.
2. David Batty, "NYU Set to Compensate Thousands of Migrant Workers on Abu Dhabi Complex," The Guardian (April 24, 2015), http://tinyurl.com/o6juy2f.
3. Mostafa Heddaya, "Louvre Abu Dhabi Admits Worker Death After Gulf Labor Letter," *BlouinArtinfo* (July 16, 2015), http://tinyurl.com/pty9m65.
4. Gulf Labor, "A Letter to the Louvre," at http://gulflabor.org/2015/letter-to-louvre/

Overview

In the summer and fall of 2014, the GLC decided to extend its program of "in-country" investigative research. A series of field trips were planned, to India in December 2014, and to the UAE in March and May 2015. In the fall, in the course of planning these visits, the GLC was invited by curator of contemporary art Okwui Enwezor to participate in the Venice Biennale. In our response to Enwezor's invitation, we shied away from creating a physical installation or work of art, and proposed instead that our research, field visits, and resulting report would constitute our contribution to the exhibition.

These field visits built on the knowledge gathered during Gulf Labor's March 2014 trip, allowing our 2015 teams to follow up on lines of inquiry initiated at that time. Like our May 2014 report (published in this volume), the objective of this report was to document the findings in the field. Interviews with workers and visits to labor camps served three main purposes. First, they added to the growing picture and store of data on local working conditions. Secondly, they reinforced our capacity to investigate and rebut, with our own first-hand data, many of the sanguine claims and assertions that the Guggenheim, Louvre, NYU, TDIC, and various state officials have made about worker treatment. Thirdly, they helped establish new lines of communication between Gulf Labor and workers, migrant worker organizations, and activist groups based in sending countries.[5]

The decision of the UAE authorities to deny entry to Andrew Ross in March 2015, and to Walid Raad and Ashok Sukumaran in May 2015, also shifted the tenor of Gulf Labor's engagement in the region. The UAE crackdown on speech and assembly, which was heightened after the Arab Spring and resulted in the jailing of dozens of dissenting residents (citizens and non-) now extended to our own ranks. Officially, our Gulf Labor members had been denied entry "for security reasons." The invocation of this hazy catchall term parallels its broader use by government authorities and

---

5. In addition, Gulf Labor West (an offshoot of the GLC comprised of artists from cities in the US, Canada, and Mexico) interviewed workers, especially women in domestic services and maquiladoras in the US–Mexican border region of Tijuana and San Diego.

security managers all around the globe, and not solely in the UAE, to limit reporting on a variety of politically sensitive issues.

These outcomes were not entirely surprising. Raad, Ross, and Sukumaran were on the field research team that had been invited to meet with TDIC officials and tour the Saadiyat Accommodation Village in March 2014, and they had been followed while visiting other Abu Dhabi labor camps. Other investigators of UAE migrant labor conditions have also recently been barred or deported.[6] Media coverage of these Gulf Labor bans was singularly extensive, and brought an ever larger public into the orbit of the campaign. Professional organizations in the educational academy and in the artworld produced strong statements of support for us and condemnation of the UAE's censorious actions. Allied labor organizations stepped up their advocacy campaigns. So, too, the further announcement of criminal investigations into corruption at FIFA brought added scrutiny of migrant labor conditions in the Gulf, in advance of preparations for the 2022 World Cup in Qatar.[7]

In March 2015, exactly four years after the Gulf Labor campaign went public with the call to boycott the Guggenheim Abu Dhabi, we presented the museum foundation with a three-point proposal. We offered to lift the boycott if our recommendations were taken up and positively acted upon. These recommendations were reimbursement of recruitment fees through a debt settlement fund, establishment of a living wage, and worker representation.[8] The Guggenheim failed to respond by our deadline, even as the release of the Nardello report, commissioned by NYUAD and its Emirati partner Tamkeen, confirmed allegations of labor violations brought forth by the media and human rights groups—including the GLC—and verified that the university's monitoring system had been badly flawed.

By the beginning of the summer, urgent questions about the tenability of the museum's Abu Dhabi branch were being asked in the Guggenheim Foundation board-

---

6. Nicholas McGeehan, "Art and Hypocrisy in the Gulf," *New York Times* (May 28, 2015), http://tinyurl.com/p62amze; and Zoe Schlanger, "Under Surveillance in Abu Dhabi" *Newsweek* (March 30, 2015), http://tinyurl.com/qh8hvzy.

7. Matt Apuzzo, Stephanie Clifford, William Rashbaum, "FIFA Officials Arrested on Corruption Charges," *New York Times* (May 26, 2015), http://tinyurl.com/mljssj5.

8. Gulf Labor, "Letters to Guggenheim" (March 16 and April 18, 2015) http://gulflabor.org/2015/glc-03-04/

room. After the pressure exerted by the two G.U.L.F. occupations—the first on May Day in New York, at the Guggenheim's flagship Fifth Avenue museum, and the second a week later at the Venice branch of the museum during the Biennale opening—the Guggenheim Foundation trustees finally agreed to a meeting. This meeting between GLC and Guggenheim board members was convened in early June, and, after several hours of discussion, a joint commitment to work together on a set of common goals was generated. These goals were tied to the Gulf Labor proposal delivered to the museum officials in March 2015.

In the course of our five-year campaign, we have kept up a dialogue with the museum's artistic directors, and with TDIC officials, as well as with international organizations such as Human Rights Watch, International Trade Union Confederation (ITUC), and the International Labour Organization (ILO), among others. Despite repeated assurances that the Guggenheim Foundation and TDIC shared our goals, they have yet to deliver any tangible results on behalf of workers. The new meetings with the trustees extend our longstanding efforts to try every avenue available to us in engaging the museum. In this case, since the board is ultimately accountable for the Abu Dhabi project, we have the assurance of speaking with a group that has the power to significantly improve the lives of the workers building the museum.

In the report that follows, we summarize our recent field research in India and Abu Dhabi (based on interviews with more than 50 workers) and reflect on the implications of the travel bans placed on our members in order to explain why we must extend our campaign to include the Louvre Abu Dhabi, and other Saadiyat projects by calling for broader support from the artworld. The report is being issued in the months before the commencement of the final construction phase of Guggenheim Abu Dhabi, and during a period of increased leverage and critical importance for the campaign. Gulf Labor's first report in 2014 already contained several recommendations about Saadiyat Island that are now topics of discussion with the trustees. In the following pages, we provide further support for these recommendations, and also expand the scope of our inquiry to the villages, towns, and cities in India and across South Asia where migrants begin their journey to the Gulf.

In the Field—India

The first field trip, to India, between December 2014 and January 2015, took Gulf Labor researchers to several regions across the country. Migration to the Gulf from India has a long history that predates the first oil boom of 1973. However, it is only in the aftermath of the oil and real estate booms of the last four decades that there has been a mass migration of Indian workers to the region. There is a significant amount of research on this topic that we consulted in setting up our study.[9] The original goal was to make contact with, and interview, workers who had been deported from Abu Dhabi as a consequence of the strikes of 2013 and 2014. But in the course of travels to Kerala, Telangana, Uttar Pradesh, and Bihar, while stopping off to interview in the industrial zones around Delhi, we also gathered stories about the circuits of internal migration within India. Economic restructuring over the last two decades has accelerated the uprooting of rural populations and set them in motion toward industrial zones and megacities where their contingent labor is often employed to undercut the security of local workforces.[10]

Some of the conditions of work and life for these internal migrant communities are shared by those who go overseas to pursue the "Gulf Dream." While the aspirations of those who traveled to the UAE may be perceived to be on a grander scale, the two circuits of migration are not disconnected; economically distressed workers from West Bengal, Jharkhand, and Bihar, for example, migrate to the south of India to fill the jobs vacated by Gulf-bound Keralites. The socio-economic segregation and the hyper-exploitative labor conditions for internal migrants engaged in construction, manufacturing, and a range of low-wage services have generated spontaneous protest

---

9. The scholarship is most extensive on migration from Kerala to the Gulf. For example, see the reports by the Research Unit on International Migration at the Centre for Development Studies http://www.cds.edu/research/research-units-and-endowment-funds/union-ministry-of-overseas-indian-affairs-research-unit-on-international-migration/

10. The factors affecting rural migration are numerous and vary from place to place. They include the impact of climate change on traditional livelihoods, devaluation of traditional forms of agricultural cultivation, and policy changes at federal, state, and local levels that adversely affect small-scale agricultural production or subsistence-based farming. The rise in remission-based economies in areas of high migration also adds to this dynamic of the devaluation of traditional forms of agricultural work and land use.

movements and other organized efforts by labor and social movement activists. We found that activists working on labor issues within India see a natural connection to transnational migrant labor activism—especially in relation to advocacy for the millions of Indian workers in the Gulf.

Turning to the interviews with returned migrants, all the workers we spoke with went to the Gulf in search of better opportunities for paid work, expecting higher wages than what they could earn at home. Regardless of the outcome, most were proud of how hard and long they had worked during their stints in Qatar, the UAE, Saudi Arabia, and elsewhere, and wished only that they had been paid fairly and treated with dignity. It became clear from our interviews that caste, class, and ethnic networks had reproduced hierarchies of privilege within the terms of work and wage levels in the Gulf. Outside of a small number of "semi-skilled workers" we spoke with in Kerala, few of the "unskilled" managed to deliver substantial improvements in the economic situation of their families, or even come out of their multi-year stints in the Gulf with savings of any kind after repaying recruitment debts and covering household expenses and children's schooling.

Most workers reported that their wages had been significantly lower than promised and that they had routinely been deceived about the terms and conditions of the employment on offer, both by recruiters and employers. They also reported a "dual contract" system whereby the contract they signed in India meant little in practice on arrival in the Gulf. Typical outcomes included sudden changes in type of work, longer hours, unpaid overtime, lengthy stints without pay, and unexpected expenses incurred from illness and work-related injuries. The emotional toll of being separated from their families for several years weighed heavily against whatever financial returns had been eked out. This was particularly the case with unskilled Dalit migrants from Telangana. As is also common in Nepal and Bangladesh, they borrowed against their small land plots to get to the Gulf and often found themselves pursuing work in the informal economy as day laborers. Routine wage theft and underpayment, coupled with, in many cases, informal high-interest loans left them with little extra to show for their time and labor in the UAE. Yet, in some cases, even workers who had very negative experiences were willing to try their luck again in a different Gulf country, hoping for a better outcome.

Returnee Indian migrant workers (Credit: Gulf Labor)

In the regions of Uttar Pradesh and Bihar, there is currently an upsurge of worker militancy and Dalit and Adivasi (indigenous community) uprisings. We speculated that this may help to explain why we found that migrants from these "backward caste" communities were more likely to resist the cruel and unjust work conditions they encountered in the Gulf, and to participate in informal actions and strikes. (Alternately, we found evidence that the experience of hardship in the Gulf was cause enough to politicize workers, regardless of their origin.) However, in contrast to Kerala and Telangana, these Northern states have not seen the emergence of migrant worker organizations through trade unions or NGOs, and so aggrieved workers have little recourse. Moreover, it became clear from our interviews that Indian government officials, such as the POE (Protector of Emigrants) in the Ministry of Overseas Indian Affairs (MOIA), or the Indian Embassy and the IWRC (Indian Workers Resource Center) in the UAE, do very little to protect the migrants. As a result, the overwork, poor safety standards, and work-site conflicts in the Gulf inevitably resulted in a pattern of wage theft, detention, and deportation. Additional research conducted by Gulf Labor members in Nepal has yielded nearly identical patterns of migrant worker experiences.

In the Field—Abu Dhabi

On Saadiyat Island itself, our team was able to talk to a variety of workers engaged on the Louvre, NYUAD, Saadiyat Villas, and the Manarat Al Saadiyat, which was also serving as a temporary exhibition structure for the Guggenheim and Louvre. Counter to the TDIC rule that all workers must live in the Saadiyat Accommodation Village (SAV), our team found and interviewed Al Jaber workers who were being housed in Mafraq Workers City, on the outskirts of Abu Dhabi. Their daily commute of three hours or more meant that their workday stretched well beyond the eight-hour maximum (not accounting for overtime) and left them little time for themselves. Since the food in Mafraq was unacceptable to them, almost all of that non-work time was devoted to finding and cooking costly alternatives, which sliced into their wages. Food strikes are common; many of the Arabtec workers deported for striking in 2013 were demanding a monthly food allowance of 340 dirhams ($92) as an alternative to the food on offer in the camps. According to workers housed in the SAV, food quality continues to be a contentious issue and does not seem to have improved substantially since our visit in 2014, even though the camp is under new management, and a new caterer has been employed. Workers complained about rumored chemical additives, stale chapatis, and undercooked meals in much the same way as they had done the previous year.

Even aside from these chronic problems with food, the SAV itself was not a popular choice. Because of the night curfew, social isolation, and constant surveillance, some of the interviewees said that they would actually prefer to be housed in Mafraq, in spite of the commute (a "gift" of extended working hours to their employers), because they could access a range of informal commercial and social activities—from "alternative" food to haircuts and shaves, gym facilities, and mosques—outside the residential compound. They reported that it felt more like a city, and, despite the distance, it was still easier to access Abu Dhabi from there. On our visit to the Manarat, a public relations official overseeing the "Saadiyat Experience," an interactive exhibition promoting the cultural district, blithely informed us that although "activists claim the workers are badly treated," he himself had played cricket tournaments in the SAV with the Manarat's security guards, and that the living standards were so good that even he would like to live there. As it happens, we also interviewed the guards he mentioned, and they told us that, contrary to TDIC policy, they lived in Mafraq Workers City.

These findings added a new dimension to the observations in our first report about whether the mass labor camp, increasingly favored by the UAE authorities and their GCC counterparts, is wholly in the interests of workers. Tens of thousands of Abu Dhabi laborers live in each of the Mafraq Workers City compounds, while Qatari authorities are building seven cities to house more than a quarter-million World Cup worker. One of them, called "Labor City," will house 70,000 people in 55 buildings, and will include a mall, a jumbo mosque, and a 24,000-seat cricket stadium.[11] The building of these vast complexes is typically promoted in a high-profile way as the

---

11. "Qatar Builds Seven 'Cities' to House 258,000 World Cup Migrant Labourers," *The Guardian* (May 6, 2015), http://tinyurl.com/nau94wl.

On the Road to Mafraq Workers City (Credit: Gulf Labor)

government's good faith response to international criticism of worker conditions. While the accommodations and infrastructure are more shipshape than the existing labor camps (the rent that contractors are charged for each employee housed in the SAV is more than the salary that worker earns), the level of security is much higher. This further restricts access to friends, family, and investigators, and enables such camps to function as detention facilities—as happened at Jebel Ali's Camp 42 after the 2014 BK Gulf strike.

The camps tend to be in remote locations, so the chances of any interaction, let alone integration, with other classes of migrants from South Asia and elsewhere—much less with Emirati society—are non-existent. It was not uncommon for us to find workers who had spent many months in the UAE whose only experience of Abu Dhabi was through the road they traveled between their camp and their work site. On the other hand, the mass co-existence of workers in one place is a spur to collective organizing—these conditions make it easier to communicate about grievances and strike actions, and to bolster the shared perception that strength and mutual protection lies in numbers.

On a less orchestrated tour of a labor camp in the Jebel Ali industrial area, one camp boss revealed how his company specifically employs workers left in the lurch by defaulting or bankrupt companies (a common occurrence in the UAE due to the recent, and general, slowdown in construction projects). His firm pays special attention to the quality of food, and keeps an open door for one-to-one counseling and collective redressing of complaints. He reported that employers had a free rein when it came to deciding wage hikes and bonuses; for example, a one-time bonus issued at the time of Eid could go a long way toward repayment of workers' recruitment debts.

Worker advocates, media organs, and the interested public tend to focus unduly on the quality of labor camp accommodations. The grisly spectacle of substandard housing gets good press because it is visible or tangible, and because it violates norms of decency, hygiene, and propriety. Yet our field interviews continue to show that the quality of accommodation ranks well below other factors in workers' own priorities. Underpayment is far and away the primary concern. Migrants come to the Gulf to earn as much as they can, and their grievances are sharpened when compensation is discounted and promises are broken, and when back pay and paid leave is denied outright. Reimbursement of recruitment fees, which is required of Saadiyat Island contractors under the terms of the TDIC's Employment Practices Policy (EPP), rarely occurs. As part of its 2014 monitoring report, PricewaterhouseCoopers (PwC) recorded that 93 percent of the workers interviewed did not receive reimbursements while the remaining 7 percent received partial payments at best.[12] According to the Nardello report, although 85 percent of NYUAD workers said they had paid recruitment fees (making more than 25,000 workers potentially eligible for repayment), Tamkeen's interpretation of the university's Statement of Labor Values disqualified almost all the workers from receiving any reimbursement.

Estimates of how much workers are paid vary greatly. Skills, seniority, ethnic differences, countries, and region of origin are all taken into account. For example, laborers from Bangladesh and Nepal are generally worse off than most Indian or Pakistani migrants, and their average recruitment debt is significantly higher. The minimum wage of 800 dirhams ($217) set by the Indian embassy in 2011 was put into practice only last year, and multiple violations were noted in our 2014 report. Unlike Filipino workers who had access to some protection and services from their embassies, South Asian workers across the board know they can expect very little from their own national representatives in the region.

In June 2015, in what is positioned as an effort to minimize fraud and exorbitant recruitment fees, the MOIA announced an "e-migrate portal" mandating all foreign employers from GCC countries who employed 25 to 150 workers to recruit exclusively via this portal. According to the new rules, approved employers will have to outline the terms of work, and these will be held as conditions for a work contract. It remains to be seen if this newly transparent process will result in a significant change in recruitment patterns, or mitigate the many problems faced by workers once they arrive in the UAE.

Similarly, in July 2015, the Department of Foreign Employment (DOFE) in Nepal established a controversial zero-cost migration policy, which demands written guarantees that the employer will provide air tickets and cover visa fees. However, according to Gulf workers we interviewed in Mumbai, officials at the Indian Embassy in the

---

12. Saadiyat Island Third Annual Monitoring Report (December 22, 2014), http://tinyurl.com/qe93265.

UAE themselves are known to exhort workers to amicably "settle" grievances with their *kafeels* (sponsors), with embassy officials often playing middleman. Many workers we spoke with, both in Mumbai and UAE, reported that the Philippines Embassy was known to be the most supportive; case files were regularly sent to Ministry of Labor by a representative from the Embassy. One UAE-based Pakistani worker, who had prepared his own case file with copious receipts and proof of underpayment for his work in the UAE for over 19 years, expressed more confidence about self-representing his case to the Dubai Ministry of Labor than if he were to hire a lawyer or go through the Embassy. Another interviewee—a young Bangladeshi lawyer—spoke of handling a lot of cases for Bangladeshi workers at the Abu Dhabi labor court, and confirmed that none of them were *pro bono*; the worker would have to bear full costs of legal counsel. He mentioned that cases for Saadiyat workers were often summarily dismissed by the courts: "Saadiyat is a touch-me-not island," he observed, "there are many powerful people behind its development at every stage."

Employers and managers strategically manipulate ethnic and religious differences (over food preferences, for example) to divide workers within camps. Most workers we spoke with were paid less than $300 per month. This is consistent with the Nardello report, which reported that the average wage for the 30,000 workers employed on the NYUAD site was $217 per month. Asked what a fair basic wage would be, workers we spoke with responded with an estimate, on average, of between $450 to $500, or what would amount to a 60 percent increase on the current median. Needless to say, the best way to assess what constitutes a living wage is to allow workers to determine this for themselves. Just as employers and state officials speak for themselves without intermediaries, it makes sense for workers to determine and express for themselves the bases of their financial, physical, and emotional well-being. Implementing a living wage policy transnationally is already a core component of the ILO's ongoing campaign in sectors like construction, domestic work, garment manufacturing, and more.[13]

---

13. Asha D'Souza, "Moving Towards Decent Work For Domestic Workers; An Overview of the ILO's Work," (2010, International Labour Organization, Bureau for Gender Equality), http://courses.itcilo.org/A906119/documentation/ilo-studies-papers/Moving%20towards%20DWDW%20Overview%20of%20ILOs%20work.pdf

Yet hiking pay to the level that meets workers' perception of what is fair would still not fully account for the wage depression generated by the *kafala* system. In its complaint to the ILO, the ITUC described *kafala* as a system of "forced labor,"[14] while a neoclassical economist might call it an "extreme distortion" of the market wage. So would the workers' estimate be a bona fide living wage? Experts on the topic argue that a living wage should cover not just basic necessities, but also provide for recreational needs. More generous, or high-minded, estimates assume that a certain level of freedom from want is a requirement for exercising political liberty, through the ability to participate in civic life without fear of reprisal.

In the case of the UAE's non-citizens, especially low-wage laborers, who are included in civic accounting only as non-participants, and who have minimal access to the courts and judicial process, this kind of political liberty may be no more than a mirage in the desert. Even if non-citizens had access to the courts, the UAE's judicial system "faces challenges that negatively affect the delivery of justice, the enjoyment of human rights and the public's confidence in the judiciary," as stated in the 2015 Mission Report of the UN Special Rapporteur on the independence of judges and lawyers in the UAE.[15]

Operating under a crushing debt burden and threat of deportation, any legal avenues for claiming, let alone exercising, basic rights are slender. Under these circumstances, the security of getting paid fairly and on time is a minimum condition of a dignified life for migrant workers. But the very concept, and the reality, of a living wage suggests a surplus, or margin, beyond the subsistence level of compensation. For migrant workers, and not just in the Gulf, there is an intrinsic social worth to being valued at a higher level than the marketplace price for their labor, and especially when that price has already been driven down by the restrictive, if not indentured, conditions of the visa sponsorship system. If they are merely earning the "efficient wage" regarded by managers as the price that guarantees a steady labor supply, then

---

14. Nir Elias, "UN Investigating Slavish Treatment of Migrant Workers in UAE," Reuters (November 30, 2014), http://apflnet.ilo.org/news/un-investigating-slavish-treatment-of-migrant-workers-in-uae

15. Mission Report of the UN Special Rapporteur, 29th session of the Human Rights Council (2015). See A/HRC/29/26/Add.2 at http://www.ohchr.org/EN/HRBodies/HRC/RegularSessions/Session29/Pages/ListReports.aspx

that is how they are viewed—as a demand good, even a commodity. Higher-paid workers have more of a claim to recognition from the host society as is evident with tailors, small-time entrepreneurs (e.g., cafeteria owners), higher paid clerks and office workers, and professionals and business people who make up the significant number of the more privileged South Asian, Arab, and European migrants in the region.

How that recognition gets parlayed into a rights claim is less certain. So, too, piecemeal worker welfare reforms in the *kafala* system, which we have seen in Bahrain, Kuwait, Saudi Arabia, and Qatar, do not always deliver meaningful legal changes, much less even economic effects.[16] For example, a 2011 UAE reform allowed workers to transition to a new employer upon contract expiration without permission from the initial sponsor. According to a study by labor market economists, the reform produced an increase in incumbent migrants' earnings, from 50% below the market wage before 2011 to 25 percent below in the years since.[17] But the changes proved detrimental to new migrant workers, who faced a higher entry bar, and whose overall earnings did not budge. Omnibus reforms are needed to avoid these uneven impacts. That is why our three-point proposal to the Guggenheim combined debt relief, wage increases, and the right to independent worker representation (ideally, with workers electing their own representatives), in the understanding that these provisions are interdependent.

In the meantime, and not surprisingly, given the lowering of wages and deteriorating work conditions, workers continue to take action for themselves. The BK Gulf strike covered in our 2014 report made headlines this year in a *New York Times* front-page story about labor violations at NYUAD.[18] Just before our team visited in March, over 200 workers broke the barricades of the construction site near the Downtown Dubai mall, and blocked traffic on Financial Center Road when overtime pay rates

16. Priyanka Motaparthy, "Undestanding Kafala," *Migrant-Rights.org* (March 11, 2015) (sidebar) at http://tinyurl.com/lqjytvf.

17. Suresh Naidu, Yaw Nyarko, Shing-Yi Wang, "Worker Mobility in a Global Labor Market: Evidence from the United Arab Emirates," NBER Working Paper No. 20388 (August 2014), at http://www.nber.org/papers/w20388

18. Ariel Kaminer and Sean O'Driscoll, "Workers at N.Y.U.'s Abu Dhabi Site Faced Harsh Conditions," *New York Times* (May 18, 2014), http://www.nytimes.com/2014/05/19/nyregion/workers-at-nyus-abu-dhabi-site-face-harsh-conditions.html

Gulf Labor member with Arabtec worker, Jebel Ali, Dubai (Credit: Gulf Labor)

"For Security Reasons" 321

were cut. In April, workers in Ras Al Khaimah protested by destroying their construction site equipment and torching 17 cars after an Indian worker fell to his death. Just after our team left Abu Dhabi in March 2015, a strike occurred at Saadiyat Beach Villas in the northeastern part of the island. These workers (who were housed in Mafraq and not in the SAV—again contrary to TDIC policies) had numerous grievances. An independent researcher reported to us that they were owed back pay and were not receiving overtime pay, their health insurance cards had expired, their passports were held by the employer, none of their recruitment debts had been paid, and the food on offer was often past the expiration date. Many suffered recriminations as a result of their strike participation, the strike leaders were effectively "turned" into management allies, and the promises made to end the strike were not kept.

Spontaneous actions like these are common, but are almost never reported. In a rare occurrence, the Dubai strike was mentioned in the UAE press, but probably because it involved a highly visible protest in a downtown location.[19] Police abuse of strikers is never acknowledged in the press, even though it has been a routine response to work stoppages. Notably, the Nardello report had nothing to say about the violence meted out to the BK Gulf strikers. Breaking the silence about this use of force is a way of acknowledging, and directing attention to, the courage and determination shown by workers in the face of such brutal measures. Forging solidarity with them to achieve real worker agency is a step further.

Restricted Movements

What are the consequences of the UAE state's decision to exclude Gulf Labor members? On the one hand, the travel bans on us were no different from the prohibitions on others: Firstly the South Asian, Southeast Asian, and Arab and African workers who were arbitrarily deported with little recourse. Next, the numerous Arab "stateless

---

19. Mary Sophia, "Workers Stage Strike In Downtown Dubai Over Wage Issues," *Gulf Business* (March 10, 2015) http://gulfbusiness.com/2015/03/workers-stage-strike-downtown-dubai-wage-issues/#.Vawvp_mzmxY

citizens" and activists living in the UAE who were deported in the wake of the Arab Uprisings of 2011.[20] Lastly, more high-profile European journalists like Sean O'Driscoll, and investigators like Nick McGeehan from Human Rights Watch and James Lynch from Amnesty International, all of whom were barred or deported recently from the UAE for reporting on migrant labor abuses. Excluding labor advocates from access to workers or workplaces is a commonplace response of employers and complicit officials everywhere, and it is only the least extreme—the historical record of labor organizing is littered with assassinations, torture, and lifelong imprisonment well beyond the Persian Gulf.

But the Gulf Labor bans attracted an extra layer of public attention. They were widely seen as a direct curtailment of artistic and academic freedoms that are fundamental to the cultural institutions trying to establish themselves in Abu Dhabi. For example, Sukumaran had not only been invited to the Sharjah March meetings in March 2015, but also had been invited by an NYUAD professor to mentor students in an Art course for a collaborative project engaging with the concerns of NYUAD workers. The invitation to attend the concluding week of the course was suddenly withdrawn, as perhaps both NYUAD students and faculty anticipated limits to their own academic and artistic freedoms. This news was soon followed by the denial of a visa to Sukumaran.

Gulf Labor was founded on the demand that the rights of those who construct the museums and classrooms ought to be secured at the same time as those of the artists, teachers, and students who use those buildings. From the outset, administrators at the Guggenheim or NYU had to be pushed hard to acknowledge any responsibility for the laborers' rights, but they were openly confident that their Emirati partners would respect the artistic and academic freedoms at the core of the respective missions. The travel bans proved how ill-founded this optimism had been. Nor did these institutional leaders take strong positions against the restrictions, further reinforcing the appearance of complicity in the UAE's illiberalism. Not only had the core freedoms been infringed, but the UAE authorities seemed to have thought very little about

20. Katie Cella, "The U.A.E.'s Brewing Crisis," *Boston Review* (February 3, 2014), http://bostonreview.net/world/katie-cella-united-arab-emirates-stateless-citizens

embarrassing the Guggenheim and NYU, leaving their administrators in the inconvenient position of conceding that they had no influence over decisions about whose freedoms would be sanctioned or censured.

In May 2015, 60 leaders from cultural institutions around the globe, including MoMA and the Tate, signed a letter protesting the entry bans on Gulf Labor members. The letter followed several other statements from museum and artist associations: the International Committee for Museums and Collections of Modern Art (CIMAM); the Association for Modern and Contemporary Art of the Arab World, Iran, and Turkey (AMCA); *L'Internationale*, a European confederation of six modern and contemporary museums; six high-profile Documenta curators; and a petition signed by almost all of the participating artists in Sharjah Biennial 12. Academic organizations, including the American Association of University Professors, the Committee for Concerned Scientists, and the Middle Eastern Studies Association issued similar letters after the ban on Ross.

Unless there is a concerted effort by those within the UAE, including the newly developing cultural institutions, to resist this pattern of direct censorship, the crackdown on any reporting of violations of human and labor rights will continue, and may well intensify. Yet we hear anecdotal evidence about power struggles within the ruling families over the exact course of UAE's development, and can only assume that there is a tug of war between factions who favor liberalization and the hardliners who want to retain tight control over all aspects of nation-building in the Gulf states.

State managers have their own priorities to pursue, but liberal academic and artistic institutions depend, for their long-term reputation, on the promotion of critical thought and debate. The ability of NYU and the Guggenheim to operate in illiberal Abu Dhabi has been closely watched on account of the common suspicion that the university and museums would be there to serve simply as window-dressing. No doubt, the Gulf Labor bans have gratified those who never believed otherwise. But there is no reason for self-satisfaction on our part, not when the result directly obstructs our capacity to be in the field to promote support for workers. Nor can we ignore that the speech being targeted for censure is so categorically tied to a cause. In the academy, advocacy research of this kind is often demarcated as sub-legitimate, and in the artworld, as beyond the usual vocational concerns. All the more easy to

Louvre Abu Dhabi dome under construction (Credit: Gulf Labor)

portray it as falling outside of the typical range of intellectual and artistic inquiry, and therefore somehow less deserving of the speech protections at the core of these professions.

A similar kind of boundary marker is used in the cultural industries to separate creative labor—"the talent"—from "below-the-line" technical and manual workers who can display craftsmanship at best. These are class-bound partitions, arguably the most difficult for activists to span, and, in the case of low-wage workers migrating from afar and transferable from week to week, even more challenging. In this regard, the travel bans came as a mixed blessing. On the one hand, the widespread condemnation of the UAE's heavy-handed restriction of free inquiry threatened to divert attention from the much more extreme hardships confronted by workers and those residing in the UAE whose speech is being restricted. On the other hand, the bans highlight the key links between the curtailment of expressive freedoms of cultural workers and the minimal rights of migrant workers who are building homes for art and culture on a desert island.

Coda

Five years into our campaign, and after hundreds of meetings and interviews, it remains quite clear to us that workers on Saadiyat Island (let alone elsewhere) know their interests best. The existing regulations, policies, and laws that curtail workers' abilities to represent their own interests can be dissolved. Examples of how to do so abound, and there are many partners available and willing to help bring this about. Before the final phase of museum construction begins, the Guggenheim Foundation and its Emirati partners have the opportunity to do the right thing, and avoid further tarnishing their name.

The place in the Louvre building where a young Pakistani worker died on June 8, 2015 (Credit: Gulf Labor)

AUGUST 2015

SHARE YOUR EXPERIENCES 🍵 teabreaknow.com

7 BILLION CRACKS

There is a war waging in the imagination. Our response is: more cracks. Cracks are all those attempts, big and small, to challenge the logic of power and capitalism and imagine possibilities for different worlds. These may be big (like the Arab Uprisings, Indignados in Spain or the Occupy movement in the US), medium (a factory or land de-occupation, or undocumented migrants seeking citizenship), small (a community of friends turning to sustainable farming, or neighbors standing together against police brutality), even tiny (a chat during tea break). They may be organized around a particular place (Tahrir Square), or time (a week of rioting a month of occupation) or dedicated to a specific activity (campaigning against caste/racial violence or the privatisation of water). In their difference, we might not at first recognize that these are in fact, related. The important thing in the first instance is not to judge, but to recognise: to recognise that the world is full of cracks, that being human is a constant moving against a dehumanising system. A system that punishes, then blames the brown, black and dispossessed as necessary, even just. It is only when we see that anti-capitalism is deeply rooted in the experience of living in a capitalist society that it makes sense to talk of creating a different world.

Tea Break brings the experiences and struggles of workers who have left their villages, homes and regions seeking paid work wherever work is available. This might be in the hundreds of factories outside of Delhi, or flyovers and malls and office buildings of Gurgaon or in building the world's most famous museums in Abu Dhabi or World Cup stadiums in Doha.

India and its neighbors—Bangladesh, Pakistan, Nepal and Sri Lanka along with the Philippines—supply the oil rich countries of the Persian Gulf with tens of millions of workers who build the towering skyscrapers, care, feed and clean for the Arab, European and South Asian elites and middle classes who live in relative luxury and keep the oil fields pumping to hold up the region's wealth and political importance to the world. Like their brothers and sisters in Gurgaon, gulf migrant workers are part of a growing global workforce of permanent and temporary workers, whose wages are below the paltry minimum wages set by local government, living far from their families with no job security.

Our approach, diversity of tactics amongst a coalitions of equals, whose liberation is understood as either collective or non-existent. Recurring themes across China, the United States and back to South Asia and the Middle East, include the constant precarity and insecurity of life for most workers, untenable debt, and low and lower wages.

In these conditions, we must continue to generate cracks. Of course, better wages, better accommodations, longer breaks and shorter work hours. But beyond that, our cracks are both a negation-and-creation. The world points in one direction, tells us that for something to be meaningful it must generate money, profit. And we say No and walk in the opposite direction, doing what we consider to be desirable and necessary, generating a meaning that has nothing to do with money. It is a refusal to conform to the rule of capital and, at the same time, a creation of something else, a self-determination. We say No and sow what could be the seeds of a different world. Therein, in agency, lies the power of the powerless. ■

Tea Break is a broadsheet newspaper produced for circulation among migrant workers in Abu Dhabi and India

Tea Break (Selections)

A Conversation With Faridabad Majdoor Samachar
Editors: *Nitasha Dhillon, Paula Chakravartty, Sher Singh and Amin Husain*
Production Team: *Zak Greene and Kristina Bogos*

7 Billion Cracks

There is a war waging in the imagination. Our response is: more cracks. Cracks are all those attempts, big and small, to challenge the logic of power and capitalism and imagine possibilities for different worlds. These may be big (like the Arab Uprisings, Indignados in Spain or the Occupy movement in the US), medium (a factory or land deoccupation, or undocumented migrants seeking citizenship), small (a community of friends turning to sustainable farming, or neighbors standing together against police brutality), even tiny (a chat during tea break). They may be organized around a particular place (Tahrir Square), or time (a week of rioting a month of occupation) or dedicated to a specific activity (campaigning against caste/racial violence or the privatisation of water). In their difference, we might not at first recognize that these are in fact, related. The important thing in the first instance is not to judge, but to recognise: to recognise that the world is full of cracks, that being human is a constant moving against a dehumanising system. A system that punishes, then blames the brown, black and dispossessed as necessary, even just. It is only when we see that anti-capitalism is deeply rooted in the experience of living in a capitalist society that it makes sense to talk of creating a different world.

Tea Break brings the experiences and struggles of workers who have left their villages, homes and regions seeking paid work wherever work is available. This might be in the hundreds of factories outside of Delhi, or flyovers and malls and office buildings of Gurgaon or in building the world's most famous museums in Abu Dhabi or World Cup stadiums in Doha. India and its neighbors—Bangladesh, Pakistan, Nepal and Sri Lanka along with the Philippines—supply the oil rich countries of the Persian Gulf with tens of millions of workers who build the towering skyscrapers, care, feed and clean for the Arab, European and South Asian elites and middle classes who live in relative luxury and keep the oil fields pumping to hold up the region's wealth and political importance to the world. Like their brothers and sisters in Gurgaon, gulf migrant workers are part of a growing global workforce of permanent and temporary workers, whose wages are below the paltry minimum wages set by local government, living far from their families with no job security.

Our approach, diversity of tactics amongst a coalitions of equals, whose liberation is understood as either collective or nonexistent. Recurring themes across China, the United States and back to South Asia and the Middle East, include the constant precarity and insecurity of life for most workers, untenable debt, and low and lower wages.

In these conditions, we must continue to generate cracks. Of course, better wages, better accommodations, longer breaks and shorter work hours. But beyond that, our cracks are both a negationandcreation. The world points in one direction, tells us that for something to be meaningful it must generate money, profit. And we say No and walk in the opposite direction, doing what we consider to be desirable and necessary, generating a meaning that has nothing to do with money. It is a refusal to conform to the rule of capital and, at the same time, a creation of something else, a selfdetermination. We say No and sow what could be the seeds of a different world. Therein, in agency, lies the power of the powerless.

We Are Leaderful

Mani is a carpenter from Kunnur District in Kerala who helped organise a work-stoppage in the UAE. He traveled to the Gulf for a dream of being able to build a house and support his family in Kerala. After 12 years in the UAE, Mani eventually became a foreman. In the Summer of 2012, he was working for a company in Dubai named Al Reyami at the construction site of New York University two hours away on Abu Dhabi's Saadiyat Island. Working for this company, Mani rarely received the salary he was promised. There were delays in payment to him and other workers, sometimes up to four months without salary. Delayed salary meant problems for Mani, because he could not send money as he planned to his wife, three small children and parents back in Kerala. For weeks, the boss kept telling Mani that the company didn't have money to pay him. With frustration mounting, Mani and his co-workers talked things over on the bus to and from the construction site and at their camps, in the evening over tea. Others joined in having heard about what was happening from friends and on WhatsApp. One early morning in June 2012, Mani along with 300 of his co-workers decided not to board the bus to the construction site. Three-hundred workers protested having to work without pay by refusing to go to work that morning. As a self-organised strike, the bosses did not know who to target to send a message to the workers to behave. So they did what they normally do: single out as "leaders" of the strike those who stood at the front of the work stoppage line. Mani told the company that if they only delayed the salary of a few office workers, they would be able to pay him and the other 25 workers their unpaid back salaries. Two days later, and less than 24 hours after refusing to get on the bus, Mani's employer cancelled his visa and work contract, and Mani along with 7 other strikers were driven to the airport and deported to India. Later Mani would tell us that he would return to the Gulf to work, but only if the wages were higher and his family could join him.

We Live, Work and Grow with Dignity

Siddramlu is a 54 year old man from Telangana who spent 13 years of his life in Dubai as a construction worker. When his small ancestral land no longer provided sustenance, Siddramlu went to the Gulf illegally. He is one of many workers in Telangana that pay agents to go to the Gulf on a tourist visa and then look for work on a daily wage basis. Siddramlu went to improve his livelihood and acquire new skills. While in Dubai, Siddramlu fell ill and his salary was drastically reduced. To survive on a monthly salary of $191 USD, Siddramlu borrowed money from friends and family. He considers himself one of the fortunate ones, as he knows of other workers who died after getting hurt or falling ill, because they could no longer earn enough money for food and shelter. Siddramlu told us the most important things while working illegally is to "stay together and collectively pay rent." This allows workers to find one person who is legal who can rent, and the rest remain undetected. Also, if something happens, or if someone is hurt or arrested, the group can assist. In 2007, he arranged his return to India by out-pass after "losing valuable time and money." Coming home, Siddramlu threw his passport in the dustbin, saying to us he will never return to the Gulf for work and that he can do better working in agriculture in Telangana. Siddramlu wants conditions for Indian workers improved in the UAE, and suggests that governments should take action against the agents and sub-agents who prey on workers' desire for a better life. He also wants employers to treat workers with dignity and pay them well, suggesting that governments should set salaries before work begins. He strongly recommends that employers offer workers the opportunity to improve their skills, for example, by offering training in operating new machinery. Contrary to his wishes, he didn't learn any new skill while in the Gulf. "We were born as labourers and we would die as labourers," it seems. In Telangana there are many like Siddramlu who've returned from the Gulf only to throw their passports away, vowing never to return.

We Are Not Insects

Thirty-two-year-old Mohammed Muazzam is from the Janpad-Azamgarh district in Uttar Pradesh. He worked in Doha, Qatar, for 8 years as a driver and labourer in three different companies. Before going to Qatar, Mohammed worked as a driver and farmer in his home state. Mohammed sought work in the Gulf for a better living standard and "betterment of life" for his family like so many others. When a friend in the Gulf told him about a job opportunity, he jumped on the opportunity and his friend sent him a visa. In Doha, Mohammed first worked as a driver in charge of transporting construction workers to and from the worksite and labour camp. His shifts were for as long as workers worked during the day and they almost always worked extra hours. Mohammed was never paid overtime, and when he complained to his kafeel (sponsor) he was ignored. In his third job in Doha, Mohammed's employer told him that he would be a house driver but then forced him to work in construction. Then after working for 15 months in construction, his company wanted him to change work, but Mohammed refused. He says he returned to India because employers treated workers like insects not human beings. Mohammed does not want to return to the region because they do not treat workers with respect. He would prefer to remain at home in India and live with less money.

Our Labour Is Worth More Than What They Pay Us

Kareem is 24 years old from the Azad Kashmir district in Baloch, Pakistan. He paid $1,721 USD in recruitment fees in 2013 to work in the UAE after being recruited to work as a carpenter for $300 USD a month, food included. However, after reaching Dubai with his brother, he was given the work of a rigger and was told to sign a document that stipulated his wages to be $109 USD a month instead. Kareem debated whether or not to sign the contract for 2 to 3 days. He decided to sign so that he can pay off his debt, something he could not do if he chose to return immediately to Pakistan. When we met Kareem, he was working on a scaffolding project on the construction site of the Louvre Museum on Saadiyat Island. He told us that one day at work a supervisor told him and 10 others to work on the stars of the museum's umbrella dome. But after waiting 2 to 3 days, the work never came. Soon after, they were transferred to do another type of work, and only after a month there would they be able to return to perform their original work. Kareem and the other men from Bangladesh and India refused and demanded to be sent back to their original jobs. They told the manager, "go ahead and terminate us." They were then returned to their original work. Kareem told us that living and working in the UAE you do not make money in the end. The salary is too low. It took him 22 months to pay off his debt, for example. Rather than work more or work overtime for almost nothing, Kareem does the bare minimum and plays cricket with his friends whenever he can until he can return to Pakistan. "The amount of labour we do here, day and night is not worth it. If you work the same amount in Pakistan, we can make about 30,000 [$471 USD] a month. At least we will be with family," he told us. As a labourer, Kareem thinks that a worker like him should at least $245 to $272 USD a month. With that wage, he could survive abroad and send money back home to his family. As of the date of this publication, Kareem paid off all of his debt and because he taught himself how to operate a crane on his own.

Movements Beyond Unions: Temporary Workers Protest

Mazdoor Samachar has covered a campaign led by workers in the Asti Electronics factory that began in early 2014. In May of 2015, a group of young workers involved in the campaign discussed their experiences with the newspaper and we present a short overview of the events as they unfolded. This campaign is an example of how temporary workers overcame obstacles to forge alliances with permanent workers, who together fought for justice despite the company's repeated attempts to divide the smaller group of permanent workers from the larger group of temporary workers. It also shows how organized labor unions often fall short in representing the interests and voices of workers in India's factories today, as in other places around the world.

Responding to efforts by temporary and permanent workers to come together to form a new union in early 2014, the company dismissed two temporary workers on 10th February. When the union could not get their jobs back, the fired workers asked for help.

On 18 February all temporary as well as permanent workers left their workplaces and gathered in the open place inside the company. Management was disturbed to see that the work had stopped. Around 2:30 in the afternoon, a settlement was reached to pay for the sitting days along with taking back those two dismissed workers.

More than 1 lakh ($1500.00) was raised by the contractual and regularized workers after they got their February salaries. By March 2014, the union had collected 9 lakh rupees ($14 000).

The company changed its stance. It had a talk with the union body. Two leaders of the union started visiting Chandigarh with the plant head in his car. The company called three human resource professionals to train the fulltime workers on how to make their lives better; how to move ahead in life; what should be the nature of relationship between workers and management.

Contractual workers objected to this. They said this has been organized to create a rift among the workers. The company was trying to brainwash permanent workers. But the leaders would say this company's policy and union cannot do anything about it.

The union had presented a memorandum of their demands to the management who said they were operating at a loss. In order to exert pressure, the union advised the workers to slow down the work. The company recruited 150 new workers through contractors for a new 12 hour shift at night. When the workers asked the union to stop this recruitment, the union said the company has the right to bring in workers from outside.

The company then shifted most of its production out of the factory. It started receiving the production from Japan, China and Vietnam and collected 4 month's stock in its godowns (warehouses). When the workers objected, the union leaders said they cannot do anything as the company has every right to get goods manufactured from elsewhere. In July 2014, management and union reached an agreement for 3 years.

In the beginning of October a rumor spread that all the contractual workers shall be removed from their jobs. A discussion on 31 October night: The contractual workers shall be removed any moment. On 1 November morning when the workers caught hold of top union leader and asked him about this, he said it is false news being spread and the union is with you. The same day, the temporary workers held a meeting with some prominent fulltime workers and the union body. There was no resolution.

A shift ends at 3:30 pm. The company put up a notice at 3:28 pm, but then another notice within a minute read: "due to paucity of work in the company for the time being, the company announces a 7 days break for all the temporary workers appointed through contractors and that they all should settle their salary accounts to their respective contractor's office on the 8th day."

Later that day, the management blocks workers from coming inside for the Bshift. Regular workers in the Ashift walked out silently but the contractual workers of Ashift did not come out. About 180 women and 70 men workers sat at men production line. Then, a contractor came along with a police inspector. No one moved from their places and 25 to 30 police came with lathis (sticks).

On 4 November 2014, all the contractual workers reached the factory at 6 am. Police persons, bouncers, company officers did not allow us to go inside the gate. We started erecting tent there to protest. They showed us a paper of court's notice asking to maintain distance of 150 meters from the factory—it was fake. The temporary workers tried to talk with permanent workers and the union but their attempts met with failure.

Contractual labour stood on their own feet and guts. Union leaders with ties to both the Congress (AITUC) and the Communist party (CITU) came and tried to hijack the movement, but we did not pay heed to them. On the first day we had made it clear to them with folded hands accepting or refusing their advice would be entirely our choice.

When the trumpeters arrived, the revolutionaries opposed them. Why did they come here? They should be given time to address from the platform.

Contractual labourer: This is a platform of the contractual workers. We will decide as to who will speak and who will not.

In the hope of creating pressures 2 men and 5 women sat on hunger strike from 25 November to 11 December. But had to call back the strike without any settlement.

A request was submitted in Chief Minister's public meeting, but to no avail. Government bureaucrats and leaders from political parties including the ruling BJP came to meet with us, but could offer little support.

Agitation continued near the factory even after the strike was called off. Here, we made a mistake. Contractual workers approached 4 to 5 sarpanches (elected village leader) to mediate. They went inside the factory saying, how dare this company management remove so many employees in our area. When they came out they said when there is no work how can they employ you? Sensing our weakness they even threatened us, saying move away from strike, otherwise we will forcefully make you move.

After three days goons removed our tents.

Then we sat on strike at ALC office of the Labour Department in Gurgaon. On the second day we protested along with the permanent workers of Munjal Kiriu factory, who had been protesting for the last three months. Permission was granted to us by police to sit for protests till 4:30 pm everyday.

Only contractual workers of Asti would sit on strike everyday. In the meanwhile, the company, ultimately agreed to pay 25 thousand rupees ($400.00) for unpaid wages. We had taken the decision after discussing amongst ourselves. 250 among us took salaries; other 35 including 22 women and 13 men have chosen to extend their fights to the court.

(Credit: Elizabeth Knafo)

View the full Tea Break *PDF at teabreaknow.com*

Gulf Labor Bibliography

"All Over Arts: news from around the globe," *ABC* (February 27, 2014), http://www
.abc.net.au/radionational/programs/booksandartsdaily/all-over-arts/5284942

"Anti-Guggenheim groups launch competition for South Harbour location," *YLE* (September
9, 2014), http://yle.fi/uutiset/anti-guggenheim_groups_launch_competition_for_south_
harbour_location/7460869

"Artists threaten boycott over Abu Dhabi worker welfare," *BBC Business News* (March 22, 2014),
http://www.bbc.com/news/business-26681166

Batty, David, "Artworld protest over 'mistreatment' of migrants at Abu Dhabi cultural hub,"
Guardian (November 2, 2013), http://www.theguardian.com/world/2013/nov/02/abu-
dhabi-culture-guggenheim-louvre-workers-rights

Batty, David, "Call for UN to investigate plight of migrant workers in the UAE," *Guardian*
(September 13, 2014), http://www.theguardian.com/global-development/2014/sep/13/
migrant-workers-uae-gulf-states-un-ituc?CMP=twt_gu

Batty, David, "Migrants building UAE cultural hub 'working in prison conditions,'" *Guardian* (April 4, 2015), http://www.theguardian.com/global-development/2015/apr/04/
migrant-workers-uae-saadiyat-island-abu-dhabi-battery-hens

Batty, David, "Modern Day Slave Labor: Conditions for Abu Dhabi's Migrant Workers Shame the West," *Alternet/Guardian* (December 23, 2013), http://www.alternet
.org/world/modern-day-slave-labor-conditions-abu-dhabis-migrant-workers
-shame-west

Buck, Louisa, "Artist interview, Walid Raad: a mediator between worlds," *The Art
Newspaper* (January 15, 2013), http://www.theartnewspaper.com/articles/Artist
-interview-Walid-Raad-a-mediator-between-worlds/28352

Campbell, Bradley, "Protesters take over the Guggenheim on behalf of workers
a world away," *PRI's The World* (February 25, 2014), http://www.pri.org/
stories/2014-02-25/protesters-take-over-guggenheim-behalf-workers-world
-away

Chen, Michelle, "Activists Invade the Guggenheim," *The Nation* (May 26, 2014), http://www.thenation.com/blog/180009/activists-invade-guggenheim-how-creative-campaign-holding-us-institutions-accountable-la

Christensen, Nate and John Warner, "The Art of Resistance: Labor, Debt, and G.U.L.F.'s Guggenheim Campaign," *Jadaliyya* (May 16, 2014), http://www.jadaliyya.com/pages/index/17723/the-art-of-resistance_labor-debt-and-g.u.l.f.s-gug

Chute, James, "Artists and workers unite," Exhibition review, *The San Diego Union Tribune* (March 12, 2014), http://www.utsandiego.com/news/2014/mar/12/doris-bittar-labor-migrant-gulf/

Cotter, Holland, "Door to Art of the World, Barely Ajar," *New York Times* (March 19, 2014), http://www.nytimes.com/2014/03/20/arts/artsspecial/door-to-art-of-the-world-barely-ajar.html

Crabapple, Molly, "Slaves of Happiness Island," *Vice* (August 4, 2014). http://www.vice.com/read/slaves-of-happiness-island-0000412-v21n8

Davis, Ben, "Artist Sneaks Into Future Guggenheim Abu Dhabi Site to Interview Workers," *ArtNet News* (August 13, 2014).

Davis, Ben, "What's Really Going on at Abu Dhabi's Saadiyat Island?" *ArtNet News* (March 3, 2015).

Downey, Anthony, ed., *Uncommon Grounds: New Media and Critical Practice in the Middle East* (London: I.B. Tauris, 2014).

Downey, Anthony, "Saadiyat and the Gulf Labor Boycott," *Ibraaz* (May 8, 2013), http://www.ibraaz.org/essays/62

Fitch, Asa, "Abu Dhabi Labor Record Sparks Guggenheim New York Protests," *Wall Street Journal* (February 25, 2014), http://blogs.wsj.com/middleeast/2014/02/25/abu-dhabi-labor-record-sparks-guggenheim-new-york-protests/

Fitch, Asa, "Labor and Culture Collide in the Gulf," *Wall Street Journal* (November 5, 2013), http://blogs.wsj.com/middleeast/2013/11/05/labor-and-culture-collide-in-the-gulf/

Fuchs, Martina, "Artists boycott Guggenheim Abu Dhabi in labor row," *Reuters* (March 17, 2011), http://af.reuters.com/article/ivoryCoastNews/idAFLDE72G03M20110317

Gehi, Reema, "Art in Protest," *Mumbai Mirror* (March 22, 2015), http://www.mumbaimirror.com/others/sunday-read/Art-in-protest/articleshow/46648168.cms

Gehi, Reema, "Artist Protests Labor Conditions, UAE Denies Him Visa," *Mumbai Mirror* (May 12, 2015), http://www.mumbaimirror.com/mumbai/others/Artist-protests-labour-conditions-UAE-denies-him-visa/articleshow/47241200.cms

Ghani, Mariam / GLC, "Notes from a Boycott," *Manifesta Journal* 18 (2014).

Gilbert, Helen, "Poor working conditions continue for starchitect projects in Abu Dhabi," *The Architects' Journal* (May 12, 2014), http://www.architectsjournal.co.uk/news/daily-news/poor-working-conditions-continue-for-starchitect-projects-in-abu-dhabi/8662463.article?blocktitle=Latest-news&contentID=7896

Gonzalez, Jime Reyes, "Criticism of Guggenheim Ad Escalates With Fake Website," *The Gazelle* 36 (April 19, 2014), http://www.thegazelle.org/issue/36/news/global-guggenheim/

Goodman, Matthew Shen, "Protesting the Guggenheim in Abu Dhabi: An Interview with G.U.L.F.," *Art in America* (February 26, 2014), http://www.artinamericamagazine.com/news-features/interviews/protesting-the-guggenheim-in-abu-dhabi-an-interview-with-gulf/

Halperin, Julia, "Abu Dhabi Museums Face Further Scrutiny by Gulf Labor," *The Art Newspaper* (August 1, 2015), http://theartnewspaper.com/news/museums/158076/

Heddaya, Mostafa, "Activists Picket Guggenheim Gala over Labor Abuses," *Hyperallergic* (November 7, 2014), http://hyperallergic.com/161602/activists-picket-guggenheim-gala-over-labor-abuses/

Heddaya, Mostafa, "Counter-Competition Seeks Alternatives to Controversial Guggenheim Helsinki," *Hyperallergic* (September 11, 2014), http://hyperallergic.com/148434/counter-competition-seeks-alternatives-to-controversial-guggenheim-helsinki/

Heddaya, Mostafa, "Gulf Labor Monitoring Report Finds Ongoing Violations At Guggenheim Abu Dhabi," *Hyperallergic* (May 2, 2014), http://hyperallergic.com/123873/gulf-labor-monitoring-report-finds-ongoing-labor-violations-at-guggenheim-abu-dhabi/

Heddaya, Mostafa, "Labor Activists Occupy Guggenheim New York," *BlouinArtinfo* (May 1, 2015), http://www.blouinartinfo.com/news/story/1146947/labor-activists-occupy-guggenheim-new-york-link-to-live#

Holmes, Helen, Ari Lipsitz, and StudentNation, "Reports of Worker Abuse Continue at NYU's Newly Completed Abu Dhabi Campus," *The Nation* (May 20, 2014). http://www.thenation.com/blog/179933/reports-worker-abuse-continue-nyus-newly-completed-abu-dhabi-campus#

"Island of happiness? Artist Mariam Ghani on art and exploitation in Abu Dhabi," *Art Radar* (August 12, 2013), http://artradarjournal.com/2013/12/08/island-of-happiness-artist-mariam-ghani-on-art-and-exploitation-in-abu-dhabi/

Jaffe, Sarah and Michelle Chen, "Art, Academia, and Labor Struggles in Abu Dhabi" (with Andrew Ross), *Belabored Podcast* #53, "Dissent" (May 30, 2014), http://www.dissentmagazine.org/blog/belabored-podcast-53-art-academia-and-labor-struggles-in-abu-dhabi-with-andrew-ross

Kaminer, Ariel and Sean O'Driscoll, "Workers at N.Y.U.'s Abu Dhabi Site Faced Harsh Conditions," *New York Times* (May 18, 2014), http://www.nytimes.com/2014/05/19/nyregion/workers-at-nyus-abu-dhabi-site-face-harsh-conditions.html?hp

Kerr, Simeon, "Gulf Labor calls on Abu Dhabi to pay off museum workers' debts," *Financial Times* (May 2, 2014), http://www.ft.com/cms/s/0/eaa8605e-d200-11e3-8ff4-00144feabdc0.html#axzz3Sijj3x6u

Kerr, Simeon, "Labour abuse claims overshadow Guggenheim Abu Dhabi Show," *Financial Times* (November 3, 2014).

Kimball, Whitney, "Protestors Take Over the Guggenheim With Giant Projections," *ARTFCITY* (March 25, 2014), http://artfcity.com/2014/03/25/protestors-take-over-the-guggenheim-with-giant-projections/

Lütticken, Sven, "Cultural Revolution: From Punk to the New Provotariat," *New Left Review* 87 (May-June 2014).

Mathias, Christopher, "Protest Breaks Out at the Guggenheim in New York Over 'Slave Labor'," *Huffington Post* (February 24, 2014), http://www.huffingtonpost.com/2014/02/24/guggenheim-protest-new-york-abu-dhabi-labor_n_4843947.html

Milliard, Coline, "Gulf Labor Launches Year-long Campaign to Support Abu Dhabi Workers," *Blouin ARTINFO, UK* (October 22, 2013), http://uk.blouinartinfo.com/news/story/974888/gulf-labor-launches-year-long-campaign-to-support-abu-dhabi

Miller, M. H., "Artists Launch '52 Weeks' Campaign to Protest Labor Conditions at Art Institutions in Abu Dhabi," *New York Observer* (October 18, 2013), http://observer.com/2013/10/artists-launch-52-weeks-campaign-to-protest-labor-conditions-at-art-institutions-in-abu-dhabi/

Moynihan, Colin, "At Guggenheim, Protesters Renew Criticism of Abu Dhabi Expansion Plan," *New York Times* (November 6, 2014), http://www.nytimes.com/2014/11/07/nyregion/guggenheim-plan-renews-concerns-over-labor-in-abu-dhabi.html?ref=nyregion&_r=3

Partesotti, Vega"Gulf Labor Hips Venice Biennale Visitors to UAE Labor Abuses," *Hyperallergic* (July 31, 2015), http://hyperallergic.com/226498/gulf-labor-hips-venice-biennale-visitors-to-uae-labor-abuses/

Pizzi, Michael, "Protesters 'occupy' New York's Guggenheim over Gulf labor abuses," *Al Jazeera* (May 1, 2015), http://america.aljazeera.com/articles/2015/5/1/protesters-occupy-new-yorks-guggenheim-over-gulf-labor-abuses.html

Polacek, Jeremy, "Guerrilla Protestors Storm the Guggenheim With a Message the Museum Can't Ignore," *Arts.Mic* (April 2, 2014), http://mic.com/articles/86745/guerrilla-protestors-storm-the-guggenheim-with-a-message-the-museum-cant-ignore

Rauch, Joseph, "Protest night at the museum: The Guggenheim is disrupted by demonstrators throwing fake money in the rotunda," *Time Out New York* (March 31, 2014), http://www.timeout.com/newyork/art/protest-night-at-the-museum-the-guggenheim-is-disrupted-by-demonstrators-throwing-fake-money-in-the-rotunda

Robbins, Christopher, "Photos: Labor Protesters Disrupt Guggenheim To Shame Trustees By Name," *Gothamist* (May 25, 2014), http://gothamist.com/2014/05/25/protesters_target_guggenheim_truste.php

Ross, Andrew, "Degrees of Danger: In the United Arab Emirates," *The Baffler Magazine* 26 (2014), http://www.thebaffler.com/salvos/degrees-danger

Ross, Andrew, "High Culture and Hard Labor," *New York Times* (March 28, 2014), http://www.nytimes.com/2014/03/29/opinion/high-culture-and-hard-labor.html?_r=0

Ryzik, Melena, "Guggenheim Closes for the Afternoon as Workers' Advocates Escalate Protests," *New York Times* (May 1, 2015), http://artsbeat.blogs.nytimes.com/2015/05/01/on-may-day-protesters-at-the-guggenheim-vow-to-occupy-the-space/?_r=0

Saul, Stephanie, "N.Y.U. Professor Is Barred from United Arab Emirates," *New York Times* (March 16, 2015), http://www.nytimes.com/2015/03/17/nyregion/nyu-professor-is-barred-from-the-united-arab-emirates.html?_r=0

Schlanger, Zoë, "Protesters Sneak Into the Guggenhiem, Make It Rain False Bills," *Newsweek* (March 31, 2014), http://www.newsweek.com/protesters-sneak-guggenheim-make-it-rain-false-bills-238877

Shaw, Matt, "Architizer Exclusive: Michael Sorkin Talks Alternative Guggenheim Competition," *Architizer* (September 9, 2014), http://yle.fi/uutiset/anti-guggenheim_groups_launch_competition_for_south_harbour_location/7460869

Sholette, Gregory, "A Response to Okwui Enwezor on Gulf Labor," *Artforum* (June 3, 2011), http://artforum.com/talkback/id=69907

Sholette, Gregory, "The Return of the Artist as Social Activist from the Abu Dhabi Guggenheim Boycott to the Occupy Wall Street Movement," *Springerin Magazine* (2011), http://www.springerin.at/dyn/heft_text.php?textid=2570&lang=en

Sutton, Benjamin, "May Day Occupation at Guggenheim Closes Museum #Gugg-Occupied," *Hyperallergic* (May 1, 2015), https://hyperallergic.com/203794/breaking-may-day-occupation-at-guggenheim-closes-museum-guggoccupied/

The Stream Team, "Guggenheim protesters 'make it rain' to highlight poor labor practices," *Aljazeera America* (March 31, 2014), http://america.aljazeera.com/watch/shows/the-stream/the-stream-officialblog/2014/3/31/guggenheim-protestersmakeitraintohighlightpoorlaborpractices.html

Thompson, Nato, Laura Diamond Dixit, Naeem Mohaiemen, and Andrew Ross, "Who's Happy About Abu Dhabi's 'Island of Happiness'? It's Not the Construction Workers," *Creative Time Reports* (August 18, 2014), http://creativetimereports.org/2014/08/18/abu-dhabi-saadiyat-island-construction-workers/

Vartanian, Hrag, "Artists Launch "Letter for Palestine" Campaign at Venice Biennale," *Hyperallergic* (August 13, 2015), http://hyperallergic.com/229304/artists-launch-letter-for-palestine-campaign-at-venice-biennale/

Vartanian, Hrag, "New Abu Dhabi Museum Island Report Paints Troubling Picture for Workers," *Hyperallergic* (August 4, 2014), http://hyperallergic.com/141581/new-abu-dhabi-museum-island-report-paints-troubling-picture-for-workers/

Vartanian, Hrag, "Protesters Stage Intervention at Guggenheim's Futurist Exhibition," *Hyperallergic* (May 25, 2014), http://hyperallergic.com/128514/protesters-stage-intervention-at-guggenheims-futurist-exhibition/

Vartanian, Hrag "G.U.L.F. Occupies Israeli Pavilion in Venice, Calls for Cultural Boycott," *Hyperallergic* (August 3, 2015), http://hyperallergic.com/226941/g-u-l-f-occupies-israeli-pavilion-in-venice-calls-for-cultural-boycott/

Vartanian, Hrag, "Gulf Labor and Other Arts Groups Occupy Venice's Guggenheim," *Hyperallergic* (May 8, 2015), http://hyperallergic.com/205465/breaking-gulf-labor-and-other-arts-groups-occupy-venices-guggenheim-guggoccupied/

Vartanian, Hrag, "The Guggenheim and Protesters Both Respond to #GuggOccupied in Venice," *Hyperallergic* (May 9, 2015), http://hyperallergic.com/205821/the-guggenheim-and-protesters-both-respond-to-guggoccupied-in-venice/

Wainwright, Oliver, "Helsinki v Guggenheim: the backlash against the global mega brand is on," *Guardian* (September 11, 2014), http://www.theguardian.com/artanddesign/architecture-design-blog/2014/sep/11/helsinki-guggenheim-outpost-battle

"Who's Building the Guggenheim Abu Dhabi?," *Asia Pacific Forum* (radio broadcast) (January 14, 2013), http://www.asiapacificforum.org/show-detail.php?show_id=292

"Working the global art market: labour, galleries, and activism in the Gulf," *LeftEast* (April 9, 2014), http://www.criticatac.ro/lefteast/working-the-global-art-market-gulf/

Wyma, Chloe, "1% Museum: The Guggenheim Goes Global," *Dissent* (Summer 2014), http://www.dissentmagazine.org/article/1-museum-the-guggenheim-goes -global

Wyma, Chloe, "Escape from Parametric Island: Guggenheim Abu Dhabi," *Architectural Review* (January 10, 2014), http://www.architectural-review.com/escape -from-parametric-island-guggenheim-abu-dhabi/8674388.article

Contributors

Haig Aivazian is an artist and writer currently based in Beirut, Lebanon. He is a member of the Gulf Labor core organizing committee.

A Minnesotan transplant from Saudi Arabia, **Hend Al-Mansour**'s work reflects her Arab upbringing. While thematically it makes references to the gender politics in Arab society and in Islamic teaching, it borrows aesthetics from Arabic and Islamic art forms. Al-Mansour has participated in regional, national, and international art shows, given speeches about Arab art and her personal journey, and curated exhibitions featuring Middle Eastern artists.

Mounira Al Solh (1978), born in Beirut, lives and works in Amsterdam and in Beirut. Her visual practice embraces video, painting, embroidery, and performance, and her work has been displayed in exhibitions in Beirut, Lisbon, New York, Munich, Murcia, Mumbai, Amsterdam, Bahrain, and at the Venice Biennial and Manifesta 8. In 2003 she was awarded the Kentertainment Painting Prize in Lebanon and her video *Rawane's Song* received the 2007 jury prize at VideoBrasil. She is Uriôt Prize winner at the Rijksakademie.

Alien Abduction Collective (AAC)'s current active members are Todd Ayoung, a visual artist and art professor based in the USA, Jelena Stojanović, an art historian and professor based in the USA and Serbia, and Heather Davis, a writer and post-doc student at Penn State University, PA, USA. AAC has participated in art and politics projects with Greg Sholette and Gulf Labor.

Ayreen Anastas and Rene Gabri's collaborative projects have evolved through their work at 16 Beaver group, an artist community that functions as a social and collaborative space in downtown Manhattan, where the group hosts panel discussions, film series, artist talks, radio recordings, reading groups, and more. Their Radioactive Discussion series was a physical counterpart to their fictional Homeland Security Cultural Bureau project. The artists recently had a solo exhibition at Kunstverein Arnsberg (2011). Other collaborations include: Camp Campaign, Artist talk, Radio Active, United We Stand, What Everybody Knows, Eden Resonating, 7X77, and Case Sensitive America.

Mieke Bal is a cultural theorist, critic, and video artist. Her interests range from classical and biblical antiquity to 17th century and contemporary art and modern literature, feminism, migratory culture, mental illness, and the critique of capitalism. Her many books include: *Endless Andness* (on abstraction) and *Thinking in Film* (on video installation), both 2013, *Of What One Cannot Speak* (2010, on sculpture), and *A Mieke Bal Reader* (2006). Her most recent video project is *Madame B*, with Michelle Williams Gamaker.

Zanny Begg is a Sydney-based artist. Her work uses humor, understated drawings, and found cultural artifacts to explore ways in which we can live and be in the world differently. Her work is dialogic and often collaborative, inviting engagement with key themes such as resilience, financial disobedience, and unthinking borders. Begg has an experimental and research-driven practice that works across cinema, performance, installation, activism, and drawing.

Doris Bittar's interdisciplinary projects examine decorative motifs and how they intersect with historical and geopolitical legacies. Related activities include teaching, curating, writing, and activism. Bittar's art is housed in several public collections in the United States and abroad. She works with the American Civil Liberties Union, is a core member of Gulf Labor, and is co-founder of Gulf Labor West. Bittar teaches at California State University, San Marcos.

CAMP was founded in November 2007 by Shaina Anand, Sanjay Bhangar, and Ashok Sukumaran. CAMP is not an "artists collective" but rather a studio, in which ideas and energies gather and become interests and forms. In this process they try to move beyond binaries of art vs. non-art, commodity markets vs. "free culture," or individual vs. institutional will to think and to build what is possible, equitable, and interesting, for the future. CAMP's current members are Ashok Sukumaran, Sanjay Bhangar, Shaina Anand, and Zinnia Ambapardiwala.

Carole Condé and **Karl Beveridge** live and work in Toronto. They have collaborated with various trade union and community organizations in the production of their staged photographic work over the past 40 years. Their work has been exhibited across Canada and internationally in both the trade union movement and public art galleries and museums.

Paula Chakravartty is an Associate Professor at NYU's Gallatin School and the Department of Media, Culture and Communications. She is the co-editor of a special issue on *Modi and the Media: Indian Politics and Electoral Aftermath* (2015), co-editor of *Race, Empire and the Crisis of the Subprime* (2013), co-author of *Media Policy and Globalization* (2006), and co-editor of *Global Communications: Towards a Transcultural Political Economy* (2008). Her writings have been published in a number of journals, including *Economic and Political Weekly, American Quarterly, International Journal of Communication, Media Culture,* and *Society and Political Communication*.

Sam Durant is a multimedia artist whose works engage a variety of social, political, and cultural issues. His work has been widely exhibited internationally and is included in numerous public collections including the Tate Modern, London, the Museum of Modern Art, New York, and Project Row Houses, Houston, Texas. Durant teaches art at the California Institute of the Arts in Valencia, California.

Sarah Farahat and **Aaron Hughes**'s collaboration emerges from a two-year conversation about art, life, activism and politics. Hughes is a teacher, organizer, and Iraq War veteran whose work seeks out poetics, connections, and moments of beauty in order to construct new languages and meanings out of personal and collective traumas. Farahat is an Egyptian American artists, activist, and teacher fiercely and joyously committed to working in solidarity with local and international social justice organizations.

Claire Fontaine, founded in 2004, is a collective artist based in Paris. After lifting her name from a popular brand of school notebooks, Claire Fontaine declared herself a "readymade artist" and began to elaborate a version of neo-conceptual art that often looks like other people's work. A monograph about the artist was published in 2012 by Walther König, entitled *Foreigners Everywhere*. She has published, with Mute, *Human strike has already begun and other texts* (2012), with One Star Press *Some instructions for the sharing of private property* (2011), and with Dilecta Vivre *vaincre* (2009).

Andrea Fraser is Professor of New Genres at the UCLA. Her books include *Andrea Fraser: Works 1984–2003* (Dumont, 2003); *Museum Highlights: The Writings of Andrea Fraser* (MIT Press, 2005); and *Texts, Scripts, Transcripts* (Museum Ludwig, 2013). Her recent performance "Not just a few of us" was featured in *Prospect.3: Notes for Now, New Orleans.* Retrospectives of her work will be presented at the Museum der Moderne, Salzburg in 2015 and the Museum of Contemporary Art, Barcelona in 2016.

Charles Gaines (b. 1944) was the subject of a solo exhibition at the Studio Museum in Harlem, 2014, traveling to the Hammer Museum in 2015. In 2015, his work was featured in the 56th Venice Biennial and a solo exhibition at Art+Practice, Los Angeles. In 2013, he received a Guggenheim Fellowship and presented a solo exhibition, *Notes on Social Justice*, at Paula Cooper Gallery, New York.

Michelle Williams Gamaker (1979) is an artist and researcher working with performance and renderings of reality via documentary, fiction, and video installations. With Mieke Bal (Cinema Suitcase), Gamaker has completed several films and installations, including the recent *Madame B.* Her current project, *Black Matter Earth*, is a post-colonial, post-romantic exploration of the female protagonists of British directors Powell & Pressburger, scheduled for 2017 at the BFI. She works as a Senior

Lecturer at Kingston University and Goldsmiths College, University of London in Fine Art and is an arts educator at Tate Britain and Modern.

Mariam Ghani is an artist and writer based in Brooklyn. Her work has been exhibited internationally and her writing has been published online by *Creative Time Reports, Foreign Policy, Ibraaz,* the *New York Review of Books,* and *Triple Canopy,* and in print by *Manifesta Journal, Pavilion,* the *Radical History Review,* and the *Sarai Reader.* She teaches at Queens College and is part of the Gulf Labor Working Group.

Maryam Monalisa Gharavi is an artist, poet, and theorist. Her work in film, video, text, sound, photography, performance, and critical writing appears in a wide variety of exhibitions and publications. Forthcoming books include *American Letters* (ZerO) and a translation of Waly Salomão's *Algaravias: Echo Chamber* (Ugly Duckling Presse). She writes the blog *South/South* and is an editor at *The New Inquiry.*

The Global Ultra Luxury Faction (G.U.L.F.) is a direct action group affiliated with the Gulf Labor Coalition (GLC). Beginning in February 2014, G.U.L.F. has staged a number of high profile actions at the Guggenheim Museum in New York with the intention of pressuring the museum's director and its board to accede to GLC's demands for fair working conditions on Saadiyat Island in the UAE. G.U.L.F. was formed by members of Occupy Museums, MTL, and Gulf Labor.

Jim Goldberg's long-term projects include Rich and Poor (1977–85), Raised by Wolves (1985–95), and Open See (2003–2011), for which he was awarded the Henri Cartier-Bresson Award and the Deutsche Börse Photography Prize in 2011. Goldberg's works are in numerous collections including Museum of Modern Art, Whitney Museum of American Art, Getty, LACMA, National Gallery of Art, Alinari National Museum of Photography in Florence, Le Musee de la Photographie, Belgium, and Museum für Kunst und Gewerbe, Hamburg, Germany.

Paul Graham (b. 1956) is an English fine-art and documentary photographer whose work has been exhibited, published, and collected internationally. In 2009, he won the

Deutsche Börse Photography Prize. He is also a Winston Churchill Memorial Fellow (1983) and a Guggenheim Fellow (2010). In 2012 he received the Hasselblad Award and the Paris Photo prize for the best photographic book of the past 15 years.

Matt Greco is a sculptor, photographer, and maker living and working in Queens, New York. His exhibitions include the Telfair Museum of Art (Georgia), Desoto Row Gallery (Georgia), the Dorsky Gallery (New York), the NY Studio Gallery (New York), Gallery 126 (Ireland), the Beacon Gallery (California), and the Baron Gallery (Ohio). He is adjunct faculty at Queens College, CUNY as well as the director of their 2D/3D Digital Imaging Laboratory.

Hans Haacke, born Cologne, Germany 1936. Lives in New York since 1965. Taught at Cooper Union, New York 1967 to 2002. Solo-exhibitions: Tate Gallery, London, 1984; New Museum of Contemporary Art, New York, 1986; Centre Georges Pompidou, Paris, 1989; Deichtorhallen, Hamburg and Akademie der Künste, Berlin, 2006; Museo Nacional Centro de Arte Reina Sofía, Madrid, 2012; 4th Plinth, Trafalgar Square, London, 2015. Works included in four Documentas and in Biennials of Tokyo, Sydney, Saõ Paulo, Venice, Johannesburg, Whitney, Gwangju, and Sharjah. Shared Golden Lion award with Nam June Paik for best pavilion of 1993 Venice Biennial.

Rawi Hage was born in Beirut and resides in Montreal. His first novel, *De Niro's Game*, won the IMPAC Dublin Literary Award, the McAuslan First Book Prize and the Paragraphe Hugh MacLennan Prize for Fiction. *Cockroach*, his second novel, also won the Paragraphe Hugh MacLennan Prize for Fiction. His writing has appeared in *Walrus*, *Granta*, *Tin House*, *Brick*, *Five Dials*, *TOK*, and *The Kenyon Review*. His latest novel *Carnival* (2012) was a finalist for the Writers' Trust Award and won the Paragraphe Hugh MacLennan Prize for Fiction.

Pablo Helguera is a visual artist living in New York. He has performed or presented his work at MoMA, BAM, the Guggenheim Museum, Reina Sofia, and other major museums, and participated in the Havana and Liverpool biennials among many others. He is the author of 20 books, including *The Parable Conference* (2014), *Art*

Scenes (The Social Scripts of the Art World) (2012), and *Education for Socially Engaged Art* (2011).

Thomas Hirschhorn was born in 1957 in Bern (Switzerland). His work has been shown in numerous museums, galleries, and exhibitions, including the Venice Biennale (1999, 2011), Kassel Documenta11 (2002), 27th São Paulo Biennale (2006), 55th Carnegie International, Pittsburg (2008), and Manifesta 10 in Saint Petersburg (2014). In 2013 he presented the "Gramsci Monument" in the Bronx, New York. "Flamme éternelle," his most recent "Presence and Production" project, took place at Palais de Tokyo, Paris, in 2014.

Ashley Hunt uses image, object, word, and performance-based strategies to engage the ideas of social movements, modes of learning, and the relationships between our artworlds and the larger worlds in which they sit. His work is often concerned with questions of power, the ways that some people have more and others have less, and what can be done about that.

The Illuminator Art Collective is a group of like-minded individuals—artists, activists, technologists, filmmakers, and a biologist—who came together around the banner of Occupy Wall Street in New York City in February and March of 2012. The collective formed following the popular "bat signal" projection onto the Verizon building seen by thousands of marchers crossing the Brooklyn Bridge on the night of the three-month anniversary and simultaneous eviction of Zuccotti Park in downtown Manhattan.

JAŠA was born in Ljubljana in 1978. He studied at the Accademia di Belle Arti in Venice. One of Slovenia's most prolific contemporary artists for almost two decades, JAŠA has created a rich and remarkable body of work that includes multiple solo shows and projects in Europe and the US.

John Suleiman Jurayj lives in Brooklyn, New York, and is a professor at The School of Visual Arts at Cornell University in NYC. Recent solo shows include "2013: What's left" at Walter Maciel Gallery in L.A., 2011: "No Paradises," Alberto Peola Gallery, Turin, Italy; and "Undead, Participant Inc.," New York, New York. Recent group shows include "Light from the Middle East: New Photography," Victoria & Albert Museum, London, UK (2012); "(Space): Translation/Tarjama" at the Herbert Johnson Museum at Cornell University and the Queens Museum of Art, New York (2009); and "Exposure 2009," Beirut Art Center, Beirut, Lebanon (2009).

Janet Koenig is a New York–based artist and writer. Her work has appeared in numerous exhibitions and publications, including MoMA's *Committed to Print* (1988). She has participated in the artist collectives PAD/D (Political Art Documentation/ Distribution), RepoHistory, and the catalog committee of Artists Meeting for Cultural Change, which produced *An Anti-Catalog* (1977). She translated and annotated *L'enfant perdu et retrouvé; ou Pierre Cholet* by J.-B. Proulx as *Lost and Found Again, or Pierre Cholet* and *Les mots qui font peur* by Hsi Huan-Wou and Charles Reeve as *Who's Afraid of the Big Bad Words* (2013).

Silvia Kolbowski is a New York–based artist working with time-based media. Her work has been exhibited in many international venues and contexts, including the Taipei Biennial; the Villa Arson, Nic; the Whitney Biennial, New York; and the Hammer Museum, Los Angeles. She has had one-person exhibitions at the Museum of Modern Art, Ljubljana; the Center for Contemporary Art, Warsaw; the Secession, Vienna; and LAX<>ART. She currently writes a blog as an extension of her art practice to another platform, at silviakolbowskiblog.com.

Pedro Lasch (Mexico/US) teaches at Duke University and leads ongoing projects with immigrant groups and 16 Beaver in New York. Solo projects include Open Routines (Queens Museum of Art, 2006), Black Mirror (Nasher Museum, 2008), and Anthems for Four Voices (The Phillips Collection, 2014); his work has also been shown at MoMA PS1, MASS MoCA, Walker Art Center, CAC New Orleans (US), Royal College of Art, Hayward Gallery, Baltic (UK), MUAC, Centro Nacional de las Artes (Mexico), Museo Reina Sofía (Spain), The Singapore Art Museum, Documenta 13 (AND AND AND), Gwangju Biennial (2006), and 12th Havana Biennial.

Lynn Love is a writer who lives in New York City.

Guy Mannes-Abbott is a London-based writer whose work often performs in visual art contexts. This includes *In Ramallah, Running* (London 2012), a story for *Drone Fiction* (Dubai 2013), and a text series for *End Note*(s) (Rotterdam/Hong Kong 2015). He published an essay on Emily Jacir in *Archival Dissonance* (London 2015), participated in Moderation[s] at Witte de With (Rotterdam 2013), and collaborated with CAMP on *The Country of the Blind, and Other Stories* (Folkestone 2011). He once taught theory at the AA School of Architecture, London, and his cultural criticism is widely published.

Mazatl lives in Mexico City, where he partakes in several collectives seeking social/political/environmental justice; his art is inspired by the work individuals and collectives do to shake off the noose around our necks.

Pat McElnea is a media artist based in Brooklyn, New York. His practice encompasses video, painting, collage, short fiction, and drawing. His work explores the role of abstraction in public health, memorialization, and childhood. He exhibits his work internationally and teaches experimental video at Vassar College.

Mobile Irony Valve (MIV): an anagram of Emily Verla Bovino (EVB); artist, writer, historian, chiptunes-lover, yogini. Recent projects include an exhibition of the makro-scripts of Constance Schwartzlin-Berberat, a thanatographic novel on Twitter (#nimbleloveivory), the life-long epic RK-LOG (contact evbovino@gmail.com for access), and a videographic internet novel (www.mobile-irony-valve.net/index.php/nvl/nvl/). MIV is completing a dissertation in art history and anthropogeny on Aby Warburg's psychological aesthetics of corporal introjection.

Naeem Mohaiemen is a writer and visual artist working in Dhaka and New York. He uses essays, photography, film, and mixed media to research histories of the international left and the failure of utopia projects. A 2014 Guggenheim Fellow, he is author of *Prisoners of Shothik Itihash* and editor of the anthologies *Between Ashes and Hope:*

Chittagong Hill Tracts *in the blind spot of* Bangladesh *nationalism, Collectives in atomised time,* and *System Error: War is a force that gives us meaning.*

Nitasha Dhillon and **Amin Husain** are **MTL** (mtlcollective.org), a collaboration that joins research, aesthetics, and activism in its practice. Nitasha (b. 1985, India) and Amin (b. 1975, Palestine/USA) attended Whitney Independent Study Program in New York and School of International Center of Photography. They were deeply involved in Occupy Wall Street and continue to edit and publish *Tidal—Occupy Theory* (www .tidalmag.org), a strategic platform that weaves together the voices of on-the-ground organizers with longstanding theorists to explore the possibilities created by the rupture of Occupy and its aftermath. Most recently, they helped found the Global Ultra Luxury Faction (G.U.L.F.).

Marina Naprushkina, born in Minsk, Belarus, is an artist and activist who founded the Office for Anti Propaganda in 2007 to support political campaigns and protests and publish underground newspapers. In 2013, Naprushkina started a neighborhood initiative called "New Neighborhood//Moabit" (https://neuenachbarschaft.wordpress .com/) to support refugees and migrants.

Jenny Polak's background in architecture and her family's migrations inform her artwork around racial profiling, detention centers, and strategies for surviving hostile authorities. Her projects often respond to site or community, generating fictional spaces in which the dark side of design is seen and subverted. Collaborators have included Concerned Citizens of Crete, IL; Our Lady of Guadalupe, Little Village, Chicago; immigrant detainees across the US; indigenous farmers in New Mexico; and ESOL students in New York.

Walid Raad is an artist and an Associate Professor of Art in the Cooper Union (New York, USA). Raad's works include *The Atlas Group*, a 15-year project between 1989 and 2004 about the contemporary history of Lebanon, and the ongoing projects *Scratching on Things I Could Disavow* and *Sweet Talk: Commissions (Beirut).*

G.H. Rabbath has engaged in several meta-artistic interventions since 2009, including the publication of *Can One Man Save the (Art) World*. In 2011, he was curator of the Lebanese Pavilion for the 54th Venice Biennial and created "institutional void" in the Arsenale as part of a neo-Situationist project. A special edition of the *Better World Project* for Palestine was launched on November 28, 2014, at the UN/ESCWA Beirut HQ as part of the observance of the International Day for Justice for the Palestinian People. In 2015 he launched peacerunners.org, an ongoing art photography and writing project about the Beirut Marathon runners.

Oliver Ressler works as an artist and filmmaker on issues such as economics, democracy, global warming, forms of resistance, and social alternatives. Since 2000 Ressler has realized 20 films, including three films in collaboration with Dario Azzellini on political processes in Venezuela and three films on the alter-globalization movement. His films have been screened in thousands of events of social movements, art institutions, and film festivals. A retrospective of his films took place at Centre d'Art Contemporain Genève in 2013.

Andrew Ross is Professor of Social and Cultural Analysis at NYU and a social activist. Contributor to *The Nation, New York Times, Guardian*, and *Al Jazeera*, he is the author or editor of 20 books, including *Creditocracy and the Case for Debt Refusal, Bird on Fire: Lessons from the World's Least Sustainable City, Nice Work If You Can Get It*, and *Fast Boat to China*.

Jayce Salloum tends to go only where he is invited or where there is an intrinsic affinity, his projects being rooted in an intimate engagement with places, and the people who inhabit them. He has been producing art, collecting objects, making things happen and mixing it up discursively for as long as he can remember.

Rasha Salti is a writer, curator, and film programmer. She lives in Beirut, Lebanon.

Ann Sappenfield is a designer and illustrator who lives in New York City.

Dread Scott makes revolutionary art to propel history forward. In 1989, the entire US Senate denounced and outlawed his artwork and President Bush declared it "disgraceful" because of its use of the American flag. His work is exhibited/performed internationally, including in the Whitney Museum, MoMA/PS1, Pori Art Museum (Finland), BAM Fisher, and galleries and street corners across the country. He is a recipient of a Creative Capital Grant and his work is included in the collection of the Whitney Museum.

Gregory Sholette is a New York–based artist, writer, and cultural activist whose recent art projects include "Our Barricades" at Station Independent Gallery and "Imaginary Archive" at Institute of Contemporary Art U. Penn, Philadelphia, and Las Kurbas Center, Kyiv, Ukraine. His recent publications include *It's the Political Economy, Stupid*, co-edited with Oliver Ressler (Pluto Press, 2013), and *Dark Matter: Art and Politics in an Age of Enterprise Culture* (Pluto Press, 2011). He was a founding member of the artists' collectives Political Art Documentation/Distribution (PAD/D: 1980–1988) and REPOhistory (1989–2000). He teaches at Queens College, CUNY and Home Work Space Beirut, Lebanon.

Andreas Siekmann and **Alice Creischer** are artists based in Berlin.

Nida Sinnokrot's multi-media work has received support from the Independent Study Program of the Whitney Museum of American Art, Akademie Schloss Solitude, the Rockefeller Foundation, the Paul Robeson Fund, the Sharjah Biennial, and the Al Mamal Arts Centre in Jerusalem. Nida's work is in various collections, including the Mart Museum in Rovereto, Italy, the Nadour Collection of Contemporary Middle Eastern art, and the Sharjah Art Foundation. Nida lives and works in Palestine.

SITU Research seeks to address urgent contemporary issues—be they social, scientific, or artistic. Focused on developing innovative strategies and new tools, the practice leverages a strong foundation in architecture, materials, and digital instrumentation to collaborate with and contribute to a diverse array of fields. A core value of SITU Research is the applied nature of its work. Most recently, SITU Research has been engaged with work that explores applications of spatial analysis and instrumentation in the fields of human rights and international law.

Anna Stump is an artist and arts educator living in San Diego. She was a Senior Fulbright Scholar in the Fine Arts Department at Anadolu University in Eskisehir, Turkey. She teaches studio and art history courses at San Diego City College and Grossmont College and is represented by Sparks Gallery and Sergott Contemporary Art Alliance in San Diego.

Jaret Vadera is an artist and cultural producer working between New York, Toronto, and India. Through his interdisciplinary practice, Vadera explores how different social, technological, biological, and cognitive processes shape and control the ways that we see the world around and within us. His paintings, prints, photographs, videos, and installations have been exhibited and screened internationally. In parallel, Vadera has also worked as an organizer, programmer, curator, researcher, writer, editor, educator, and designer.

John Pitman Weber, Chicago-based muralist and printmaker, co-founded Chicago Public Art Group, 1971. Traveling shows have included the Museum of Modern Art's *Committed to Print*; the Jewish Museum's *Bridges and Boundaries*; *Kunst und Krieg* (Berlin, 1989); the recent *Poetic Dialogue Project*; and *Windows and Mirrors*, from the AFSC Cultural Envoy, Spain, 2010. Studied: School of Art Institute, Chicago; Beaux Arts & Atelier 17, Paris; Harvard University. He learned intaglio printmaking with S.W. Hayter at Atelier 17, Paris.

Sarah Leah Whitson is executive director of Human Rights Watch's Middle East and North Africa Division and is a member of the Council on Foreign Relations. She has led dozens of advocacy and investigative missions throughout the region, focusing on issues of armed conflict, accountability, legal reform, migrant workers, and political rights. She has published widely on human rights issues in the Middle East in international and regional media, including the *New York Times*, *Foreign Policy*, the *Los Angeles Times*, and *CNN*.

Who Builds Your Architecture? (WBYA?) is an interdisciplinary advocacy group that works to educate architects and other allied fields about the effects of globalization on architecture labor. WBYA? promotes fair working conditions and sustainable building practices at building sites worldwide. See www.whobuilds.org (Kadambari Baxi, Jordan Carver, Laura Diamond Dixit, Beth Stryker, Mabel O. Wilson).

Acknowledgments

This book, like the Gulf Labor initiative, is a collective effort. Those who have participated and contributed over the past five years include the following:

Walid Raad, Rene Gabri, Ayreen Anastas, Gregory Sholette, Shaina Anand, Ashok Sukumaran, Naeem Mohaiemen, Haig Aivazian, Mariam Ghani, Hans Haacke, Amin Husain, Nitasha Dhillon, Noah Fischer, Paula Chakravartty, Guy Mannes-Abbott, Doris Bittar, Emily Jacir, Tania Bruguera, Natascha Sadr Haghighian, John Pitman Weber, Joseph Roach, Mabel Wilson, Kadambari Baxi, Jordan Carver, Yates McKee, Rana Jaleel, Michael Rakovitz, Doug Ashford, Sam Durant, Paul Pfeiffer, Kristina Bogos, Astha Pokharel, Beth Stryker, Scott Berzofsky, Judith Barry, Kyle Goen, Marco Barravalle, and Csaba Nemes.

Andrew Anastasi provided world-class research assistance, Courtney Andujar and Jamie Stern-Weiner did their magic on design and editing, and we owe a great debt to Colin Robinson (and John Oakes) for pursuing, and executing, the publication of this volume.

Thanks are also due to the Vera List Center for Arts and Politics, Creative Time, the Ford Foundation, and the International Trade Union Confederation for supporting our work.

About the Editor

Andrew Ross is Professor of Social and Cultural Analysis at New York University, and a social activist. A contributor to *The Nation*, the *Guardian*, *New York Times*, Al Jazeera, and *Artforum*, he is the author of many books, including, most recently, *Creditocracy and the Case for Debt Refusal*.